OLD ABE THE WAR EAGLE

OLD ABE
THE WAR EAGLE

*A True Story of the Civil War
and Reconstruction*

RICHARD H. ZEITLIN

★

MADISON
THE STATE HISTORICAL SOCIETY OF WISCONSIN
1986

Dedication

For my family.

LIBRARY OF CONGRESS
CATALOGING IN PUBLICATION DATA
Zeitlin, Richard H.
Old Abe the War Eagle.
Bibliography: p. 108.
1. United States—Army. Wisconsin Infantry
Regiment, 8th (1861–1865)—Mascots.
2. Wisconsin—History—Civil War, 1861–1865—
Regimental histories.
3. United States—History—Civil War, 1861–1865—
Regimental histories.
I. Title.
E537.5 8th.Z45 1986 973.7'475 85-26126
ISBN 0-87020-239-1

FRONT COVER ILLUSTRATION: "The Union Forever," a diorama depicting Old Abe and the color guard of the Eighth Wisconsin Infantry, designed and created by Sheperd Paine and photographed by Lane Stewart. Reproduced by special permission of the Kalmbach Publishing Company, 1027 North Seventh Street, Milwaukee, Wisconsin 53233, in whose publication *How to Photograph Scale Models* the illustration earlier appeared. Sheperd Paine's diorama is now in the collection of Andrew Wyeth in Chadds Ford, Pennsylvania.

Preface

THIS is the story of a famous bird, of the men who bore him off to war, and of what happened after the guns fell silent. It is in many respects an incredible story, but it is true—as true, at any rate, as a careful sifting and winnowing of official documents, contemporary letters and diaries, newspapers, and eyewitness accounts can make it. It is the story of Old Abe, Wisconsin's War Eagle, mascot of the Eighth Regiment of Wisconsin Volunteer Infantry, living symbol of the Union at war.

Old Abe's life contained so many imagination-capturing experiences that storytellers, both at the time and later, have outbid one another by turning the eagle into a legendary hero possessed of amazing attributes. Old Abe has become a creature of folklore and fairy tale, and the historical facts surrounding his existence have gradually become encrusted with sheerest fantasy. Over the years, Old Abe has received acclaim for saving the day at certain battles, for delivering crucial "airmail" messages, for disrupting enemy attacks, for leading his invincible comrades to victory, and even serving as the objective of Confederate strategy.[1]

Old Abe stories have appeared and reappeared in a wide variety of publications, beginning in the 1860's and extending to the present day. Journals as diverse as *Natural History* and *True Magazine* have carried features on his exploits. Poems and songs celebrated Old Abe's imaginary feats. He is a staple with newspaper feature writers and authors of children's stories. Discussions supposedly proving that the eagle was female, and therefore an important contributor to the women's rights movement, began in 1889 and have continued to this day.[2] As a general rule, the greater the attention paid by storytellers to Old Abe—to the exclusion of the men whom he accompanied—the more unrealistic the tale.[3] In some works, especially those written for children, the eagle becomes virtually the central figure of the Civil War.[4] Clearly, there is something in the Old Abe legend that interests people.

In some ways, of course, Old Abe was a pitiable creature. Secured by a strong cord to a crude perch atop a wooden pole and carried to dangerous locales by a succession of "eagle-bearers," Abe did not have much say about his own itinerary. People clipped his wings repeatedly, and the captive bird could never fly any great distance. Old Abe was never free to soar as eagles do. For sixteen years after the Civil War ended, he dwelt in a cage in the basement of the Wisconsin State Capitol in Madison—hardly an example of liberty.

Yet Old Abe was also a veteran of thirty-seven battles and skirmishes. Along with the Wisconsin boys of his regiment, he participated in the campaigns which opened the Mississippi River and assured Federal domination of the nation's watery highways. Along with nearly three million largely volunteer citizen-soldiers from the North, Old Abe fought a determined, valiant foe in a titanic four-year conflict that ended slavery, preserved the Union, and helped to usher in the modern industrial age. The agony of the Civil War, its enormous sacrifices and its terrible human costs, were borne willingly by most Northerners, including the people of Wisconsin. Old Abe became a symbol of those momentous events, capturing the imagination of his own and of subsequent generations. He become a symbol for bravery and sacrifice, first in Wisconsin and then in the North as a whole. At a time when telegraphic communication was new, and radio nonexistent, Wisconsin's war eagle became what would later be termed a "media hero."

But what made Old Abe so famous and so much-beloved? He was not the only animal or even the only eagle that went to war. A Minnesota regiment and the Twelfth Wisconsin Infantry both had half-grown bears as mascots. The Forty-Ninth Illinois Infantry had two gamecocks "of the first class breed." Badgers and raccoons, stuffed and otherwise, were dragged along as mascots by Civil War soldiers. A wildcat accompanied a Confederate regiment from Arkansas to the Battle of Shiloh in the spring of 1862. The Forty-Ninth Wisconsin Infantry acquired a golden eagle when it garrisoned a post in the Far West at the close of the war. Numerous dogs followed both armies.[5] But, as one Illinois veteran pointed out, while "other regiments had dogs, bears, cows, goats . . . there was only one Old Abe!"[6] A bald eagle—the official national bird—obviously had advantages over dogs and bears, no matter how amusing or ferocious the latter may have appeared. The eagle had long symbolized American hegemony. With fierce eyes and outstretched wings it proclaimed the Union on posters, broadsides, letterheads, buttons, coins, signs, and the mastheads of newspapers. In a metaphorical sense, the eagle *was* (in Daniel Webster's words) "the Union, one and inseparable, now and forever."

Also significant is the fact that Old Abe's fame grew after the war. Adopted and supported by the State of Wisconsin, he traveled back and forth across the country, borne now by members of veterans' organizations. Like the so-called "bloody shirt" and a generation of ex-soldiers with missing limbs and eyes, Old Abe reminded all who saw him of what the North had fought for in 1861–1865, and who the enemies of the Union had been. He became Wisconsin's ambassador at national celebrations such as the Centennial Exposition in Philadelphia (1876); he was an extraordinarily successful fund raiser for health-care facilities as well as for the preservation of historic buildings and landmarks; he was a fixture at parades, conventions, and political rallies. Talented artists (and some manifestly untalented ones) painted his likeness. Photographers discovered him early in the war; it took sculptors a bit longer to begin immortalizing him. Even in death, Old Abe continued his storied existence, thanks to the taxidermist's art. And of all Wisconsin's heroes of the Civil War—Edward Bragg, doughty commander of the Iron Brigade; Joseph Bailey of Red River fame; Frank Haskell, chronicler of Gettysburg; Lucius Fairchild, the one-armed governor—Old Abe remains the best known, the most fondly remembered, even a century afterward. It brings a smile to the historian's face to say it, but, as a historical figure, Old Abe has impressive credentials.

He is significant, however, mainly in the context of human affairs. The story of Old Abe the War Eagle is properly the story of the men among whom he lived: the farmers, loggers, clerks, and immigrants who flocked to the colors in 1861. Therefore, this work focuses on the Eighth Regiment of Wisconsin Volunteer Infantry, a body of about one thousand officers and men embedded in the vastly larger mechanism of the Union Army in the Western Theater of Operations. These citizens-turned-soldier—most of them young, not all of them brave—experienced much the same things that members of other Union regiments did: boredom, fatigue, endless marching and countermarching, the agonies of disease and sickness, the sudden terror and exhilaration of combat. What differentiated the Eighth Wisconsin from all the other regiments was their eagle, and their eagle helps make their story worth telling. A century ago, Old Abe's notoriety called attention to their accomplishments as soldiers. Today, Old Abe's lasting fame provides a window through which to view the fiery drama and tragedy of the Civil War and its aftermath.

MANY people helped me complete this book. By its generous and unhesitating encouragement, the Wisconsin Department of Veterans Affairs ensured that the state's most famous Civil War veteran would be remembered as we approach the 125th anniversary of the sectional conflict. I particularly want to thank Executive Secretary John Maurer, as well as his predecessors in that office, John Ellery and John Moses. Other helpful members of the WDVA included Cliff Wills, Robert Shaver, Harvey Stower, Sue Crouch, and Karen Emery.

My colleagues at the G.A.R. Memorial Hall Museum also deserve recognition. Alan Friedlander, Jeff Schultz, Wayne Sayles, and Mark Lopp all helped. Lynnette Wolfe merits special mention, for through all the revisions and corrections she provided a sure and loyal hand. Materials relating to Old Abe and to the post-1865 rise of the veterans' movement are well represented in the museum's holdings and constitute a significant body of primary source materials that, until recently, have gone unused.

Other individuals contributed to this history of Old Abe. Dr. Paul and Charlotte Allen of Markesan preserved an important collection of Civil War and G.A.R. manuscripts. The descendants of Dan and Margaret McCann shared information about their family through Mrs. Dorothy Fischer of Holcombe. Mrs. Margaret Burdick of Milton provided diaries of Hosea Rood, her grandfather. Dave McLain of Middleton related data about the Eighth Wisconsin's most famous eagle-bearer. Alberta Rommelmeyer of the Chippewa Valley Museum assisted in my research. Gordon Cotton, Director of the Old Court House Museum, Eva W. Davis Memorial, at Vicksburg, Mississippi, extended genuine hospitality to the author when he visited the battlefield. The curators of the manuscript, archival, and library collections of the State Historical Society of Wisconsin provided a wealth of information. Paul Hass, the Society's senior editor, assisted with the shaping and revision of the manuscript.

Finally, and perhaps most importantly, I want to acknowledge the support and devotion of my wife Elizabeth, without whose help and good cheer this book might never have appeared.

R. H. Z.

Madison, Wisconsin

1

Old Abe and the Coming of the War

THE bird that became Old Abe spent the earliest months of his life at the log home of Dan and Margaret McCann, on the northwestern side of the Chippewa River, across from the tiny community of Jim Falls.[1] The McCanns obtained the eaglet in 1861 when Mrs. McCann exchanged a bushel of corn with a group of the Flambeau band of Chippewa Indians. O-ge-ma-we-ge-zhig (Charley or Chief Sky), the Indian leader, had shot Old Abe's mother and captured a pair of helpless eaglets after cutting down the tall white pine containing the eagles' nest. The other bird died.[2]

The exact location of Old Abe's nest remains a mystery. Chief Sky, however, identified the area for Reverend J. O. Barrett when the latter prepared the bird's first biography in 1865. Barrett noted the location on a map as being "in or near Town 40 North, Range 1 East, four miles from the [1865] eastern boundary of Chippewa County," at the headwaters of the Flambeau River. Old Abe's birthplace is not far from the community of Park Falls, in the area where Price, Iron, and Ashland Counties join. Indians often traveled through the region, as the Flambeau River afforded a navigable route uniting Lake Superior and Eau Claire via the Montreal and Chippewa Rivers.[3]

The McCanns treated the eaglet as a pet. Mrs. McCann tied a blue ribbon around its neck and the family set up a barrel to serve as its bird cage. The McCanns clipped the young eagle's wings and tied his foot to prevent escape. Feeding the healthy young bird became quite a chore. Two of the McCann children spent considerable time providing the carnivorous eaglet with rabbits, mice, and partridges.[4]

As the bird matured, so his strength and abilities increased. "Beak and talons came more into use," remembered a local citizen, and the eaglet grew "fat and saucy."[5] Once he escaped and re-

mained at large for four days. The large blue ribbon around his neck, the fact that his flight was not up to eagle standards, and his familiarity with humans linked him with the McCanns. After his escape, heavier cord replaced the fishing line which tied the bird to its barrel home. The eagle had become a problem. It was not that the McCanns lost affection for him, for they had not, but taking care of a growing eagle with an increasingly adolescent disposition was more of a responsibility than they desired.

The eagle, on the other hand, liked most aspects of family life. Dan McCann was physically handicapped, and often had time to make music. The bird liked to listen to him play the fiddle, hopping up and down and fluttering his wings when the fast part of "Bonaparte's Retreat" filled the air.[6]

The Civil War began in the spring of 1861, and

WHi(W6)11591

Ah-ga-mah-we-ge-zhig (Chief Sky) of the Lac du Flambeau band of Chippewa Indians, captor of Old Abe in early 1861.

1

not long after, President Abraham Lincoln called upon the governors of northern states to raise troops. Wisconsin's Governor Alexander Randall, who had foreseen that the nation's sectional problems would develop from crisis into war, had strengthened the state's militia system to supply troops to the national army. Mobilization in 1861 took the form of voluntary enlistments into militia companies (some existing, some newly formed), which were based on cities, towns, and villages throughout Wisconsin.[7] Typically, volunteers formed a company of seventy to ninety men by attracting the manpower of a specific community or region, electing their officers, and selecting a name. Eventually, each militia group became incorporated into a body of ten companies, called a regiment. The regiment was the basic and best-remembered unit of the Civil War era. Each contained about 1,000 men at full strength. Because of local recruiting practices, most Wisconsin soldiers campaigned alongside their neighbors and friends during the Civil War. In this "war between the states," fighting men and politicians both North and South were very conscious of their states' identities.

When Dan McCann heard of a militia company forming in Chippewa Falls, he brought his eagle to town and tried to have the men adopt the young bird as a mascot. The Chippewa Falls company rejected McCann and his bird. Undismayed, McCann went to Eau Claire where another company was organizing. Captain John E. Perkins, a real estate broker, lawyer, insurance salesman, and politician, commanded the Eau Claire Badgers. Born in upstate New York, Perkins stood over six feet tall. With his gawky frame and bearded countenance, he resembled President Abraham Lincoln. At fifty, Perkins was the oldest man in his company. When Lieutenant James McGuire told Perkins that he wanted to buy Dan McCann's pet eagle as a company mascot, Captain Perkins approved.[8] Mills Jeffries, an Eau Claire tavern owner whose establishment was patronized by the Badgers, donated $2.50 for the purchase of the eagle.[9] Dan McCann's pet had a new home.

On September 7, 1861, the Eau Claire Badgers embarked on the steamer *Stella Whipple* for Madison, where they would join nine other companies and form a regiment. The trip began at the steamboat landing in Eau Claire and continued for two days. The men transferred from ship to railroad at

WHi(X3)14021
First known photograph of Old Abe, made in 1861.

La Crosse and then on to Wisconsin's capital city. Somewhere along the way, the Eau Claire Badgers became the Eau Claire Eagles, and Captain Perkins named the company's young feathered mascot Old Abe.[10]

Upon arriving in Madison, the Eau Claire Eagles marched into Camp Randall, the training facility that transformed most of Wisconsin's Civil War volunteers into soldiers.[11] To the tune of *Yankee Doodle* the company, joined by Governor Randall, marched through Camp Randall's gate. Old Abe, aroused by the music, the trip, and the attention of the citizens who lined the streets, grasped the end of the company's flag with his beak. Flapping and stretching his wings, he created a sensation. Madison's *State Journal* described the event as a "majestic sight" and a "favorable omen."[12]

Captain Perkins' men became Company C of the partially formed Eighth Regiment of Wisconsin Volunteer Infantry. The Seventh Wisconsin had nearly completed its course of instruction and would soon join the Army of Potomac, where it gained immortality as part of the Iron Brigade. The Eighth Wisconsin completed its muster on

September 17, five days after the Seventh Wisconsin departed, and began intensive training at Camp Randall.

Old Abe received a new perch to replace the beribboned one donated by the Ladies of Eau Claire. The regimental quartermaster, Francis L. Billings, a thirty-year-old Oshkosh merchant, constructed a shield-shaped wooden plate above which rested a crosspiece for Old Abe to roost on. Billings had the shield painted with the stars and stripes, placed three wooden arrows along each side of the roost, and attached the device to a five-foot pole. At the base of the shield was inscribed "8th Reg. W.V."[13]

2

Meet the Eighth Wisconsin

OLD Abe's regiment began its official career on September 4, 1861, when Captain William B. Britton, a thirty-two-year-old New Jersey-born furniture manufacturer, led members of the Janesville Fire Zouaves into Camp Randall. They became Company G of the Eighth Wisconsin Infantry. Two weeks later, Captain William P. Lyon, speaker of the Wisconsin Assembly and future chief justice of the state supreme court, completed the regiment's muster by joining his company from Racine with the nine others that had arrived earlier.[1]

The men of the Eighth came from all over. While recruitment and membership in specific companies was generally a local phenomenon, volunteers could, and often did, join whichever units had vacancies. Captain Perkins, for example, enlisted Sol Fuller and Dighton Smith, laborers from [Lake] Pepin, into the Eau Claire Badgers during a business trip he made to Prairie du Chien. William Naumer, thirty-three, joined the Sheboygan County Independents—overwhelmingly composed of men from the Town of Greenbush—even though he listed Syracuse, New York, as his residence. Naumer became Company B's, and the regiment's, first deserter.[2] There would be fifty-nine others.

Backgrounds, skills, and professions or trades varied among members of the regiment. Lumberjacks could be found in Company F, largely recruited in Grant, Crawford, and Vernon counties;

in Company A, raised in Waupaca, Portage, and Waushara counties; in Company I from the La Crosse area; and in Company C from the Eau Claire region.[3] Woodsmen Philip Gould, a twenty-year-old Prairie du Chien resident, and Edward Cronon, nineteen, of La Crosse, had both traveled extensively in the South, rafting down the Mississippi River while engaged in the lumber business.[4] (Neither would forget their next visit to the South, where Gould died of wounds and Cronon lost an arm.)

Mechanics, laborers, and carpenters existed in every company. Company B boasted a tailor. Several blacksmiths served in the Eighth Wisconsin. The regiment had two watchmakers, Edward C. Dwight, twenty, of Company F and Owen White, forty-seven, of Company K. Dwight contracted a disease and received a discharge in 1863. White died of typhoid.[5]

John M. Williams, seventeen, of Belleville; Thurlow W. Lacy, sixteen, of Prairie du Chien; Augustus Weissert, seventeen, of Racine; George W. Driggs, twenty-five, of Fond du Lac; and T. B.

This portrait of Old Abe was made when the bird was less than a year old.

GAR Memorial Hall

William B. Britton, last commander of the Eighth Wisconsin. A resident of Janesville, he was wounded at the Battle of Nashville in 1864.

Chippewa Valley Museum, Eau Claire

William P. Lyon of Racine was Speaker of the State Assembly in 1860 and became Chief Justice of the Wisconsin Supreme Court after the war.

GAR Memorial Hall

John E. Perkins of Eau Claire gave Old Abe his name and was the first officer in the Eighth Wisconsin to be killed in action.

Coon, twenty-one, of Eau Claire all had been printers before volunteering. Two later published books about their experiences in the war, as did the newspaper editor who led Company F, a clerk in Company C, a Walworth County youngster who transferred to another regiment in 1863, an unidentified staff officer, and Chief Justice Lyon. Hometown newspapers had steady correspondence from men in the ranks of the Eighth Wisconsin during 1861–1865.[6]

Private Phil Currie, a twenty-one-year-old Dane County resident who joined the Rough and Ready Guards at Fitchburg, possessed special skills. Currie received credit for the repairing and handling of railroad engines damaged by Confederate cavalrymen near Tuscumbia, Alabama, in 1862. Like the vast majority of enlisted men and officers, however, Currie was a farmer.[7]

Ethnic and nationality differences also existed within the regiment. Men from Norway and Germany could be found in all companies, and in significant numbers. Company B contained a largely Yankee and Anglo-Saxon membership, even though it had been raised in Sheboygan County where numerous settlements of recently arrived German immigrants existed. Company I from La Crosse had many Irish and Norwegian volunteers as well as a smattering of French

Canadians, as did Companies C and F. On balance, the Eighth Wisconsin was dominated, though not overwhelmingly, by people of Yankee extraction who comprised the majority of the Wisconsin population.[8]

Governor Randall appointed the regimental commanders. Surprisingly, the governor selected men whose political backgrounds differed from his own Republicanism. Robert C. Murphy, a St. Croix Falls Democrat, for example, was named as Colonel of the Eighth Wisconsin. Murphy, an Ohio-born lawyer, had acquired military experience in the Mexican War. At thirty-four years of age, he had crossed the North American continent twice, had served on the Mexican Boundary Commission of 1850, and had been a U.S. consular agent in China. A short, thick-set man with dark eyes and a light complexion, Murphy earned a reputation for being a strict disciplinarian.[9]

George W. Robbins, a slender twenty-three-year-old farmer from the Town of Madison, became Lieutenant Colonel. Robbins was popular, competent, and New England-educated. He gained command of the regiment when Colonel Murphy was dismissed for "cowardly and disgraceful conduct" in December, 1862. Robbins fell wounded at Corinth, and experienced a horse-related accident at Vicksburg a year later which seriously affected his health. He resigned the service in 1863, physically broken, returning eventually to Massachusetts.[10]

John W. Jefferson, another Democrat, grew up in Virginia before settling in Madison. The twenty-six-year-old Jefferson had red hair, dark eyes, and a reputation for being a hearty eater. He engaged in business and politics in Wisconsin's capital city, where he became a member of the socially elite Governor's Guard militia unit. Governor Randall appointed him Major of the Eighth Wisconsin. He rose to command the regiment upon Robbins' departure. Wounded at Corinth, and again at Vicksburg, Jefferson left the military when his three-year term expired in 1864. He went into the cotton business in Memphis, became a Republican, and made a fortune.[11]

Three chaplains attended to the spiritual needs of the Eighth Wisconsin during their four years of southern travel. William McKinley, twenty-seven, of St. Croix Falls was the first. He lasted one year, resigning just after the battle of Corinth. John Hobart, a tall, gray-eyed minister of fifty-three from Darien in Walworth County, replaced McKinley and served until the end of the war.[12] A Methodist minister, James T. Temby of Batavia, joined the ranks of Company F as a private. The thirty-seven-year-old Temby, who was only 5'3"tall, carried a musket during the daytime and "held singing and prayer meetings at night in his tent."[13] He received a discharge in less than a year.[14]

Old Abe remained with Company C. Four members of the company served as his bearers during the war. James McGinnis, nineteen, a farmer from the Town of Burnside in Eau Claire County, carried the eagle until May, 1862. McGinnis died of disease at Iuka, Mississippi. Thomas J. Hill, twenty, of Eau Claire, became Abe's next bearer. Hill's abilities with wagons, however, destined him for duties with the Quarter Master's Department in August of 1862. David McLain, twenty-four, a 5'7", sandy-haired carpenter and farmer from Gilmantown, Buffalo County, became Old Abe's best-remembered bearer. McLain carried the eagle during the fiercely contested two-day battle of Corinth in October, 1862. McLain resigned his position in November of that year, and twenty-three-year-old Vermont-born Edwin Homaston, an Eau Claire blacksmith, became Old Abe's closest human associate. Homaston carried the eagle through the Vicksburg campaign, until he was assigned to duty as the regimental blacksmith in September, 1863. Jacob Burkhardt, a

GAR Memorial Hall

George W. Robbins rose to command of the Eighth Wisconsin in 1862. He was wounded at Corinth and injured during the Vicksburg campaign.

GAR Memorial Hall

John W. Jefferson of Madison, a major in 1861 who rose to command of the Eighth Wisconsin in 1863. He survived wounds at Corinth and Vicksburg and remained in Tennessee after the war.

GAR Memorial Hall

Surgeon Joseph E. Murta of Racine labored valiantly but often unsuccessfully against disease, sickness, and the effects of modern weaponry.

Area Research Center, UW-La Crosse

David Cronon of La Crosse, a member of Company I of the Eighth Wisconsin. His brother Edward is pictured on page 42.

GAR Memorial Hall

Augustus Weissert of Racine, shown here in the state-issue gray uniform of 1861, was just eighteen when he joined Company K.

US Army Military History Institute

John Phillips of Company K. He was promoted to sergeant in 1864 and, like Augie Weissert, was wounded at the Battle of Nashville.

thirty-three-year-old German immigrant from Eau Claire, bore Old Abe from Homaston's resignation until August, 1864. John F. Hill, Thomas' sixteen-year-old brother, who had been wounded at Corinth, carried Old Abe back to Madison, and muster-out, in September of 1864.[15] The position of "eagle-bearer" was not an official one in the Army hierarchy, but it was considered a rank of honor in the Eighth Wisconsin.

3

The Making of Soldiers

STATE officials distributed uniforms to the volunteers as they arrived at Camp Randall. The State of Wisconsin's standard enlisted man's issue was a non-colorfast gray uniform of dubious quality. James H. Greene, a twenty-eight-year-old newspaper editor from Prairie du Chien and captain of Company F, wrote to his wife after arriving at Camp Randall: "You should see us in our new uniforms. . . . The uniforms are made of gray cloth, which is not regulation. Blue is the color which we should have, but the State furnishes us our uniforms and it has no blue cloth so it made

them of gray."[1] Officers supplied their own uniforms as well as accessories. Lieutenant Jeremiah Baker of Company A, formerly the Waupaca Union Rifles, spent $150 on his hand-tailored wardrobe, with accouterments. Since officers' pay started at a rate nearly ten times that of the $13 a month received by privates, the expense of providing for themselves could not have been unduly burdensome. In fact, most officers had two uniforms, one blue and one gray.

During 1861, the differences which existed between the uniforms of one unit and another were accepted as normal. Throughout the North (and the South as well), state uniforms varied widely in regards to color, cut, quality, and utility. It was not uncommon for companies within the same regiment to have different uniforms and even different equipment. The Eighth Wisconsin, for example, went off to war with the men clad in gray and the officers in both blue and gray. Not until January, 1862, did the blue uniform appear in the ranks of the enlisted men of the Eighth, and then it arrived only in stages. First came the hat. Private Edward C. Dwight, the watchmaker from Prairie du Chien, noted in his diary, "We all received new blue caps which puts quite a different appearance to the reg't." Two weeks after the hats, John M.

Williams, an eighteen-year-old private in Company H, noted that while stationed in Cairo, Illinois, the men drew blue uniforms. Unfortunately, they were of such poor quality that they soon disintegrated in the rain and weather. Several days later, a new shipment of blue uniforms arrived. In early February, blue jackets became available.[5]

Throughout the war, there continued to exist a variety of uniforms among the members of the Eighth. Trim-looking shell jackets of the cavalry and artillery were popular articles of clothing—although they were non-regulation for infantrymen. Lined sack coats became common, but they never completely replaced frock coats. The stiff, uncomfortable black Hardee hat competed with the French-style kepi, or forage cap, as late as 1864.[6] As much from choice or individual whim as from anything else, American soldiers of the Civil War era seemed to wear whatever they preferred or whatever was available within a range of generally acceptable articles of clothing.

Government-issue shoes were popular. In fact they were so comfortable that Corporal James E. Brown of Milwaukee marched in his pair without wearing stockings, thereby cutting down on laundry work. Robert Burdette of the Forty-Seventh Illinois, who served throughout the war alongside

the Eighth Wisconsin, extolled army shoes: "The shoes were not dancing pumps. But of all the things that ever went on a man's pedals, the old army shoe was the easiest, most comfortable and comforting thing that ever caressed a tired foot. . . . Affection could not make that shoe beautiful. But prejudice could not make it uncomfortable."[8]

Shortly after arriving in Camp Randall, the men received muskets. As with clothing, the State of Wisconsin provided a variety of weapons to the early volunteer regiments. The Eighth received Harper's Ferry Model 1822 muskets of .69 caliber. These weapons had been converted from flintlock to percussion locks at the Springfield Arsenal, and mounted clasp bayonets. The weapons had smooth bores and no rear sights. They threw a large ball, but were not accurate.[9]

While in Madison, the volunteers fired blank cartridges to familiarize themselves with their arms, "over the hill west of the University. . . on the lake shore." In the style of the times, firing occurred by company, files, and battalion.[10] Oddly, the men were not instructed in marksmanship, but instead were given firearms training which would accustom them to firing in unison, on order, and in formation.

Area Research Center, UW-La Crosse

James Mellor of La Crosse was mortally wounded at the Battle of Nashville in December, 1864.

GAR Memorial Hall

David McLain of Gilmantown, pictured in 1861. McLain was Old Abe's eagle-bearer at the Battle of Corinth in October, 1862.

Milwaukee Public Museum

Emerson H. Webster of Company B. He was promoted to lieutenant in mid-1862 but resigned the service not long afterward.

More difficult than firing, the men needed practice in the rapid reloading of their arms. Muzzle-loading weapons were slow to charge, especially under battlefield conditions when one might be advancing, retiring, or carrying out a maneuver under fire. Reloading the cumbersome musket was taught in a drill-like fashion. First the hammer would be drawn to half-cock for safety. Next a paper cartridge containing powder and ball would be bitten off by the soldier. The gun powder would be poured into the barrel followed by the projectile, the paper wrapper being discarded. After that the charge would be sealed in the firing chamber by compressing the wad with a ramrod attached to each musket. Finally, the percussion cap—which ignited the charge—would be fitted to the hollow nipple of the lock. The weapon could now be fired after drawing the hammer to full-cock.

Another difficulty encountered with Civil War longarms was the fact that the muzzle-loading weapon measuring fifty-six inches was most easily loaded when the user stood up—and thus was liable to be in plain view. Eventually, soldiers learned to accomplish the feat of quick reloading—even while lying on their backs. Three shots a minute became the standard rate of fire for veteran Civil War infantrymen.

The question of marksmanship is difficult to assess, even a century afterward. The Harper's Ferry muskets had never been intended for precision work, because military experts believed that sheer weight of fire, rather than accuracy, would be crucial in determining the outcome of infantry combat. Members of the Eighth Wisconsin came overwhelmingly from rural backgrounds. They were familiar with firearms, but not with sightless weapons of large caliber. In March of 1862, for example, a group of Eighth Wisconsin men demonstrated their inability to hit an easy target at very close range. Edward Dwight, the watchmaker in Co. F noted: "Today several soldiers were out on the levee, shooting at a duck, which boldly came within . . . pistol shot but although some fifty shots were fired none succeeded. . . ."[11]

In November of 1862, the Eighth received new arms. These included the .58-caliber U.S. Springfield Model 1861 and the English-made .577-caliber Enfield rifle-musket. The weapons fired interchangeable ammunition and had adjustable rear sights. Both delivered reasonably precise fire at 500 yards, and at 250 yards were deadly accurate. The Enfield proved itself to be an exceptionally fine rifle, and members of the Eighth sniped at

Union regiment (these are Michigan men) drawn up in line of battle for the cameraman. Such rigid linear formations produced tremendous firepower, but were vulnerable to enemy artillery and musketry.

Union army corps formed in combat array at Blue Springs, Tennessee, c. 1863. Note the arrangement of skirmishers in front, dense line of battle behind, and artillery pieces on the flank. The flags (barely visible at center and right-center) served as guides and rallying-points.

US Army Military History Institute

Confederates from ranges of three-quarters of a mile during the siege of Vicksburg in 1863. So great became the reputation of the Enfield that many of the men obtained captured Confederate Enfields after Vicksburg surrendered, and traded in their Springfields.[12] By 1864, Enfields became a three-to-one favorite among soldiers of the Eighth Wisconsin.[13] In spite of the great improvements in weaponry, however, it still took over 900 pounds of lead to drop each soldier hit by either army during 1861–1865.

Training at Camp Randall involved more than obtaining uniforms and muskets. Civil War infantry tactics had evolved from European practice, and demanded that great attention be paid to drilling. Because the infantry officer was expected to be able to maneuver his men in precise linear formations without cover and under fire, it became imperative that the soldiers be able not only to follow orders, but also to be familiar with the various formations. Moving from a column of four abreast, so useful while marching along a road or in covering ground quickly, to the horizontal line of battle—which typified the combat formation of the 1860's—was difficult, time-consuming, and continually practiced. The transformation of ordinary citizens into polished veterans took time and experience. Both officers and enlisted men were to gain their military skills at the sharp end, on the battlefield, after leaving Camp Randall.

The Eighth Wisconsin spent more time at Camp Randall than some regiments which used the state's major training facility during the crisis-filled years of 1861–1862. The Eighth was not fully mustered in until September 17—and stragglers from the Sugar River Rifles did not finally join their company until the following week. The men departed for war on October 12, which left not quite four weeks for regimental training.[14] Of course, several of the companies had practiced drilling as militia units before their arrival in Madison. The Sheboygan Independents (Company B) had been drilling since June. The Fox Lake Volunteer Rifles (Company D), the Rough and Ready Guards (Company E), the Janesville Fire Zouaves (Company G), the La Crosse County Rifles (Company I), and the Sugar River Rifles (Company H), had all spent time drilling and training. The Sugar River Rifles attracted local attention with their smartness and proficiency at a Fourth of July picnic near Belleville in 1861 which Governor Randall attended. This company also had the good fortune to have an officer with military experience—New-York-born First Lieutenant Lafayette

Munsell, forty, who had served in the Mexican War and had been wounded at the battle of Chapultepec in 1847.[15]

The men drilled three times a day at Camp Randall, and held dress parade each evening. Battalion drill commenced at 6 A.M., immediately after reveille and company roll call. It lasted one hour, after which the men ate breakfast and mounted the daily guard. Non-commissioned officers conducted squad drill until 9:30 A.M., when company drill began. By lunch time, the volunteers had drilled for five hours.[16] In the afternoon, enlisted men practiced "striking camp" by repeatedly taking down and putting up tents.[17] Officers trained at sword drill and at command drill. Guard duty was assigned before dinner. Dress parade occurred between 6 P.M. and sunset, immediately following the evening meal.[18] The regiment's twelve-piece band contributed to the liveliness and military pomp of the dress parade. Occasionally, Governor Randall or other Madison dignitaries would review the spectacle. Men had to be in their tented bunks by 9 P.M.[19]

Camp Randall's food appealed to some and repelled others. Captain Greene wrote his wife that "our grub is good, plain and wholesome—no luxuries—and well cooked. . . ."[20] On September 24, however, young John Williams of Company H noted, "some of the boys who were tired of rye coffee and mop soup made a raid on the cook house and nearly chopped both it and the dining hall to pieces."[21] Captain Lyon of Company K felt the same way, although he did not participate in the destructive mischief. Lyon wrote to his hometown newspaper that Camp Randall food was "poor," with its "stale bread, rancid butter, and lean tough beef." The training camp's coffee, Lyon continued, was "a villainous liquid," and the mess hall stank.[22]

After the volunteers' militant protest over camp food, men were obliged to cook their own meals. This worked well for only a short while. By the time the Eighth Wisconsin departed, they were thoroughly ready for a change.[23] What the men thought about Camp Randall food after several years of campaigning on army rations is not recorded.

Wisconsin's citizen-soldiers adapted readily to life at Camp Randall. "I like camp life so far," wrote Lieutenant Jeremiah Baker of Company A to his brother. "I have always had an itching to be in the military and now I am there . . . I can furnish a . . . greater amount of means to support my family, besides displaying my patriotism."[24] Visitors who were friends or relatives of the soldiers, noted Captain Greene, "are frequent here every day."[25] Formal religious services took place on Sunday, just as home, and many soldiers brought their own pocket testaments to the gatherings.[26] Refreshment stands sprouted around Camp Randall, as well as several "picture-taking establishments" and barber shops.[27] Once the ladies of Madison held a picnic for the regiment.[28]

Old Abe had become a part of the color guard of the Eighth Wisconsin, and his presence attracted numerous curiosity-seekers ranging from schoolchildren to Governor Randall. His place for the next three years remained to the left of the regiment's flags. Company C received the honor of being the color company, so Old Abe served at the very head of the regiment on parade or in line of march.[29]

At the end of September, orders arrived directing the Eighth Wisconsin to ready itself for departure for Missouri and the war. "Greatest joy prevails in the camp," Captain Greene wrote to his wife. "Men are cheering all around. . . ." Noting that morale was high, Greene explained that he had become "much attached to the regiment" and "would not be willing to go to another."[30]

How well prepared were the 973 men of Old Abe's regiment when they departed from Camp Randall? Probably they were as good as most citizen-soldiers of 1861. But Lieutenant Thomas Priestly of the Eleventh Wisconsin, which began to muster as the Eighth Wisconsin concluded its stay at Madison, disparagingly noted that he had not much respect for the regiment's proficiency: "The 8th now quartered here don't amount to much. . . they are so poorly drilled—and make so many mistakes. They do not understand the drill but little. . . . I am afraid that in case that regiment gets into an engagement they will be cleaned out."[31]

4

To the Front

OLD Abe and his regiment began their southward journey from Madison by rail on October 12, 1861. Governor Randall accompanied the Eighth as far as Chicago. The railroad journey was enlivened by a lengthy stop at Janesville, home of

To the front! Scenes such as this were common throughout the North during the early days of the Civil War. Here, an Ohio regiment sets off for war, led by the regimental band.

Captain Britton and most of Company G. The citizens of Janesville hosted a picnic lunch for the regiment.[1] In Chicago, the Eighth Wisconsin marched from the Northwestern Railway station to that of the Illinois Central. People gathered to see the regiment and Wisconsin's governor pass through the city. The presence of Old Abe naturally excited interest, and the local newspapers were filled with classical allusions concerning eagles. "The eagle," noted Private John Williams, was "more important than the [Eau Claire] Eagles" who bore Old Abe.[2] Captain Lyon wrote to the editor of the *Racine Advocate* dry-humoredly: "We had what newspapers call a brilliant reception in Chicago. It consisted mainly in being stared at by a large number of people, some few of whom cheered us as we marched through the city."[3]

Another day passed before reaching Alton on the Illinois side of the Mississippi River near St. Louis. After ferrying across the river, the Eighth Wisconsin regiment became the first Wisconsin unit to arrive in Missouri and to participate in the Western Theater during the Civil War. The overwhelming majority of Wisconsin's soldiers followed the Eighth, and served in the West.[4]

Secretary of War Simon Cameron, Adjutant General Lorenzo Thomas, and representatives of Missouri's pro-Union governing element met the regiment at St. Louis and gladly welcomed the Wisconsin troops to the troubled, sharply divided border state. Wisconsin's citizen-soldiers gave the dignitaries three cheers after a brief ceremony. Old Abe joined in by outstretching his wings approvingly. Colonel Murphy described the scene to Governor Randall: "The Eagle joined by flopping his wings most laboriously, a trick the bearer had taught him, but which never fails to elicit the greatest enthusiasm."[5]

The Eighth Wisconsin then paraded through St. Louis en route to Benton Barracks, about seven miles away. During this proceeding, the gray State of Wisconsin uniform caused more than a little confusion. Members of the city populace—generally pro-Union—at first mistook the Wisconsin soldiers for Confederates and began pelting them with rotten tomatoes and "hen fruit." As apprehension and fear mounted, the regimental quartermaster distributed heavy blue woolen overcoats to the men. The citizenry calmed down when the troops donned Union blue.[6]

The troops continued the march in 90° heat,

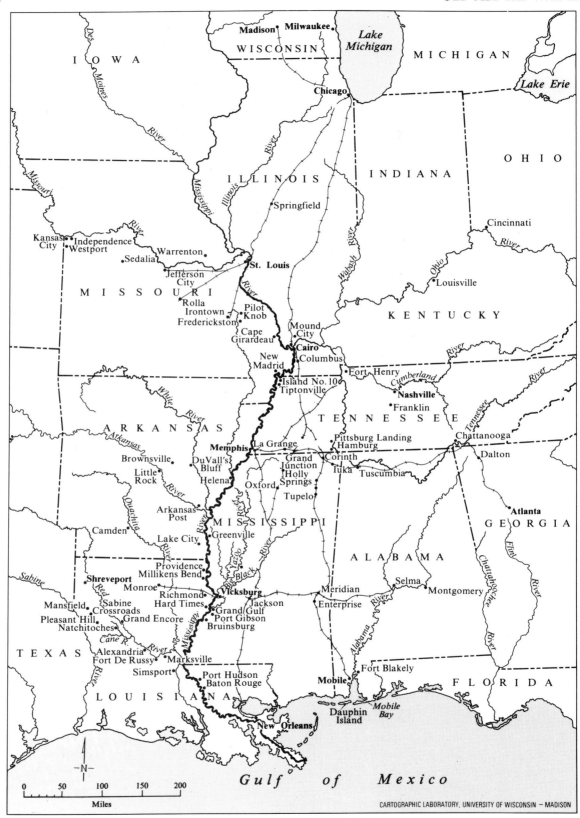

WESTERN THEATER OF OPERATIONS, 1861–1865

their gray uniforms covered by winter coats. Each man carried his musket, bayonet, cap box, haversack, canteen, knapsack—containing a wool blanket, rubber poncho, spare clothes, soap, razor, stationery, eating utensils with iron skillet, and sewing kit or "housewife"—as well as a leather cartridge box containing forty rounds of ammunition ("Forty Dead Men"). All fifty pounds of equipment hung from straps designed to support the soldier's accouterments.[7] Understandably, Private Williams remembered the march as being "exceedingly hard." Twenty sunstroke victims had to be rushed to nearby hospitals in horsedrawn ambulances.[8]

To make matters worse, Southern sympathizers taunted Old Abe and his regiment along their weary route through the city. Cries of "Wild goose!" and "Yankee crow!" pierced the air. The eagle became so excited that he managed to break free and fly off. Pandemonium then erupted. Several companies broke ranks to chase their feathered mascot "over house tops" and "through alleys and streets."[9] Colonel Murphy offered a $25 reward for the return of Old Abe. Some time later, a policeman helped recapture Old Abe when the eagle landed on a sidewalk.[10] All agreed that the Eighth Wisconsin caused a sensation in St. Louis.[11]

Immediately after arriving in St. Louis, the Eighth Wisconsin departed for "the front"—an ill-defined locale in Civil War Missouri. After a week of pursuing bridge-burning Confederate irregulars, Old Abe's regiment joined with four others and formed a brigade under Colonel William P. Carlin of the Thirty-Eighth Illinois Infantry. Carlin's brigade marched from Pilot Knob to Fredericktown, Missouri, twenty-two miles, traveling most of the night, in order to arrive on October 21.[12] At Fredericktown, they rendezvoused with another Union brigade and, much fatigued after their arduous march, stacked arms and quickly fell asleep on Fredericktown's dusty main street.[13] At noon, scouts discovered the Confederates lurking less than a mile away. Three hours later, the Union forces moved out to the assault.[14]

The men of the Eighth Wisconsin expressed great enthusiasm at the expectation of participating in their first battle. "There was never a happier set in the world," observed seventeen-year-old Augustus Weissert, describing the scene to a friend in Wisconsin. "We went along to the battlefield sing-

ing."[15] The excitement was detrimental to formation, discipline, and safety, however. As the Wisconsin boys attempted to form into line of battle, a sergeant in Company G accidentally discharged his musket. The ball struck Henry F. Illingworth of the Sugar River Rifles above the right knee, mortally wounding him.[16] Losing all semblance of order, the regiment stumbled forward and "within but a few rods of the battlefield . . . we were ordered to act as the reserve."[17]

Disappointed, the regiment moved back into Fredericktown. Others fought the indecisive battle. The Confederates escaped. Old Abe spent the day tied to the roof of the local courthouse. The rest of the regiment, according to Private Williams, "lounged around town."[18] The Eighth's baptism of fire was scarcely what the men had hoped for.

For about two months, the Eighth, and Carlin's brigade, marched around southeastern Missouri in search of Confederates. Intensive training and drilling took place during the short intervals spent in camps. Although never overtaking any of the

Old Abe on his shield, c. 1863–1864. The eagle's plumage is not yet mature; by the time he returned to the war from veteran furlough in July, 1864, his head had turned completely white.

Confederate irregulars who infested the region (they apparently represented much of the local populace), the regiment did manage to run into a measles epidemic. By December, when Colonel Carlin finally halted for winter at Camp Curtis near Sulphur Springs, over one hundred men in the Eighth Wisconsin had contracted the disease. Several died.[19] When that epidemic passed, mumps broke out, and then typhoid fever.[20] The Irish-born surgeon, James E. Murta of Racine, vaccinated the regiment against smallpox, but disease continued to deal Wisconsin's soldiers greater blows than all their battles.[21] Indeed, throughout the Civil War, disease caused more suffering, deaths, and discharges than enemy action, by a four-to-one margin.

5

The Valley of the Mississippi

IN mid-January, 1862, the Eighth Wisconsin Infantry moved to Cairo, Illinois. Strategically located at the confluence of the Mississippi and Ohio rivers (and further south than Richmond, Virginia), Cairo became a vital nerve center in the Western Theater of operations during the Civil War. From Cairo, Union forces moved to establish control over the nearby Tennessee and Cumberland rivers. At Cairo, the U.S. Navy based its gunboat fleet—the famous Mississippi River Squadron. Six miles away, at Mound City, an im-

portant ship-repair facility sprang up as well as a hospital. Cairo had railway connections linking it with Chicago, as well as the obviously favorable geographic relationship to the major navigable rivers of the Mississippi Valley.[1] Cairo could be likened to an arrow pointed deep into the mid-section of the Confederacy.

Federal domination of the inland waterways played a crucial part in the ultimate Northern victory—especially in the West. Rivers provided Union armies direct highways to the urban and trade centers of the South. Northern industrial superiority was used to great advantage against the Confederates through the construction of a large and modern river fleet. Possibly more important even than railways (for few lines ran north and south), river-borne traffic sustained the North's armies during most operations.[2] The importance of river transportation can be easily demonstrated in the case of Old Abe's regiment. Between 1861 and 1865, the Eighth Wisconsin Infantry traveled about 15,000 miles, campaigning in seven states. Of the total distance, 7,165 miles were by ship, while only 2,500 were by rail.[3]

When the Eighth reached Cairo, however, the troops did not immediately appreciate the city's strategic importance. Rather, its physical limitations seemed most striking. "I shall not try to describe. . . the appearance of this. . . city," Captain Greene wrote his wife. "It is mud, mud, mud. . . a fathomless sea of mud."[4] The Cairo barracks apparently left much to be desired. "Our

US Navy Audio Center

The Union's ability to construct and man large river fleets, such as these gunboats at Mound City, Illinois, in 1863, helped to ensure Federal domination of the nation's waterways. Many major operations depended upon waterborne transport.

City Class gunboat *St. Louis*, c. 1862: one of seven such vessels designed specifically for the Union navy by St. Louis engineer James B. Eads. Partially ironclad and heavily armed, City Class gunboats participated in all of the major river campaigns of the war.

barracks is a miserable concern," explained one soldier, "built of rough boards in a style of architecture which a respectable Wisconsin farmer would not tolerate in a common stable."[5] It should be noted, however, that the regiment itself looked shabby. The Wisconsin gray uniforms had deteriorated, and according to a newspaper correspondent, "the men presented rather a dismal appearance."[6] Even the relatively unknown Brigadier General who commanded at Cairo, Ulysses S. Grant, did not inspire confidence by his outward appearance. "He may. . . be better than he looks," wrote Captain Greene hopefully.[7]

For about two months the Eighth carried out duties in the Cairo area. Several companies were sent to guard Mound City. Confederate prisoners taken at Grant's successful attacks on Forts Henry and Donelson during the winter of 1861–1862 were escorted by other members of the regiment. The regiment chased Confederate partisans fruitlessly back into Missouri, and rebuilt the bridges whose destruction seemed to have been the irregulars' specialty.[8]

During the second week in March, General John Pope's 15,000-man Army of the Mississippi began operations to capture Island Number 10, Tennessee, and its supporting base, New Madrid, Missouri, an important Confederate stronghold located on one of the many bends in the Mississippi's channel.[9] Old Abe's regiment moved to General Pope's command where it joined a brigade commanded by Colonel John Loomis of the Twenty-Sixth Illinois Infantry. The brigade also contained the Forty-Seventh Illinois, the Eleventh Missouri, and the Second Iowa Battery. With the exception of the Twenty-sixth Illinois, which departed for another command in early 1863, the Eighth Wisconsin remained closely associated with these same regiments for the remainder of the war. Their brigade was designated the Second Brigade of the Fifth Division, under Brigadier General J. B. Plummer.[10]

The reduction of Island Number 10 involved a number of techniques which seemed new at that time, but which became standard practice as the war continued. The Confederate batteries commanded the northern approach along the river. A swamp protected Island Number 10 to the east. General Pope quickly occupied New Madrid after the Confederates withdrew from their vulnerable position on the accessible Missouri shore. But, in order to silence the artillery and open this section of the Mississippi to navigation, Pope had to move his troops across to the Tennessee shore by ship, and then attack the Confederates from the south. It was believed, however, that the Confederate guns on shore would destroy Union ships passing below Island Number 10.

Union gunboats and mortar ships bombarded the Confederate works to no avail for two weeks.

Union mortar vessel of the type that bombarded Confederate river defenses at Island Number 10 and Vicksburg.

Pope's men dug a canal through the low-lying peninsula north of Island Number 10 along the Missouri shore at New Madrid in hopes of getting gunboats and transports below the island without having to pass the Confederate guns. But the canal could not accommodate ironclad gunboats.[11] So, after three weeks of effort, the Union army manned rifle pits stretching for more than twenty miles along the river's edge, from opposite Island Number 10 to Point Pleasant, unable to come to grips with the enemy.

Captain Henry Walke of the Union ironclad *Carondelet* then daringly volunteered to run by the batteries on the night of April 3. Walke succeeded. Once past the entrenched guns of Island Number 10, the *Carondelet* silenced the less-protected Confederate artillery positions below the island. The gunboat *Pittsburgh* joined the *Carondelet* several days later, and together they covered the successful landing of General Pope's army on the Tennessee shore.

Under the guns of the *Carondelet* and the *Pittsburgh,* Old Abe's regiment crossed the Mississippi River from New Madrid at midnight on April 7. They helped capture Tiptonville, Tennessee, cutting the only route available to the Confederates for supplies or retreat. On April 8, 1862, several

thousand Confederates surrendered.[12] The running of river batteries, the dredging of canals, the amphibious nature of operations, and the importance of naval supremacy combined to distinguish Civil War military operations in the Mississippi River Valley.

While Pope's command occupied itself with Island Number 10, General Grant had been involved in a bloody and inconclusive encounter at nearby Pittsburg Landing on the Tennessee River. At the Battle of Shiloh (April 6–7, 1862), Grant's command had been surprised by 40,000 Confederates under Generals Albert Sidney Johnston and P. G. T. Beauregard, who had advanced undetected from their base at Corinth, Mississippi, twenty-two miles away. After two days of savage fighting the Confederates withdrew, leaving 10,000 of their comrades—including General Johnston—dead and wounded on the field. Grant's men had also suffered tremendous losses in what was the bloodiest battle in American history to that time, but they had recovered from their initial surprise and won a costly victory.

Major General Henry W. ("Old Brains") Halleck, the senior Union commander in the West, held Grant responsible for Shiloh's horrors. Halleck therefore assumed personal command at

Pittsburg Landing on April 11, placing Grant in a subordinate role. Federal reinforcements rushed to the scene, as Halleck prepared to follow the Confederates and crush Beauregard at Corinth. About 120,000 Union soldiers in three armies combined for the massive effort. Many of the generals who later became famous were present in Halleck's swollen force: William T. Sherman, Phil Sheridan, William S. Rosecrans, John A. Logan, George H. Thomas, John P. McClernand, Grant, and John Pope all played a role in the movement to Corinth.[13]

It had taken Johnston and Beauregard's men four days to march twenty-two miles for their strike on Grant at Shiloh.[14] Halleck took nearly four weeks to cover the same distance. His grand army moved cautiously, anxious to prevent another surprise attack. The Federal troops advanced as if undertaking a siege, bringing up heavy artillery and naval guns, constructing corduroyed roads and telegraph lines, and building continuous entrenchments.[15] As one Wisconsin enlisted man complained, Halleck was "advancing underground."[16]

As part of Plummer's Second Brigade, the Eighth Wisconsin became attached to Brigadier General Davis S. Stanley's division of General Pope's army, on the left of the Union force.[17] Stanley's division would participate in a series of actions in the vicinity of Corinth, over a six-month period, that, taken all together, decided the fate not only of this important rail junction, but of Memphis and West Tennessee as well.

6

The Eagle Regiment

MARCHING southward from Pittsburg Landing on April 24, 1862, Old Abe's regiment passed the Shiloh battlefield. For the first time, the Wisconsin men witnessed the effects of modern war's mass destruction. Rain had partially uncovered the bodies of thousands of men and animals killed in the battle. Broken guns, shattered carriages and caissons, abandoned weapons and accouterments, fragments of uniforms and personal effects littered the grim, desolate scene. The men of the Eighth Wisconsin marched southward in a somber and reflective mood.[1] Fourteen days later,

and twenty miles down the road, they got their first taste of combat.

A Confederate division struck Stanley's command in the rear as two of Pope's divisions engaged in a reconnaissance near Farmington, Mississippi, on May 9. Skirmishing began at 6 A.M., followed by artillery firing, and more skirmishing.[2] Acting under General Halleck's instructions not to bring on a full-scale engagement, Pope ordered a withdrawal. The 12,000 Federals had to utilize a single road over a creek through the swamps north of Farmington in order to rejoin the main Union force. The withdrawal took place in time-consuming stages, as inexperienced troops maneuvered from line of battle into a column by unit, and were subjected to enemy fire.[3]

Stanley's Second Brigade covered part of the Union withdrawal. During the Confederate artillery shelling, the brigade lay flat on the ground behind the brow of a small knoll, unseen and unharmed. At 4 P.M. the Confederate infantry made its first assault. "They came forward in line of battle, their flags fluttering over them and their bayonets glistening," wrote Captain Greene. "My heart was in my throat. . . ."[4]

The Twenty-Sixth and Forty-Seventh Illinois, with the Eighth Wisconsin, rose on command and fired. Five volleys from approximately 3,000 muskets, delivered at close range, checked the Confederates, who had just uttered "one of their unearthly yells."[5] The Eighth Wisconsin and Twenty-Sixth Illinois then advanced in sequence to the line of trees from which the enemy charge originated. As the Southerners fell back, Confederate field guns opened fire on the two Union regiments while a brigade of infantry "poured out of the timber on all sides, raking us with cross fire," remembered Captain Greene.[6] The Union troops retreated quickly back to their comrades, made a stand, volleyed with the rebels who followed them closely, and held their position for a while. Shortly thereafter, the Federal brigade began a withdrawal, during the course of which the Confederates out-flanked the regiment holding the Union right—the Eighth Wisconsin. With their unprotected right flank "in the air," the Wisconsinites absorbed heavy fire. In fact, Old Abe's regiment barely managed to escape.[7] The Eighth Wisconsin's first taste of battle was much like that described in Stephen Crane's *Red Badge of Courage*: complete confusion, alternating mindlessly between terror and exhilaration, with no apparent design.

Considering the exposed and vulnerable position they had occupied at Farmington, the Eighth's losses were only moderately heavy. Fourteen men suffered serious wounds. Nineteen others were superficially injured and quickly returned to duty. Five members of the regiment received mortal wounds. When the day ended, Captain Perkins, commander of the Eau Claire Eagles and the man who had named Old Abe, was among the dying.[8] The losses might well have been higher but for the fact that inexperienced troops on both sides tended to fire high and often ineffectively. Later in the war, combat became deadlier.[9]

During the battle, but before he was hit, Captain Perkins ordered eagle-bearer McGinnes to carry Old Abe to the rear of Company C for safety.[10] When the brigade took cover from the Confederate artillery, McGinnes was not exposed and did not lie down. The eagle, however, imitating the men, jumped off his perch to be close to the ground. McGinnes hoisted the tethered bird back on his perch, but again Old Abe took cover. After several more attempts the bearer gave up, and himself lay down. When the brigade rose, Old Abe leaped back onto his perch and flapped his wings. His seeming awareness of danger earned Old Abe a reputation for "sagacity."[11]

The eagle's reputation had been enhanced by his battlefield antics, as had that of his regiment and brigade. One of Pope's generals complimented the "regiment that bore the eagle," and the Eighth Wisconsin Infantry became known popularly as "the Eagle Regiment" from that day forward. The men of the Second Brigade, who had fought well and had as much to be proud of as their Wisconsin comrades, understandably adopted the unofficial name "Eagle Brigade."[12]

The Battle of Farmington had represented an attempt by the Confederates to entice the Union army into a battle before they reached Corinth and could bring their overwhelming numbers into play.[13] But General Halleck, ever cautious, declined to engage in full-scale battle, preferring instead to continue his ponderous, siege-like forward movement. It was not until May 28 that the armies clashed again. The Eighth Wisconsin once more found itself holding an exposed flank, but after a sharp forty-minute engagement in which two men were killed and five were wounded, the

Courtesy of Old Court House Museum, Vicksburg

Ulysses S. Grant, photographed in Vicksburg after the fall of that city in 1863.

Confederates withdrew.[14] That night, under cover of martial music, railroad whistles, and loud cheering, the out-numbered Confederates slipped away. Halleck entered Corinth, Mississippi, the next day without a fight. Memphis fell under Union control shortly thereafter.

President Lincoln soon ordered his massive army broken up and dispatched to other arenas, and "Old Brains" was recalled to Washington. If nothing else, Halleck had demonstrated that knowledge of military theory did not necessarily make a successful general. In the Western Theater, control of Mississippi and West Tennessee was given back to quite another type of general: Ulysses S. Grant.

7

The Battle of Corinth

THE Eagle Brigade went into summer quarters at Camp Clear Creek, near Corinth, after the Confederate withdrawal. Intensive training took place under the strict tutelage of Colonel Murphy of the Eighth Wisconsin. The entire brigade, about 3,500 effectives at this point, drilled as a unit for the first time. The troops spent twice as many weeks drilling in Mississippi as they had in Madison, and Camp Clear Creek was as important as Camp Randall in transforming the volunteers of the Eighth Wisconsin into soldiers.[1]

Confederate cavalry became active as September approached. Union infantrymen marched in pursuit, the Eagle Brigade, Colonel Murphy commanding, covering the sixty miles between Corinth and Tuscumbia, Alabama, in four days. Splitting up, regiments marched off to guard and reinforce various posts. The Eighth Wisconsin, the Fifth Minnesota, part of the Second Iowa battery, and a company of cavalry moved to Iuka, Mississippi, an important Federal supply depot about twenty-five miles east of Corinth. Finding the garrison abandoned and the telegraph cut, Murphy suspected trouble, and he soon found it. On the morning of September 13, 1862, he was attacked by some 2,000 mounted Confederates.[2]

Correctly believing that the cavalry force would be followed by enemy infantry, Murphy immediately ordered a retreat towards Farmington by way of Burnsville, Mississippi. The day went badly. Heavy skirmishing took place until late af-

ternoon, followed by a forced night march. Confederate horsemen struck repeatedly at the rear of Murphy's column. Thousands of slaves, seeking freedom and protection, fled along the same road, causing delays and wild confusion.[3] The scene was, nevertheless, a memorable one, and one Wisconsin soldier wrote:

> I wish I could describe the scene I witnessed, as we marched out . . . that moonlight evening. It will live forever in memory. . . . In the advance . . . the Army of the Union and of Freedom, with gleaming muskets, serried ranks, and steady tramp. In the rear came the army of contrabands, all ages, sexes, and shades of complexion. On foot and in wagons, mounted on horses, mules, and jackasses, loaded down with the sum total of their worldly goods; on through the moonlight came that strange procession . . . there was something strangely sublime in the spectacle of these thousands of human beings fleeing from bondage to freedom. . . .[4]

Fifteen members of the Eighth fell wounded during the retreat. Another twenty-four were captured when they failed to keep pace with Murphy's rapidly withdrawing force. Private Sam Miles of Company E lagged behind with swollen feet, and Confederate cavalrymen made him prisoner. The captives were paroled shortly thereafter, however,

"Contrabands"—meaning slaves making their way to freedom—followed the Union armies as they advanced into the South. Many black men formed Union regiments and fought against their former masters.

and Miles returned to the Eighth in February after being exchanged.[5] General Stanley censured Murphy for retreating and allowing the Federal supplies to fall into rebel hands.

The entire Eagle Brigade was then ordered back towards Iuka after reuniting at Farmington. Colonel Joseph A. Mower of the Eleventh Missouri led the force.[6] Born in Vermont, raised in Massachusetts, a Mexican War veteran, and an "Old Army" regular, Mower entered the Civil War as a captain of volunteers with Company A of the Eleventh Missouri Infantry, mostly composed of citizens from Illinois. Mower distinguished himself in every campaign, rising quickly to regimental, brigade, and then divisional command. He finished the war at the head of the XX Corps at thirty-six years of age. Bold and impetuous, Mower was described by Captain Britton of Janesville as "all fight from head to foot." Mower merited his nickname, "Fighting Joe."[7]

During two days of inconclusive skirmishing, during which he was wounded, Mower slowly fell back from Iuka until reuniting the Eagle Brigade with the 9,000-member Army of the Mississippi, now comanded by Major General William S. Rosecrans, on September 18.[8] The next day, Rosecrans advanced to Iuka and struck at the Confederates with one of his divisions. Losses on both sides were high, considering the limited number of troops actually involved in the fighting on September 19. "The musketry fire was not in volleys, but in one tremendous roll," recorded Private Williams of the Eighth Wisconsin.[9] The Eagle Brigade acted as the divisional reserve, except for the Eleventh Missouri, which suffered casualties during a bayonet charge they delivered when ammunition for their newly issued Enfield rifles ran out. Dusk ended the battle of Iuka. The Confederates slipped away that evening, leaving nearly 1,000 dead, wounded, and sick in Federal hands. The North lost 790 in killed and wounded, including three wounded from the Eighth Wisconsin.[10]

After Iuka, Confederate forces under Generals Sterling Price and Earl Van Dorn united near Ripley, Mississippi. On September 28, with their 24,000 well-armed, experienced troops, they prepared to drive the Federals from Corinth, recover West Tennessee, and, thereby, support the Confederate campaigns for Chattanooga and Kentucky.[11] Rosecrans, not knowing where or when Price and Van Dorn would attack, spread his

National Archives

Joseph A. Mower, pictured in 1865 when he was a corps commander. Previously, he commanded the Eagle Brigade.

forces out in an attempt to protect the railroad line to Memphis. When Price and Van Dorn finally appeared to be moving in the direction of Corinth, he ordered his troops to concentrate.[12]

Price and Van Dorn attacked Corinth on October 3, 1862. Striking from the northwest, instead of from the south where they had been expected, the Confederates managed to surprise General Rosecrans.[13] The Federal position consisted of three concentric lines of earthen defense works, each closer to Corinth with its rail juncture and precious supply depot, and each stronger. Price's men captured the outer works in a single coordinated assault. At the second defensive position, however, the Federals made a determined stand, pulling in reinforcements from outlying posts.[14] By mid-day, Rosecrans had assembled about 23,000 men. The Union center now bore the weight of the main Confederate thrust. At the juncture where two Union divisions were supposed to be connected, a gap existed. The gap drew the attention of a Confederate division as Price ordered his men to strike at the opening.[15]

The Eagle Brigade had marched to Corinth early that morning, covering the fifteen hot, dusty miles by 2 P.M. General Stanley directed Colonel Mower to close the gap in the Union center and stem the enemy tide. The Fifth Minnesota remained behind; the rest of the brigade advanced at the double quick to the critical area with fixed bayonets. Arriving at an open field, Mower's brigade exchanged a murderous fire with Confederate infantry, while aligning with the other Federal units.[16]

Mower's line of battle formed a shallow V or salient. The Twenty-Sixth and Forty-Seventh Illinois held the right of the brigade's three-quarters-mile front, the Eleventh Missouri and the Eighth Wisconsin the extreme left.[17] Two columns of Southern infantrymen attacked each end of Mower's line simultaneously, successfully outflanking the Eagle Brigade on both sides. The Forty-Seventh Illinois suffered heavy casualties as they attempted to bend back (or "refuse") their section of the line to prevent a deadly flanking fire or enfilade. The regimental commander was killed, as were several other officers and thirty enlisted men. A hundred other members of the Forty-Seventh Illinois fell wounded.[18]

At the same time, Lieutenant Colonel Robbins of the Eighth Wisconsin found his unit flanked on its left. Then Robbins fell wounded, and Major Jefferson assumed command. Jefferson ordered Company B to bend back its section of the line to the left.[19] Newly promoted Captain Albert E. Smith, a twenty-six-year-old farmer from Walworth County who had distinguishd himself at Farmington, began carrying out the Major's command. The Confederates, meanwhile, had just completed overrunning the brigade further to the right. They poured continuous fire into the disintegrating Forty-Seventh Illinois, whose fleeing survivors interfered with the bending back of the Eagle Regiment's left. Smith remembered the moment he was hit: ". . .We were subjected to a withering fire . . . men seemed to fall under this fire as snowflakes melt in an April sun . . . when I looked around, our lines were broken and in retreat. But few of our men were in sight. . . ."[20]

Major Jefferson ordered a retreat just as he was hit in the hand and shoulder. For about two minutes, the Confederates subjected the left of the Eagle Regiment to a murderous enfilade. Captain William J. Dawes of Company D remembered those "exceedingly destructive" moments before he fell: "Of 35 men which I took in, I lost 14 killed and wounded, and other companies lost in a like proportion. Our field officers were all wounded. . .

Mower had his horse killed the moment I fell, and his adjutant. . . was shot. . . . The same volley. . . cut the cord of Old Abe. . . ."[21]

Old Abe took off when the bullets severed his leash. Eagle-bearer David McLain chased after him as the bird went gliding down the Federal line, nine or ten feet off the ground. Confederate bullets saturated the air, knocking men down right and left, obliterating the Union formation. McLain's shirt and trousers were riddled, and Old Abe lost several tail and wing feathers.[22] McLain caught the eagle after running another fifty feet, just as the Eighth Wisconsin and the rest of the brigade dissolved under the devastating musketry. McLain picked up Old Abe, and—according to Captain Greene, who witnessed the scene—held the unprotesting eagle under his arm and ran, "as fast as he could run."[23]

Captain Nelson T. Spoor's Iowa artillerymen covered the Eagle Brigade as the men retreated in disorder towards Corinth. "Behind each tree we found men from different regiments of the brigade," recollected Captain Smith of Company B.[24] Captain Britton of Janesville finally reformed the surviving members of the Eighth Wisconsin on the outskirts of the city.[25] At dusk, General Van Dorn reported that his Confederate forces were "within 600 yards of Corinth, victorious so far."[26]

By midnight, Union troops had withdrawn behind their third and final defensive line. The Federal perimeter was well-engineered, with mutually supporting, detached earthen fort-like redoubts covering all the roads and rail lines entering Corinth. Each redoubt mounted three heavy guns, and an attack on any redoubt could be resisted by the combined fire of supporting forts.General Stanley placed three regiments of the Eagle Brigade left of Fort Williams, and his entire Ohio Brigade to the right of Fort Robinette, the two central redoubts. The Eleventh Missouri was in reserve immediately behind Fort Robinette, the Fifth Minnesota near General Rosecrans' headquarters on the northernmost street of Corinth.[28] October 4 dawned cloudless and extremely hot.

Van Dorn's attack that morning did not go according to plans. He hoped to carry the Union line by delivering a single assault along a 2½-mile front with 21,000 men in three divisions. Delays occurred on the Confederate left, and by the time Van Dorn's flanks were in motion, the center had become engaged prematurely.[27] The ensuing battle was characterized, however, by incredible displays of courage on the part of the Confederates.

The Union right was first assailed by Price's men. The Confederates, although subjected to a heavy fire, penetrated the Union line and came pouring into northern Corinth. Reduced in number by the enfilading fire of Federal heavy guns and rifle fire, the Confederates slowed to reform their lines near General Rosecrans' headquarters. Colonel Lucius Hubbard of the Fifth Minnesota found his reserve regiment of the Eagle Brigade in a perfect location, lying exactly across the Confederate right flank. "From the position it occupied, the right flank of the penetrating force of the enemy was presented in easy and unobstructed range of our guns," Hubbard explained, "and as it passed across the front of the regiment it was given a volley under deadly aim, that seemed to cut a swath through the Confederate mass."[30]

The Confederates retreated, and directed their next efforts at the Federal center. Massing in columns, charging down the Chewalla Road, and without firing, the Southerners advanced on Fort Robinette and Fort Williams, in the face of heavy and accurate crossfire from the supporting forts. After two assaults failed, a third was mounted by a joint force of Texans, Mississippians, and Arkansans under Colonel William P. Rogers of Texas. In the best tradition of the Rebel army, they came on howling, shoulder to shoulder, and actually carried the Union works at Fort Robinette.[31] A veteran of the Forty-Seventh Illinois stationed close enough to witness the assault later recounted: "The infantrymen sprang to their feet. Volley after volley of musketry helped the big guns tear the assaulting lines to pieces. But they kept on. . . . We saw the soldiers in gray swarming into the embrasures, fighting with the gunners who met them hand to hand. . . ."[32] "They swept over the ditch and into the fort like a human hurricane. . . many stands of Confederate colors appearing on the fort. . . perfect pandemonium," noted another Forty-Seventh Illinois veteran.[33]

"Corinth is ours!" shouted Colonel Rogers of the Second Texas as his men carried Fort Robinette. A bullet cut him down instantly. Then a supporting force of Union infantry rushed forward and met the Confederates at close quarters. After a short, brutal fight, the Rebels were thrown

Library of Congress

Brave Colonel Rogers of Texas lies dead at the ramparts of Fort Robinette following the Battle of Corinth, October 5, 1862.

back. By early afternoon the crisis was past and the battle over. The Confederates retreated in good order, leaving some 4,800 casualties, including prisoners. Union losses at the battle of Corinth totalled 2,520.[34]

Old Abe's regiment had not been an active participant during the events of October 4, although it had been positioned very close to where the drama at Fort Robinette climaxed. Several men were wounded. After the battle of Corinth the Eighth Wisconsin numbered 300 men present and fit for duty. The regiment had suffered 115 killed, wounded, or missing, a loss of 25 per cent.[35] The Eagle Brigade had likewise lost heavily at Corinth. Some 321 men killed or seriously wounded, including Colonel Mower, who had been shot in the neck, captured, and then escaped.[36]

Promotions, congratulations, and a bit of reflecting swept over the victorious army. All agreed that the Confederates had exhibited "matchless bravery . . . that would have honored a better cause."[37] Private Dwight, the watchmaker from Prairie du Chien, sent a piece of the dead Confederate Colonel Rogers' shirt home to his mother as a souvenir.[38] Private John Esterling, twenty, from the Town of Osceola in Sheboygan County, had been reported dead on October 3, but he turned up alive on the fifth. Although "shot through the body," Esterling made a complete recovery—only to be killed in action two years later.[39]

Among the troops, Old Abe's notoriety reached new heights. The eagle's "flight" of fifty feet on October 3 grew into the legend of Old Abe and his "aerial reconaissance" of Confederate lines, his delivery of messages, and his soaring over the regiment to encourage the men. Eagle-bearer McLain and other Eighth Wisconsin soldiers attempted to correct the sensational newspaper coverage of the events of October 3—where Company C had lost many men—but to no avail.[40]

One story which was accepted as being true involved the Confederate General Sterling Price. By October 4 the Eagle Brigade had faced Price's men on three battlefields and in numerous skirmishes. The close combat of the Civil War permitted enemies to get to know one another— often they exchanged fire at fifty yards or less— and it is likely that some Confederate units had caught sight of Old Abe on more than one occasion. McLain talked with a Confederate prisoner from Price's army at Corinth who claimed that

their General had offered to reward anyone who took Old Abe "dead or alive." McLain believed that the Confederate attack that out-flanked the lines of the Eighth Wisconsin on October 3 had Old Abe for its objective.[41]

Old Abe, meanwhile, had his wings severely cropped to prevent any chance of his flying away. His appearance changed dramatically, and not for the better. McLain resigned in protest. Ed Homaston of Eau Claire became Old Abe's next eagle-bearer on November 1.[42]

New recuits for the Eighth Wisconsin began arriving after Corinth. By November 1, the regimental roster listed 521 enlisted men and officers present and fit for duty. The men's weapons were replaced as well, and they now carried Enfield rifle-muskets instead of the old Harper's Ferry smoothbores.[43]

General Stanley praised the Eighth Wisconsin and complimented the entire Eagle Brigade for their performance at Corinth. He noted that he had always known that the "Eighth Wisconsin. . . could march a mule off his feet," and recent actions proved that "they could *fight* as well as march."[44] The regiment, with the rest of the brigade, moved off to Grand Junction, Tennessee, in November, covering fifty miles in two days.

General Grant reorganized his western armies in December of 1862, creating four Army Corps, each commanded by a major general.[45] These four corps—the XIII, XV, XVI, and XVII—became the Army of the Tennessee. The Eagle Brigade eventually became the Second Brigade (Mower's) of the Third Division (Brigadier General James D. Tuttle's) of the XV Army Corps under Major General William T. Sherman. In this last month of 1862, Grant opened his campaign against the Confederate citadel astride the Mississippi: Vicksburg.

8

Opening the Mississippi

THE Confederacy's strongest Mississippi River defense centered on Vicksburg, a small city situated along a range of irregular hills looming over the waterway some 400 river miles north of New Orleans. To the northeast of Vicksburg ran a continuation of the hills upon which the city was built, several large meandering branches of the Yazoo

River, and a wide stretch of swampy bayou country. It was an impressive position.

The Confederates had planted heavy guns along the Walnut Hills towards Haines's Bluff, ten miles northeastwards—thereby anchoring Vicksburg's right flank on the Yazoo. To the south, along the Mississippi's rugged banks, six miles of fortifications connected Vicksburg with Warrenton. Forty-five miles below Warrenton, at the mouth of the Big Black River, the fortified town of Grand Gulf secured Vicksburg's left. A hundred and ninety miles below Grand Gulf, near Baton Rouge, gun emplacements at Port Hudson defended the juncture of the Mississippi and Red rivers.[1]

The area between Port Hudson and Vicksburg was critically important to the South. Food, horses, and recruits from the Trans-Mississippi West, as well as portions of the Confederacy's foreign commerce, were transported up and down the Red River. Vicksburg was also an important rail and river junction; it connected the Southern Railroad from Meridian and Jackson, Mississippi, by ferry, with Richmond, Louisiana, and the Shreveport Railway. After the Federal capture of New Orleans, Island Number 10, Memphis, and Helena, Akansas, Vicksburg, with its contributing defenses, remained the only serious impediment to complete Federal control of the Mississippi River and the forcible division of the Southern Confederacy. It is easy to see why so much attention focused on Vicksburg, the key position in the southern Mississippi Valley.[2]

Vicksburg itself was a bastion. Confederate engineers had mounted heavy guns along the crest of the 200-foot bluffs. So well placed were Vicksburg's seven river batteries that in spite of a month-long bombardment by Union gunboats, mortar ships, and Admiral David G. Farragut's salt-water fleet from New Orleans, in July of 1862, not one Confederate cannon was silenced. Moreover, the artillerists occupying Vicksburg disabled two of Farragut's warships, the *Brooklyn* and *Octorora*. Vicksburg's gunners and the Confederate ironclad ram *Arkansas* seriously damaged several other Federal vessels, including the ironclad *Carondolet*.[3]

To the rear (east) of Vicksburg, along an eight-mile arc, ran continual fortifications. At the rail and all road junctures, the Confederates had constructed earthen forts, redoubts, lunettes, and re-

dans. These emplacements were connected with a line of rifle pits complete with ramparts and parapets. Outside the line, a ditch eight feet deep and fourteen feet wide, covered by abatis (sharpened stakes), completed the engineering aspects of Vicksburg's land defenses. One hundred and two cannon, not counting the water batteries, and three divisions of troops—between 30,000 and 32,000 men—eventually manned the defenses.[4]

In December of 1862, General Grant devised a plan to capture Vicksburg. He would advance southwestward from the Corinth area with a strong force, following the line of the Mississippi Central Railroad towards Jackson. After capturing the capital of Mississippi, he would assault Vicksburg from the rear. Holly Springs became the main supply base for Grant's first Vicksburg campaign.

While he moved inland, Grant ordered General Sherman to undertake a simultaneous amphibious operation against Vicksburg. Sherman and his men were to descend the Mississippi from Memphis, steam up the Yazoo, cross the swampy territory below Haines's Bluff using Chickasaw Bayou, and carry the Confederate defenses north of Vicksburg. The Southerners, Grant believed, would be unable to defend the city against this two-pronged attack.

Unfortunately for Grant, the Confederates had plans of their own. Grant's communication and supply line ran through miles of unsubdued Confederate territory. Southern cavalrymen made life uncomfortable for the increasingly large numbers of Federal troops needed to guard the rail lines. In December, General Nathan Bedford Forrest—one of the great Southern cavalry commanders of the war—led a three-week attack on Grant's depots and rear outposts in southwestern Tennessee. And, on December 20, 1862, General Earl Van Dorn captured the Holly Springs supply depot in a lightning raid coordinated with Forrest's movements.[5]

Colonel Murphy, detached from the Eighth Wisconsin, was in command of the garrison at Holly Springs, and it fell to him to surrender the town with its $4,000,000 worth of supplies without firing a shot in its defense. Van Dorn magnanimously paroled the Union guards as well as Colonel Murphy, burned the supplies, and departed. His daring move quickly sent Grant's troops into motion rearward. The Eagle Brigade, for example,

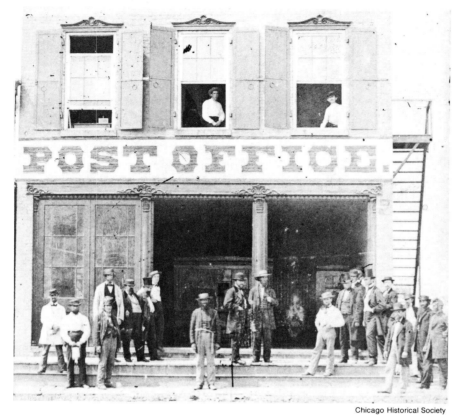

Chicago Historical Society

General Grant (center, hand in pocket) on the steps of the post office at
Cairo, Illinois, 1863. As in many photographs from the war years, it is
difficult to distinguish soldiers from civilians without close scrutiny.

marched back to Holly Springs from the vicinity of Oxford, forty miles away, arriving while the Federal supplies still burned.[6] The Eighth Wisconsin then left Holly Springs and marched all night to protect another important supply depot at La Grange, Tennessee, between Memphis and Corinth. (This rearward move of thirty-five miles took only sixteen hours!) The Eighth and the Eagle Brigade began establishing its reputation as a tough, tireless marching unit during the winter of 1862–1863, when thousands of Union infantrymen tried to keep pace with the destructive guerilla activities of mounted Confederates.[7]

Marching "in zig zag directions, day and night," the Eagle Brigade fruitlessly pursued Southern horsemen through northern Mississippi and southwestern Tennessee. To entertain themselves while on the move, regiments began sponsoring marching contests. The Ninety-Third Indiana, a new unit with a reputation for physical strength, challenged the regiments of the Eagle Brigade. Private McLain of the Eighth Wisconsin described the contest in a letter to his sister: "We ran them all day, and they got so tired towards night that we marched straight through their ranks and left them behind. . . ." On the next day, the men of Old Abe's regiment beat the Eleventh Missouri and established themselves as the champion marchers.[8] Time and again the Eagle Brigade demonstrated its ability to cover great distances quickly, and on foot.

Grant's "Central Mississippi Expedition" had gone up in smoke at Holly Springs. Sherman's move against Vicksburg failed as well. Unable to carry the Confederate positions south of Haines's Bluff, Sherman retreated after suffering heavy casualties. The Federal ironclad *Cairo* sank after hitting a torpedo along the Yazoo. The first Vicksburg campaign ended disastrously.[9]

As a final indignity, Grant cashiered Colonel Murphy, accusing the St. Croix Falls Democrat of "gross cowardice" if not outright disloyalty. Murphy hurriedly departed the war zone, a dejected man. He eventually moved to Philadelphia, where he died impoverished.[10]

9

The Vicksburg Campaign

ULYSSES S. Grant was not a man who gave up easily. Between February and April, 1863, he mounted four major operations against Vicksburg. He hoped to transport his men and supplies by ship through the malarial bayous, tortuous streams, and roundabout river network which characterized the Vicksburg environment. Union soldiers, therefore, dug canals, removed snags, built levees, improved roads, redirected watercourses, and carried out major dredging operations to improve navigation. All of their efforts failed.[1]

The Eagle Brigade received orders to move towards Memphis from Germantown, Tennessee, in March, 1863. Before the brigade could march, however, hundreds of men spent several hours chasing Old Abe, who had broken loose from his leash and tested his wings for the first time since the severe cropping at Corinth. Eventually, eagle-bearer Homaston coaxed Old Abe back to his perch. Reassured, the command marched rapidly to Memphis and shortly thereafter boarded the steamer *Empress*, heading south.[2] Second Lieutenant Charles Palmetier, a twenty-seven-year-old mechanic from Geneva in Walworth County promoted from sergeant in recognition of his bravery at Corinth, explained to his family, "There is lots of troops going to Vicksburg, and the prospects is a big fight or a big skedaddle."[3]

The *Empress* was packed with equipment, mules, wagons, ambulances, personnel, and the regimental mascot. Each regiment of the brigade rode its own steamboat. Accommodations, noted an officer in the Eighth, were the same as "all boats on our western waters—berths for a few, whiskey for all."[4] One hundred and eight miles below Memphis, the steamer docked at Helena, Arkansas, to take on fuel.

Helena had acquired an unenviable reputation as being a soldiers' graveyard. Disease and inactivity characterized duty at the river town. In the words of an Eighth Wisconsin officer, the town looked like "an old broken plate besmeared with molasses and liberally spotted with dead flies."[5] Here, men from Company A became involved in a spree of disorderliness that ended in bloodshed.

Because the Eagle Brigade had arrived on Sunday, the commander of the Helena garrison objected to the excessive noise generated by the men as they purchased goods from local sutlers. He sent a provost guard of Indiana soldiers with fixed bayonets to quiet the rowdy, half-drunken Wisconsin troops. A fusillade of coal and mud, slung by the Waupaca Union Rifles, met the Hoosiers, who retreated. Soon the Helena fortress trained its guns on the Eagle Regiment. Harsh words were exchanged, and a barrage of coal knocked down a provost officer. An Indiana soldier then discharged his rifle, the bullet striking a horse which fell on a member of Company A, injuring the man. Several Waupaca citizens ran after the soldier with the smoking gun and, according to Private Robert Rogers of La Crosse, "used knives on him."[6] More guards turned out. More coal filled the air. The Eighth Wisconsin was ordered put under arrest. Joe Mower, by now a Brigadier General, eventually arrived on the scene, and directed his men back to the ships. The steamers moved off ten miles downriver, to tiny Chuck-a-Luck Island opposite Yazoo Pass.

Chuck-a-Luck Island was so confined that no room existed to pitch tents. Driftwood provided fuel for the Eagle Brigade's campfires.[7] Two weeks passed before the brigade moved on. Clyde Bryner of the Forty-Seventh Illinois recalled: "The time spent at Chuck a Luck Island . . . was a dismal time, filled with forebodings and gloom. Crowded in narrow quarters between the Mississippi River and a black bayou were . . . wagons, cannons, mules, and men; the campaign against Vicksburg thus far a failure; small pox and measles raging; toads, lizards, and snakes infesting the soldiers quarters, everybody suffering from malaria."[8]

The Eagle Brigade participated in the last stages of the unsuccessful Lake Providence canal campaign, Grant's third attempt to take Vicksburg. After this failure, the brigade boarded steamers and traveled to Duckport, Louisiana, opposite the mouth of the Yazoo River, twelve miles above Vicksburg. During April, 1863, the Eagle Brigade carried out duties associated with the construction of yet another canal designed to enable Union ships to pass below Vicksburg without being subjected to plunging fire from the city's heavy guns.[9] Private Rogers noted, "We will have to give up soldiering and go to canaling. . . ."[10] Steam-powered dredges helped the men dig.[11]

Union troops docking at Cairo, Illinois. Cairo, with its rail and river connections and its location on the edge of the Confederate heartland, possessed great strategic value for the Union early in the war.

But the canal failed. Changes in the river's depth and silt flooded it before it could handle the deep-draft gunboats. Grant's 43,000-man army was thus left stranded along the west bank of the Mississippi, strung out for sixty miles between Young's Point and Lake Providence.[12] Grant had either to cross the Mississippi or admit failure.

On the night of April 16, Grant therefore risked the Mississippi gunboat fleet. He directed the ironclads *Benton*, *Lafayette*, *Louisville*, *Mound City*, *Pittsburgh*, *Carondolet*, *Tuscumbia*, and the ram *General Price* with three transports to run downstream past Vicksburg, and take up position below the city. Once below Vicksburg, Grant expected the gunboats to silence the enemy batteries at Grand Gulf. He could then ferry his army across the Mississippi, and transport supplies and troops up and along the Big Black River during the army's move against Vicksburg.[13]

Rear Admiral David D. Porter led the Mississippi Squadron through the Confederate barrage that eventful night. Enemy shells struck Porter's ships repeatedly, but only one Federal transport was sunk. All the gunboats arrived safely below Vicksburg. Several nights later, Grant sent six more wooden transport streamers to run the Vicksburg gauntlet. Confederate gunners sank one and damaged several others.[14] But, by the last week in April, Grant had—at last—the means to move his troops to an initial staging area south of Vicksburg, on the eastern bank of the river. Grant ordered two of his three corps to march for Hard Times Landing, opposite Grand Gulf, where the fleet would carry them across the Mississippi after eliminating the Confederate batteries.[15]

Grand Gulf's cannon, however, would not be silenced. Confederate artillerymen dueled with Porter's gunners all day on April 29, disabling the *Benton* and *Tuscumbia* and injuring the *Pittsburgh*. Grand Gulf remained Confederate.[16] So Grant ordered his already-loaded troop ships to land the men nine miles below Grand Gulf at Bruinsburg.[17] Distributing five days' rations to the men as they disembarked, Grant pushed the XIII and XVII Corps rapidly on towards Port Gibson, a garrisoned town straddling the network of bridges and roads to Grand Gulf, Vicksburg, and Jackson. Sherman's XV Corps and several ironclads made a feint against Haines's Bluff, to prevent the Vicksburg garrison from sending reinforcements to Port

Gibson. The gunboat *Choctaw* was damaged, but no reinforcements went to oppose Grant's landing, or to Port Gibson.[18]

Grant's men took Port Gibson on May 2 after a hard fight. Three days later, they took Grand Gulf.[19] Sherman's corps crossed the Mississippi on May 7 after marching down the western shore of the river, along seventy miles of difficult roads filled with supply wagons freighting goods from Millikens Bend to Hard Times Landing. Gunboats ferried the XV Corps across the river to Grand Gulf.[20]

Grant's forces were at last south of Vicksburg—and on the same side of the river. Confederate General John C. Pemberton held Vicksburg with about 30,000 troops. General Joseph Johnston at the head of approximately 25,000 Confederates was headed towards Vicksburg; his forward elements were already in Jackson. On the west side of the river, more Confederates would be able to threaten Grant's exposed supply route. Yet, as

Grant later said, ". . . I felt a degree of relief scarcely ever equalled since. Vicksburg was not yet taken . . . nor were its defenders demoralized. . . . I was now in the enemy's country, with a vast river and the stronghold of Vicksburg between me and my base of supplies. But I was on dry ground on the same side of the river with the enemy. All the campaigns, labors, hardships and exposures . . . previous to this time had been made and endured . . . for the accomplishment of this one object."[21]

Grant kept his three corps intensely busy for the next two weeks. With only five days' rations per man, Grant's troops had cut themselves off from all supplies—except ammunition—and would now subsist off the country for the first time in a major operation. It was said that General Grant carried only a toothbrush on the decisive campaign which followed.[22]

After the fall of Port Gibson and Grand Gulf, Grant swung his troops on an arc to the right, reaching eastward for Jackson, thirty miles dis-

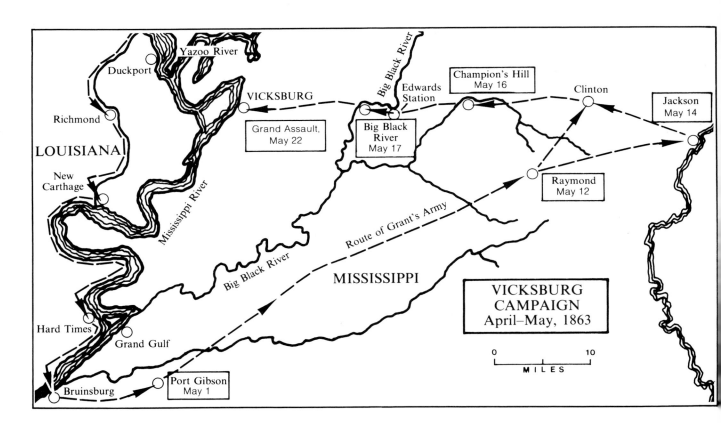

tant. General Joe Johnston's troops were fortifying Mississippi's capital city where they expected General Pemberton, with the Vicksburg garrison, to sally out and join them. United, Johnston and Pemberton would outnumber Grant's men. Grant, however, planned to keep himself between Johnston and Pemberton, and beat each of their individually smaller forces before they could concentrate. Jackson became Grant's first objective because Johnston's forces there numbered only 11,000 men.[23] Speed was essential.

After taking Grand Gulf, the Union troops marched to Fourteen Mile Creek. They drove the garrison off on May 12 and headed for Raymond, which fell on the thirteenth after a short engagement. Sherman and McPherson's corps pushed on towards Jackson immediately. Up to the capture of Raymond the weather had been dry, the roads choked with dust raised by masses of troops. Private Miles of Company E of the Eighth Wisconsin remembered the days as "hot with suffocating clouds of dust."[24] Then torrential rains turned the dust and the clayey soils into mud during the march towards Jackson.[25]

Sherman's and McPherson's men assaulted Jackson simultaneously and in overwhelming force on a rain-soaked May 14. General Sherman had spent the previous day riding alongside the Eagle Brigade, complimenting the regiments, taking off his hat to Old Abe.[26] The Eagle Brigade led Sherman's advance and participated in an assault on the half-completed Confederate trenches during the afternoon. As Sergeant Burnette Demarest of Eau Claire noted in his diary:

> This was a glad day for our troops . . . moving . . . cautiously and steadily through a heavy rain towards the city. . . . The shells bursting around us and the sharp crack of musketry mingled with the loud peals of thunder from the heavens rendered this a most grand scene. Sherman and Mower . . . order . . . charge bayonets double quick. The army is in motion our banners are unfurled . . . with a rush and yell . . . our Brigade went in . . . and captured the City of Jackson. . . . Our Brigade went charging right through the streets of the city . . . to the State Capitol. . . . We tore down the rebel flag from . . . the State House and placed our proud banner there where in triumph it floated. . . .[27]

Casualties in Sherman's XV Corps were light, and the Confederates quickly fell back. Sherman appointed Mower's brigade as provost guards to maintain order in the Mississippi capital while systematic destruction of Confederate arsenals, rail yards, and cotton factories proceeded on May 15. The Eagle Brigade could not, or would not, prevent the general anarchy and looting which soon erupted.[30] Jackson was put to the torch on the first of four occasions on May 16, as Sherman's men left the city and swung westward towards Vicksburg. Confederate cavalry immediately reoccupied the city, inflicting casualties on several members of the Forty-Seventh Illinois—killing its colonel—as they protected the rear of Sherman's departing corps.[31]

The day Sherman's XV Corps marched towards Vicksburg, the battle of Champion's Hill took place. Grant hurled a force against General Pemberton and 25,000 troops of the Vicksburg garrison who had taken a defensive position.[32] A costly engagement ensued. In six hours of fighting Grant's troops drove the Confederates from the field, capturing 3,000 and inflicting a like number of casualties upon Pemberton's men. The Confederates fell back to the Big Black River Bridge with Grant following hard on their heels.[33]

Grant's troops attacked at Big Black River Bridge on the morning of the seventeenth. The Confederates melted away, surrendering nearly 2,000 prisoners, but not before destroying the bridge. Grant ordered his engineers to construct three makeshift bridges, which they completed by the next morning. Sherman's corps laid a pontoon bridge across the Big Black River slightly north of Grant, and two divisions crossed that night.[34]

By afternoon on May 18, Grant's three corps united and moved towards Vicksburg, just behind the retreating Confederates. The Fourth Iowa Cavalry attacked Haines's Bluff, helpless from the rear, capturing it without difficulty, or casualties, the same day.[35] By evening, Sherman and Grant stood on the Walnut Hills overlooking the Chickasaw Bayou defenses where Sherman had met defeat in December of 1862. Haines's Bluff was soon transformed into a supply depot where Grant would be receiving tons of supplies and tens of thousands of reinforcements.[36]

On May 19 Grant's troops made localized attacks to improve their positions outside Vicksburg. Fighting occurred all day long. Two days later, Union troops completed a road to the Yazoo River landing at Haines's Bluff for their supplies.[37]

Grant now hoped to conclude his lightning campaign by storming Vicksburg without a pause. Unlike the independent advances of May 19, he planned a massive, coordinated Grand Assault using all available troops. Grant explained the situation to his three corps commanders and directed them to attack at 10 A.M. on May 22. Grant later recalled: "Johnston was in my rear, only fifty miles away, with an army not much inferior in numbers to the one I had with me, and I knew he was being reinforced. . . . The immediate capture of Vicks- burg would save sending me the reinforcements which we so much wanted elsewhere, and would set free the army under me to drive Johnston from the state. But the first consideration of all was— the troops believed they could carry the works in their front, and would not have worked so patiently in the trenches if they had not been allowed to try."[38]

General McClernand's XIII Corps occupied the Union left, south of Vicksburg. General McPherson's's XVII Corps held the center, and General

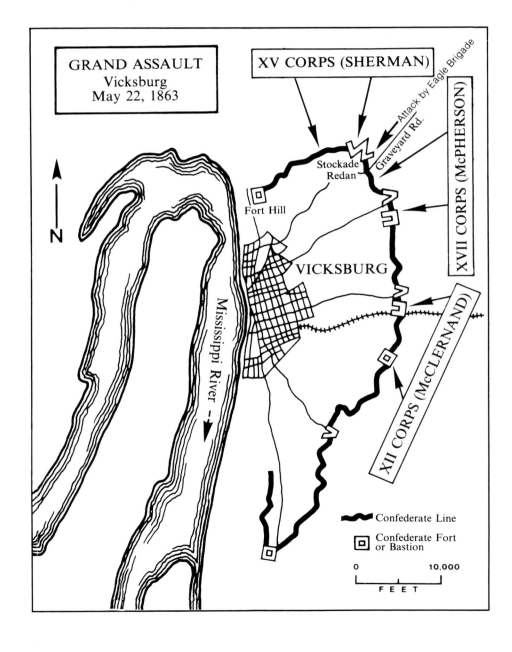

GRAND ASSAULT
Vicksburg
May 22, 1863

XV CORPS (SHERMAN)

Attack by Eagle Brigade

XVII CORPS (McPHERSON)

Graveyard Rd.

Stockade Redan

Fort Hill

VICKSBURG

XII CORPS (McCLERNAND)

Mississippi River →

Confederate Line

Confederate Fort or Bastion

0   10,000

F E E T

Sherman's men of the XV Corps held the right (to the north). After what Grant described as a "furious cannonade from every battery in position," the Federals attacked.[39] Sherman sent forward two divisions, Blair's and Steele's, holding the third, Tuttle's, in reserve. The Eagle Brigade acted as sharpshooters during the morning battle.[40] Blair's men charged along the Graveyard Road towards the Stockade Redan which dominated Fort Hill Road. Sherman reported: "The storming party reached the salient of the bastion . . . when rose from every part commanding it, a double rank of the enemy that poured on the head of the column a terrific fire. It halted, wavered, and sought cover. The rear pressed on, but the fire was so terrific that very soon all sought cover."[41]

It was Corinth in reverse. Now Union troops, like Van Dorn's and Price's gallant Confederates the previous October, tried to carry a well-manned fortified position by frontal assault. Like Van Dorn and Price, they were checked, "with terrible loss to the attacking parties."[42]

Despite this initial costly setback, at the request of General McClernand, who claimed to have breached a portion of the Vicksburg defenses, Grant ordered another attack in the afternoon. The second wave began advancing at 2 P.M.[43] Tuttle's division made the assault in Sherman's sector, General Mower leading off with the Eagle Brigade.[44] Because of the nature of the topography, Mower ordered the 2nd Brigade to advance by the flank, rather than in line of battle. This formation would subject the column to enfilading fire during their rush forward, and prevent them from firing back until they could reform into a line under the covering brow of the Stockade Redan bastion, a thousand yards distant.[45]

Under the blazing Mississippi sun, the Eagle Brigade, commanded by Colonel Lucius Hubbard of the Fifth Minnesota, with General Mower personally leading, moved down the Graveyard Road in a column of four abreast.[46] Each regiment was in file, the Eleventh Missouri closest to Vicksburg, and the first unit of the brigade to attack. Next came the Forty-Seventh Illinois, then Old Abe's Eighth Wisconsin, and lastly the Fifth Minnesota.[47]

At a point where the Graveyard Road met the moat-like ditch, the men were to turn right, enter the ravine, form line of battle and charge the Stockade Redan and its supporting works uphill across an open field of fire prepared in advance by Confederate engineers. Confederate artillery would be in range during the passage along the Graveyard Road, and musketry fire would commence at the point of entry to the ravine.

The assault of the Eagle Brigade lasted not more than a few minutes. Then it dissolved in bloody chaos. The ravine filled quickly with dead and wounded. Captain Britton related to the Janesville *Gazette*: "It can better be imagined than described how men were slaughtered as we entered the ravine; so many men were killed and wounded that the road was up so as to prevent some parts of the brigade from getting through."[49] Captain Greene of Prairie du Chien wrote his wife, "It was perfectly awful. We actually stepped on the dead and wounded in the sunken road, so thickly were they lying all around."[50]

The Eleventh Missouri and the Forty-Seventh Illinois were blasted to pieces, "literally melted down by the terrific fire," reported Col. Hubbard. The attack faltered, and losses grew.[51] Brave Colonel Mower led the charge of the Eleventh Missouri up the fire-swept open ground and to the cover of the sloping face of the Confederate redoubt. There the regiment planted its banners and remained under cover, dodging Confederate hand grenades, for the remainder of the day.

The Eleventh Missouri was the only complete regiment in Sherman's corps to attain the Confederate works during the second wave of the Grand Assault.[53] Several companies from the remainder of the Eagle Brigade successfully crossed the field, but heavy losses shattered organizational unity. The Eleventh Missouri and the Forty-Seventh Illinois experienced the highest losses in Sherman's corps, most of these occurring during the first minute.[54]

The Eighth Wisconsin dutifully climbed over the bodies clogging the sunken ravine, and left the ditch after taking a number of casualties. Converging fire from enemy artillery and musketry caused confusion. Major Jefferson fell wounded again. Captain Britton assumed command and led his own Janesville company upward across the open field, while Companies F and E followed.[55] The color company, with Old Abe and the regimental banners, simply could not advance in the face of the murderous fire. An accurately delivered charge of cannister struck Company C, breaking the ranks, scattering its formation, and preventing the balance of the regiment from going forward. As Lieutenant John Woodnorth of Company C explained many years later: "At once everthing was *chaos*. Everyone seemed to be seeking a place of safety. There was no one to give orders and if there had been it would have been useless, as it would have been impossible to keep men together under those circumstances as they had no chance to form their lines . . . we could not protect ourselves. . . . There was *no charge* as they could not *charge*. They simply stood and took the enemy's fire. . . ."[56]

Confederate shells bursting near the regimental colors knocked the flags down.[57] Color Sergeant Myron C. Briggs of Eau Claire, Corporal Ambrose T. Armitage of Oakfield, and Corporal L. B. Lathrop of Racine immediately picked them up again.[58] Shellfire splintered trees and pierced the regimental flags. Private Homiston of Eau Claire slipped and fell, carrying Old Abe to the ground with him. The eagle lunged forward, yanking Homaston, who clung to the staff, into a log where he was knocked unconscious for a moment. Confederate gunners and riflemen used the colors and eagle as their point of aim, and casualties mounted. The color guard soon lowered their banners and flattened themselves on the ground until the order to retire came.[59] Old Abe, Homiston, and the color guard, together with a "perfect jam of men," retreated into a ravine where they found adequate cover. One of the soldiers discovered a rabbit hiding in the same place, and captured it for Old Abe's dinner. As the hot afternoon wore on, Old Abe devoured his treat.[60]

After dark, those Union troops who had made it across the field to the Confederate works retreated. Colonel Mower and his men returned to the Union lines at 9 P.M. Sherman's corps experienced over 600 casualties in the Grand Assault of May 22, with Tuttle's division and Mower's brigade conspicuously represented in the grim total. The Eighth Wisconsin and the Fifth Minnesota suffered much fewer losses than the leading regiments in the brigade. The Eagle Regiment lost four killed and sixteen seriously wounded; the Fifth Minnesota lost only two men.[61] General Grant regretted the decision for this second attack for the rest of his life, and settled down to besiege Vicksburg.[62]

May, 1863, had been an eventful month. The Eagle Regiment, like many of Grant's troops, had marched four hundred miles, lived off the enemy's country with but five day's rations of hardtack crackers per man, and had not slept in a tent or changed clothes since crossing the Mississippi. In the fast-moving campaign on the east bank of the Mississippi they had fought and won an impressive series of battles—Port Gibson, Fourteen Mile Creek, Raymond, Jackson, Champion's Hill, Big Black River Bridge—as well as numerous skirmishes. Old Abe's Regiment had 479 men present and fit for duty at the end of the month. With justifiable pride, the regimental memorandum for May noted: "The discipline and efficiency of this regiment is *good* and are *well instructed* in skirmish and light infantry drill."[63]

Vicksburg had not fallen to Grant's assault, but Pemberton and 32,000 Confederates were trapped inside the city. Grant reinforced via Haines's Bluff and the Yazoo River. Thirty-five thousand fresh troops arrived in June. By mid-month, Grant ringed Vicksburg with 77,000 men and 220 guns, and he controlled the river with Rear Admiral Porter's fleet.[64] The days of Vicksburg, the Confederacy's great river bastion, were numbered.

10

Used Up: The Siege of Vicksburg

G RANT began siege operations against Vicksburg after the Grand Assault. Naval bombardment of the city continued for over a month. The city's populace took up digging and living in subterranean bunkers to protect themselves. Private Rogers of Company I wrote to Ed Cronon, who had returned home to La Crosse after being wounded at Corinth, "The way shell is going into Vicksburg is a caution. I would rather be in Hell as in there."[1]

Grant took precautions against attacks from Confederate forces outside Vicksburg who might attempt to assist the besieged garrison by raiding Union supplies or positions. The Eagle Brigade participated in three fast-moving mini-campaigns during the forty-seven-day siege. The Eighth Wisconsin marched from Haines's Bluff northeastward towards Mechanicsburg, forty miles away, on May 27. Intermittent skirmishing with mounted Confederates took place while cotton,

Officers of the Forty-Seventh Illinois, Eagle Brigade, at Oxford, Mississippi, in December, 1862. Captain George Puterbaugh (seated) became a G.A.R. activist following the war and helped coordinate Old Abe's successful appearance in Peoria, Illinois, in 1866.

corn, and cattle were burned or carried back to feed Union troops.[2]

Satartia, eighty miles up the Yazoo, was next. Embarking on steamboats, the Eighth Wisconsin and several other recently arrived regiments (including the Twenty-Fifth and Twenty-Seventh Wisconsin) marched around the countryside between the Yazoo and the Big Black River. The Eagle Regiment encountered a strong force of Confederate cavalry at Mechanicsburg on June 4, defeating them in a hot skirmish which won the regiment and Captain Greene praise, and cost two seriously wounded. Mechanicsburg was burned to the ground.[3]

The terrific heat of Mississippi in June caused a number of additional casualties. Private Rogers claimed that forty soldiers fell dead from sunstroke on the march back to Haines's Bluff. However exaggerated Rogers' figures might be, he sounded a truthful note when he explained to Ed Cronon, "They have wore us out . . . we are reported unfit for duty . . . the last two days march has come near settling us . . . there is over sixty reported sick—the new troops that went with us

gave out entirely. . . It was the hottest day ever I marched. . . ."[4]

Old Abe's regiment crossed back to the western shore of the Mississippi in mid-June. At Young's Point, Louisiana, the men rejoined their knapsacks, took a bath, and had their first change of clothes since beginning the campaign. As Private Rogers explained in a letter: "We just got our knapsacks . . . and has had a chance to get cleaned up, something I am not sorry for—for I assure you I had more company than I actually wanted and you might plant potatoes, as the saying is, on any part of my body with fair prospects of a good crop."[5]

A number of soldiers had picked up various articles of clothing during the campaign. Private Miles of Company E for example, had exchanged his "dilapidated and rather over-populated" uniform for a pair of "blue and white pepper-and-salt denim pants and blue-gray shirt."[6]

Several days after their long-overdue bath, the men of the Eighth moved west to engage the enemy once more. The Eagle Brigade marched eighteen miles to Richmond, Louisiana, where it par-

Old Abe and the Eighth Wisconsin color guard, pictured at Big Black River Bridge, Mississippi, after the fall of Vicksburg in July, 1863. Edward Homiston holds the eagle; Myron
Briggs the national colors.

ticipated in a fierce, inconclusive little battle. One
day later, the brigade returned to Young's Point
after burning the city.[7]

Young's Point, like Helena, Arkansas, became
a "graveyard." The ground was low-lying,
swampy, and mosquito-infested, and disease broke
out immediately. For six weeks the Eighth Wisconsin remained stationary at Young's Point, ostensibly to prevent the Confederates from breaking out of their doomed stronghold and crossing
the river in small boats. In truth, however,
Mower's command had been "used up"—the
Grand Assault, the swift little battles at Mechanicsburg and Richmond, the long marches,
and finally sickness had all contributed to the casualty lists. In March, Old Abe's regiment totaled
606 men present and fit for duty. By the end of
June, however, only 436 remained. Confederate
guns had eliminated twenty-two men; bacteriologi-
cal enemies had carried off or incapacitated 170.[8]

Surgeon Murta, European-trained, did the best
he could. He won praise for his efforts, which supposedly prevented more death and suffering than
would otherwise have occurred. Murta arrested
soldiers who refused to place themselves on sick
call, and ordered them to local and distant hospi-

tals.[9] But as Captain Greene explained to his wife,
"We lost as many men as we would have lost in a
big battle."[10]

When General Pemberton finally surrendered
Vicksburg and 29,491 Confederate troops to
Grant on July 4, 1863, the North had won a decisive victory. Vicksburg followed the great Union
triumph at Gettysburg by one day. Grant's forces
lost 9,362 men during the Vicksburg campaign
and siege; the Southerners lost 9,059.[11] Port Hudson fell several days later, and the Mississippi
River passed completely into Union hands. The
Confederacy had been split in two, and the South
had lost its bid for independence, though it took
the Confederate army another year to realize it.

General Sherman sent a letter commending Old
Abe's regiment to the governor of Wisconsin, Edward Salomon. Sherman apologized for the high
casualties and the sufferings occasioned by the
Vicksburg campaign. He complimented the "courage and manliness" of the Eighth Wisconsin and
thanked the governor for allowing him to use such
fine troops.[12]

The Eagle Brigade departed from Young's
Point on July 12, passing through Vicksburg for a
camp located on higher, healthier ground near

the Big Black River Bridge. Here, itinerant photographers began offering their services to the thousands of Union troops in the Vicksburg vicinity. It became fashionable to send one's likeness home to parents and friends, not seen for two years. Photographers at Camp Randall had captured the young and inexperienced Wisconsin soldiers in their gray uniforms in 1861. Now, fifteen battles and many skirmishes later, the citizen-soldiers again sent and exchanged snapshots of themselves. Old Abe and the regimental color guard made a perfect subject, and the resulting photograph became one of the most famous in Wisconsin's Civil War history. As one soldier explained to the readers of the Milwaukee *Sentinel*:

> Old Abe, our eagle, has recently like everybody else, and because it is the fashion, had his carte de visite taken. . . . His friends will of course excuse him if his coat does look a little rough for he has seen over two years of hard service. The picture includes also the regimental colors with the color guard in position around them, the flags are sadly torn and soiled, and show the marks of affection of our misguided Southern "brethren" in every fold.[13]

Captain Britton of Janesville, commanding the regiment after Colonel Robbins' injury and Major Jefferson's wounds, related that the command expected soon to return home with all its honors and "bearing with us our favorite American eagle who has participated in every engagement, exciting the admiration of both friend and foe."[14] The Wisconsin adjutant general, Augustus Gaylord, dutifully noted the experiences of the Eighth Infantry in his annual report of 1863. Gaylord went on to mention Old Abe for the first time in an official published document: "It is, perhaps, not unworthy of note, that the eagle which they took with them from the state 'still lives,' apparently in the enjoyment of excellent health and undiminished appetite."[15]

11

Camped Among the Pines

THE soldiers of 1861–1865 spent most of their time not fighting battles. As in all the wars of history, considerable activity revolved around life in camp. Camp life had its own special characteristics, and chief among these was monotony. The ability to endure it became as much the hallmark of the Wisconsin trooper as bravery in combat. Boredom reigned in all camps, regardless of the length of the stay. Comparing soldiering to a disease, Captain Greene noted that the battles, like "occasional spasms," would be followed by "exhaustion, dullness, and finally monotony" caused by idleness.[1] George Driggs of Dane County wrote that his boredom was so great "that days of the week, dates of the month, and even the year is nearly forgotten."[2]

The Eighth Wisconsin moved so often, however, that the amount of time its members spent in any particular camp was minimal. During four years of active service, the regiment experienced lengthy stays only at Sulphur Springs, Missouri; Cairo, Illinois; Camp Clear Creek not far from Corinth, Mississippi; and near the Big Black River Bridge after Vicksburg fell. The men covered so much territory in 1864 that it would be inaccurate to say they camped anywhere.

Camp routine could not provide enough diversion to occupy the minds or bodies of the young men who made up the Civil War armies. On a normal day, roll call took place at dawn, followed by breakfast, and then sick call. Drilling occupied the men for another hour or two, depending upon the weather and other circumstances. After lunch, the men relaxed until two in the afternoon, at which time they drilled for another two hours. The evening meal ended a soldier's official responsibilities, unless he had sentry duty.[3]

Some soldiers actually preferred marching to the enforced inactivity of camp life. Corporal Brown wrote to his family in Milwaukee explaining that he wished the regiment could be back in Missouri chasing Confederate partisans rather than experiencing the flies and heat of Camp Clear Creek.[4] "Waiting is more of soldiers' business than fighting," wearily observed another enlisted man.[5]

Periods of inactivity frequently coincided with and probably even brought on outbreaks of disease. Certainly, camps such as Clear Creek near Corinth, were particularly unhealthy. Overcrowding, lack of sanitary facilities, numerous insects, poor water quality, an imperfect knowledge of what caused illnesses, and the Southern climate combined to make camp life dangerous as well as boring.[6] "Typhoid and its kindred scourges," malaria, pneumonia, measles, mumps, small pox, in-

Union soldier washing clothes in camp. Note the semipermanent shelters with their mud-and-stick chimneys and the small two-man "dog" or "pup" tent at left.

fluenza, the "bloody flux" or "chronic diarrhea—a thing very prevalent among the soldiers," brought death and disability to many. According to Colonel Lucius F. Hubbard, commander of the Fifth Minnesota Infantry and eventually of the Eagle Brigade, fear of disease was "a far greater terror than rebel guns. . . ."[7]

Doctors simply could not handle the problems caused by sickness. Indeed, the medical profession was ill-prepared for the responsibilities which confronted it during the Civil War. The germ theory of disease, for example, did not emerge until just after the war. Doctors, as a result, might not bother to sterilize their instruments or even wash their hands between patients. Hospital Steward James A. Jackson, who drove the Eighth Wisconsin's ambulance, and who eventually became a prominent Madison physician, recalled that during the war it was common practice for doctors to hold sutures in their teeth while sewing up cuts or wounds. Internal medicines, moreover, were primitive and basically herbal in nature.[8]

The prevalence of disease overwhelmed regimental medical staffs and contributed to the siphoning-off of many able-bodied men to aid in caring for the sick. Large health-care facilities were set up in major cities like Memphis, Cairo, and St. Louis to treat the sick and injured who filled field hospitals to overflowing. Those who failed to respond to medical treatment were sent further north, to recover or die. Thousands of men received disability discharges because of chronic incurable bouts of sickness.

Robert Rogers of La Crosse expressed what some soldiers already knew: that a hospital was an ideal location for coming into contact with disease. Rogers wrote from Memphis in 1864, ". . .When a man has got over one disease he is apt to have several others if he stops around hospitals."[9] The Eighth Wisconsin suffered four times as many deaths from disease as from bullets, and among Western Civil War regiments this experience was typical.[10]

The Union Army contained men who possessed a wide variety of skills, and the same can be said of the Eighth Wisconsin. Their ability to improvise camp shelters out of Army-issue equipment and whatever they could scrounge illustrates the phenomenon. Typically, the men pitched their conical four-man Sibley tents over a "dug out," a semi-basement lined with rough boards for a floor. They constructed benches and tables, as well as bunks, and built "comfortable old fashioned fireplaces." Such a semi-permanent dwelling normally took two days to build.[11] Sometimes encamped troops built even more elaborate and more permanent shelters.

Soldiers laid out their camps in orderly fashion. Each company erected its shelters in a straight line, forming a "company street."[12] Improvisation, adaptability, and orderliness, however, could not overcome harsh environmental conditions or inadequate supplies. Snow and cold weather were not uncommon in Tennessee and Missouri, and it made the troops suffer on more than one occasion.[13] A chronic lack of adequate shelter equipment plagued the men of the Eighth Wisconsin especially during their first winter, there being only eighteen tents for the entire regiment.[14] Unusually cold winters in 1862 and 1863 surprised those who had expected a milder climate.[15] "This is the sunny south, but give me Wisconsin for all this," wrote James Mellor of Company I after describing the snow and bitter cold—"regular Wisconsin weather"—encountered by the regiment while camped at Germantown, Tennessee, in February, 1863.[16]

Securing and preparing food occupied the time and thoughts of most Union soldiers. The officially prescribed daily food allowance per man was generous. The lisit of requirements included: 12 ounces pork or bacon or 1 pound fresh or salt beef; 1 pound, 6 ounces soft bread or 1 pound hard bread; a helping of beans, peas, rice and/or hominy; coffee or tea; sugar; vinegar; salt and pepper; potatoes (when practicable); and a ration of molasses.[17]

In practice, such food allowance regulations provided only a guideline for commissary officials. Local conditions, the availability of supplies, enemy activity, or movement during a campaign all affected the type and quantity of military fare. Union troops at least ate regularly in camp. The quality of army rations, however, made lasting impressions on the minds of citizen-soldiers. Salt pork—or "sowbelly"—and bacon were the most commonly available meats. Pickled beef (called "salt horse") also appeared on a regular basis, and fresh beef was not unknown. The meat-packing and preservation techniques of the 1860's more

National Archives

Mess cooks at work in a Union camp. The twelve-man Sibley tents have been improved with log foundations and wood-frame doorways.

than occasionally failed to accomplish their goals. Men consumed spoiled, tainted, insect-infested meats if there was no option, and probably helped swell the sick rolls by doing so. "Stale pork and bacon that crawls" provided some of the "delicacies which are common in the camp," wrote Augie Weissert of Racine.[18]

Hard bread, or "hardtack," a flat cracker manufactured in immense quantities out of water, flour, and salt, provided the staple of the soldier's diet.[19] Tasteless and durable, hardtack crackers accompanied all Union armies on all operations throughout the Civil War. It proved to be as susceptible to insects and spoilage as any other commissary stores, however.[20] Soldiers grumbled and joked about the meat readily available in the form of "hard tack filled with worms," and some referred to their hardtack as "worm castles."[21] In general, however, hardtack, was an effective method of preserving bread and, like sailors and their sea biscuits, Union troops grew accustomed to and eventually somewhat fond of the ubiquitous crackers.

In addition to the various forms of preserved meats and hardtack, desiccated vegetables supplemented the soldier's diet. This was a primitive form of dried, processed food which the troops nicknamed "baled hay." It was never popular.[22] Among members of the Eighth Wisconsin, beans and rice were much more important sources of nutrition.[23]

Along with meat, hardtack, and beans, coffee became one of life's necessities. Whether it was prepared in large cauldrons for an entire company or in smaller pots to suit the individual's taste, coffee helped to make the war "tolerable."[24] As one enlisted man in Company K remembered, "it was our ration of coffee which we wanted more than anything else."[25]

The preparation of food varied with circumstances. Early in the war, the Eighth Wisconsin established a company cook system, which made several men responsible (on a rotating basis) for the preparation of food for a specific company. The company cook method continued to prevail in camp, but when the regiment was on the march, cooking duties became decentralized and the informal "mess" system emerged.[26] Groups of six or eight soldiers formed their own mess and improvised the cooking and other responsibilities associated with food preparation.[27]

But rotating cooking duties probably contributed to the spread of disease. So many soldiers of the Eagle Regiment succumbed at Young's Point during the Vicksburg siege, for example, that when it came time for a turn at cooking, diseases that a particular soldier already had contracted were inadvertently passed along to his comrades. The ailments that ravaged the Eagle Regiment did not disappear when Vicksburg fell and the command moved to healthier locales. Rather, many men remained in the grip of various diseases well into the fall of 1863, probably because they continuously reinfected one another.[28]

Supplements to government rations could be found at all camps. The men craved variety and were especially eager to obtain fresh vegetables. Several mechanisms existed to vary the diet; all involved money. Regular foraging parties existed in camp. They purchased fresh produce from area farmers and resold it to the men. Sergeant Major Driggs noted in mid-1862: "We are having a good living these days. Aside from our regular rations . . . we have men out foraging constantly who bring in butter, eggs, chickens, and vegetables of all kinds, which we pay high prices for in order to keep the market running."[29]

Licensed private merchants or sutlers followed the troops in the field. They extended credit to the men, charged exorbitant prices, and provided otherwise unavailable luxury items.[30] Tobacco, of course, was an important part of a sutler's stock of goods. "The weed was in general demand," recalled a Wisconsin trooper.[31] Sutlers made tobacco readily available to Northern soldiers throughout the war.[32] Sweets, cheese, butter, tea, and condensed milk likewise attracted members of Old Abe's regiment to the sutler's tent. Peaches canned in syrup were among the most available of treats.[33]

When the Army of the Tennessee embarked on its downriver expedition against Vicksburg in 1863, vast piles of sutlers' stores lined the Memphis waterfront waiting to be moved. Several men of the Eighth Wisconsin led a night raid on some boxes of cheese. "We were at swords points with all of the sutlers just then . . . and this was a rare opportunity to display that," remembered one of the conspirators.[34] The regiment apparently appreciated the cheese, and nobody was punished for the theft. As might be expected, sutlers were viewed by the troops as profiteers or worse, but they provided a genuine service to the troops—for a price.

Liquor played an important role in the lives of some soldiers. Alcohol, and the quest to obtain it, revealed much about the character and level of imagination possessed by numerous citizen-soldiers. Although officially frowned upon, spirituous beverages seem never to have been far out of the trooper's reach, and, indeed, they occupied a paramount place in his thoughts. At Camp Clear Creek, for example, Private Miles of Springdale in Dane County spent an eventful night guarding General Stanley's personal whiskey still. Under cover of darkness, Miles pried open one of the divisional commander's storage containers with his bayonet, filled a number of canteens with the illicit drink, and noted the next day that "the boys were on a spree."[35]

The men experienced "dry" as well as "wet" periods. In fact, the availability of liquor apparently helped distinguish good times from bad. "I cannot enjoy myself," wrote Irish-born Corporal Rogers to his one-armed comrade Edward Cronon back home in Wisconsin, because ". . . as for whiskey our bottle is ran dry and cannot . . . nor knows not where to get it Replenished."[36] One of Rogers' hometown friends in the Second Wisconsin Cavalry shared some whiskey with the suffering La Crosse man on an occasion. Rogers explained: ". . . O it done me good! I felt as I was a man again."[37] "Spirits in to keep spirits up . . . that would be my motto just now if I could get them," wrote Corporal Rogers during another dry spell in mid-1864.[38]

A humorous episode revealing the extent to which men would go to obtain ". . . the elixir of life" took place during Grant's abortive first Vicksburg campaign.[39] At Oxford, Mississippi, Corporal Joseph B. Huggins and Private George T. Stickney, both of Janesville, broke into a drug store at night searching for alcohol. One of their comrades in Company K recalled: "They had the faculty of getting away with as much whiskey or 'Pine Top' as it was called at that time, as any two men in the Union Army. They had been without the stimulant for a long time, and of course, longed to get a taste of it."[40] Hunting around in the darkness and sniffing various bottles to test for alcoholic content, Huggins and Stickney found what they had been seeking. After consuming most of the liquid in a glass jar which had at-

tracted their attention by its strong alcohol smell, the men were surprised to note that something more substantial was bobbing around in the container. Upon closer examination, they discovered that they had been sipping the embalming fluid used to preserve a human organ on display at the drug store. Revulsion and disgust resulted from the incident; but, as one of the men remarked, "It tasted good when I was drinking it."[41]

In addition to their incessant search for alcoholic beverages, the men of the Eighth Wisconsin Infantry, like other Civil War soldiers, entertained themselves in a variety of ways and found relief from constant association with war and disease.

Card games such as poker and "chuck a luck" found patrons among the ranks. Card playing was equated with gambling and sinfulness among some religiously oriented elements of the American population. "I am sorry to say," wrote Private Weissert in early 1864, "that many pass their time in playing cards and such like."[42] But it provided an enjoyable pastime for idle young men in blue, thousands of whom were enjoying freedom from family constraints for the first time.[43]

Other forms of gambling included the establishment of lotteries and the sponsoring of races. On one occasion just prior to the Vicksburg campaign, members of the Forty-Seventh Illinois Infantry organized a horse race. While their colonel was absent, the men of the Forty-Seventh matched his "big bay" against a fleet gray mare from the Second Iowa Battery. The whole Eagle Brigade turned out for the event. "Bets were laid without odds," remembered an Illinois soldier. "When the money was exhausted up went shirts, socks, blankets, every article of a soldiers apparel . . . until there was nothing left to bet. . . ."[44] (It is not recorded as to which horse won the race.)

Some men sang. Tunes such as "A Rocky Road to Dublin," "The Girl I Left Behind Me," "Garry Owen," and "The Death of My Poor Children" were popular in camp and on the march.[45] Corporal Brown of Milwaukee enjoyed listening to fiddle music, which reminded him of home. He explained: "Just after dark is the time I like to sit in front of my tent and smoke, hat off and shirt unbuttoned thinking of home and the end of the war . . . there is a feller over in Co. D playing on the fiddle and it sounds like home."[46]

Corporal Rogers wrote poetry. His "Ballad of the Vicksburg Canal" never reached a publisher, but several verses expressed some of his hopes and concerns:

Verse 1: You Western heroes get ready. Attention one moment I call
And I'll sing you a few words of a ditty that's made on the Vicksburg Canal.
Operations we'll make on the Stronghold, and navigate up the Yazoo,
While monitors [gunboats] float on our waters, the rebels we're sure to subdue.

Chorus: So girls don't be in a hurry,
We'll be home in a year from next fall;
Don't marry a home sick coward,
Take a Soldier here from the canal.

Verse 2: Let Irishmen flock to our standard, and foreigners come without fail!
Columbia's your land of adoption, Americans need no appeal!
Rebellion will soon crush forever, our cup of joy then will be full
And discountenance peace arbitrators, including that far-famed John Bull.[47]

Others worked at self-improvement. Private Weissert practiced arithmetic in his spare time.[48] John Williams made an attempt to stop swearing. As he noted in his diary in May, 1864, "Going to try and stop swearing. Find it hard work. Try, try again."[49]

Newspapers provided a constant source of diversion. They were important to soldiers partially because the Civil War took place at a time when the majority of participants—at least from the North—could read. Newspapers, therefore, became popular articles of mass consumption, a means of entertainment as well as of information. Private T. B. Coon of Company C wrote to his father, the editor of the Eau Claire *Free Press*, where he had been employed prior to the war, and explained that the soldiers had access to a variety of newspapers. He observed: "The daily paper is almost as much of a necessity in the camp as the daily bread, and indeed, some of the boys would much rather go without breakfast than without their morning *Tribune*, *Democrat*, or *Republican*."[50]

Mail call was the single most important event in the life of the encamped soldier. From the war's very outset, mail provided soldiers a tenuous but vital link with home and family. The men of the Eighth wrote frequently. As many as five hundred letters might be sent back to Wisconsin in a single day. Three-cent postage stamps became the means by which ties were maintained, and they became scarce and in great demand. Civil War correspondents frequently requested stamps from home because of their difficulty in obtaining them while on the move.[51]

Soldiers' letters often contained requests for information about home. Citizen-soldiers relished in the ordinary affairs of their loved ones in Wisconsin. Lieutenant Charles Palmetier, the future mayor of Delavan, for instance, wrote that he was interested in ". . . all those little things that occur around home that you do not think anything of are all news to us down here. . . ."[52] The knowledge that folks back home had not forgotten them was important to some. Private Augustus Root of Company B wrote to his ten-year-old son, "My Dear little sun . . . i got your letter. How glad i was to see that you could rite to me my Dear little one. You h'aint forgot me yet have you? You shall have all the candy and apples you can eat when i cum home."[53] Augustus Root died of disease, and his son, Muncil, later became the youngest volunteer from Wisconsin to serve in the Civil War.[54]

James Mellor of Company I sent his wife a steady stream of elaborate instructions concerning the operation of the family farm, which he had not seen for several years. "Be sure and sow the oats plenty thick. . . . I do not want you to sow more than 2½ bushels of wheat. . . . Put it on the ground that was sodded down . . . you might save a small piece in the Bottom near the house for potatoes if you wish. . . ." directed Mellor from "Camp in the field in Louisiana" during 1863.[55]

Letters also contained expressions of war weariness. Many citizen-soldiers had expected the war to end quickly when they volunteered back in 1861. It took two years of hard campaigning to convince some men that the war would not be ended by a single battle. James Mellor, for example, believed the war would end when the Union forces took Columbus, Kentucky, in early 1862; and then Island Number 10 in mid-1862; and before, during, and immediately after the battles near Corinth in late 1862; and finally, along with several others, upon the fall of Vicksburg in 1863.[56] "This war seems to hang on like the toothache," wrote Lieutenant Jeremiah Baker of Fre-

Indiana Historical Society

Western troops (these are from Indiana) had a distinctly rugged appearance after 1862, no doubt because they took part in long-range, highly mobile operations and excelled at marching and living off the land. Note the wide variety of coats, headgear, and uniform details.

mont. "I thought . . . it was nearly at an end, but the end is not yet. . . ."[57]

There were never enough letters from home. "The men wait with the greatest anxiety for the mail," observed one soldier, "and manifest the greatest disappointment when they fail to receive letters."[58] "Letters from home are more than bread and meat to us," explained Captain Greene.[59]

Sometimes the mail brought gifts from home. James Brown received a red hunting shirt from his family in Milwaukee.[60] Private Weissert helped one of his Racine schoolmates devour a cheese sent from Wisconsin.[61] Soldiers sent cash back to their wives and families. Many letters contained references to when and how much had been sent home and requested notification of its safe arrival.[62]

Some enterprising troopers had their eyes peeled for business opportunities. James Mellor concocted two schemes by which he hoped to profit. One involved the likelihood of the war's end in 1862 and the resulting huge surplus of government mules and horses. Mellor calculated that he would be able to purchase government teams cheaply, drive them back to Wisconsin from St.

Louis, and resell them in La Crosse.[63] Another hopeful venture involved Mellor's desire to pick up large numbers of winter overcoats discarded by soldiers in the spring, "for the men will not Pack them in warm weather." But Mellor could not figure out a cost-free mechanism to ship the overcoats back to La Crosse, and his scheme failed.[64]

Women haunted the minds of Wisconsin's boys in blue. Nineteenth-century Americans, for the most part, did not openly discuss sexual matters. Theirs was a reticent age. But soldiers of the 1860's experienced desire, and during the war some found ways to satisfy their wants. The availability of illicit pleasures was much greater in the South during 1861–1865 than in rural Wisconsin. Probably venereal disease was more widespread in the field as well. Southern cities such as Memphis and Nashville were famous for their red-light districts. Memphis, especially, seems to have been a haven for prostitutes who flocked to the river town from Chicago, St. Louis, and Cincinnati. Not all of the harlots were imported from the North, for many Southern "Cyprians" plied their trade after the Confederate troops withdrew from the area. A Union officer described Memphis as being "one of the first places of female prostitution on the continent. Virtue is scarcely known within the limits of the city."[65]

The soldiers of the Eighth Wisconsin enjoyed the "gayeties and luxuries" of Memphis while waiting for the steamboat *Empress* to take them to Helena and Vicksburg in 1863. Captain Duncan A. Kennedy with a group of men from Company I "went off to take a night walk through town." Corporal Rogers narrated the experience to his wounded comrade Edward Cronon: "Of course we had something to eat and something to drink and other things that is good but not Proper to mention here, and when I got on the boat I was Pretty well . . . eased. . . ."[66]

At Saulsbury, Tennessee, fifty miles east of Memphis, the Eighth Wisconsin spent time encamped in January, 1864. Private Mellor wrote to his wife describing the amorous activities of members of his company in "charming the hearts of the Secesh widows around here, and Secesh widows is very plenty here."[67]

In areas where some pro-Union sentiment existed, members of the Eighth Wisconsin attempted to fraternize politely with the female populace. In Missouri, for example, the men attended local dances, apparently conducting themselves in gentlemanly fashion, though there were never enough loyalist women. Officers faced better odds since they were fewer in number, and visits from their own wives made it easier for local females to equalize the imbalanced sexual ratio. Captain Greene was much impressed with Missouri's women. "You ought to see the Missouri women dance!" he exclaimed to his wife.[68] (The next year Mrs. Greene and the couple's young daughter visited the regiment.)

Christmas time brought visits from officers wives and women of the United States Sanitary Commission—a forerunner of today's Red Cross. These visits had positive effects on morale. Speaker of the Wisconsin Assembly Lyon and Lieutenant James O. Bartlett were visited by their wives and children in 1861. The women brought chickens and several barrels of potatoes as gifts for the men of Company K. The Bartlett and Lyon children became "great pets of the camp," recollected Mrs. Lyon.[69] Mrs. Reed of Beaver Dam visited the regiment as a respresentative of the Wisconsin Sanitary Commission in early 1862. She brought the men such presents as butter, cheese, thread, needles, and pins.[70]

Young men frequently thought about the girls back home. Corporal Rogers envied the one-armed Edward Cronon, home in La Crosse after being wounded. Rogers wrote understandingly:

> . . . glad to learn . . . you are enjoying yourself so well especially with the females—now Ed you must be careful while we are away. Do not be Hoggish—leave some of them for us . . . when we get home—still I do not Blame you, it is nothing more than any of us would do if we were there, and as you have a large Pasture to run in and none, I may say, but yourself to run over, why not have the choice bites. . . .[71]

Lieutenant Palmetier requested that his sister extend compliments to the young women at home. He closed one letter saying, ". . . in regards to the girls, give my best to *all* the young ladies. . . ."[72]

The inactivity associated with camp life encouraged discussion and debate on a wide range of topics, including the causes of the war and other political questions. Many of the enlisted men had volunteered in 1861 without understanding either the causes of the war or the hardships which

Edward Cronon, Company I, Eighth Wisconsin, pictured about 1870. Cronon lost part of his left arm at the Battle of Corinth in 1862.

awaited them. The opportunity to earn a steady income had great appeal, as did the war excitement generated in early 1861.[73] Before long, however, more realistic appraisals and a maturing level of perspective appeared as the men reflected upon the drama in which they were participating. The sense emerged that the war was indeed being fought over important issues. The Eighth Wisconsin contained men of differing ethnic and political backgrounds as well as educational levels. In camp, they shared ideas apparently in a frankly democratic and informal fashion. The distinctions between officers and enlisted men, always difficult to maintain among the volunteer citizen-soldiers, broke down when discussing current events. If few men appreciated what they were embarking on when they enlisted in 1861, at least some grew to understand the momentous events of the era, and rose to acquire an understanding of issues based on their experiences and sacrifices.

"Strange as it may seem," wrote an officer of Old Abe's regiment in 1863, "life in camp seems to have a liberalizing tendency . . . common sense has triumphed over educational predilections. Honest convictions . . . are respected and even radical utterances are listened to . . . with respectful attention."[74] What the men called the "great question" of what the war was about, became a natural topic for conversation. Many volunteers believed that the war had been caused by slavery. Private J. M. Flint of Company F wrote, "We wish to see the end of this wicked rebellion, and we hope to glory in the final triumph of freedom forever over the wicked and accursed institution of slavery, which has brought upon us this terrible war. . . ."[75] Captain Greene developed a sense of revulsion over the institution of slavery, even though he did not originally believe that slavery caused the war. "I realize from actual observation," he explained to his wife after extolling the beauty of the Tennessee River Valley, "what a blasting curse to a country . . . this forced labor is; the accumulation of all the wealth and power in the hands of a few and the grinding and crushing of the many."[76]

Captain Britton of Company G looked at the slavery issue from its human side. He was gladdened when he witnessed "slaves deserting their masters by the hundreds." Britton wrote to the Janesville *Gazette*: "I see here, every day, slaves as white as myself; and this morning I saw a child and mother at the depot—the mother had but very

WHi(X3)38387

James F. Greene of Prairie du Chien, commander of Company F of the Eighth Wisconsin, 1863. Greene was cited for bravery in action during the Vicksburg campaign.

little of the negro features, and the child was as white as the whitest child in Janesville . . . and a slave . . . thank God the time has about come when all such folks can claim their freedom. . . ."[77]

Sergeant Major Driggs felt differently. He observed in 1864, "These long faced Abolitionists . . . t'was they that provoked this war—they that first sowed the seeds of discord. Where are they? At home praying for the immortal nigger. . . . They are doing their utmost to make slavery the issue of this war. We do not propose to interfere with slavery."[78]

The men of the Eagle Regiment agreed on one fundamental principle, however: the war was necessary to preserve the Union. Whatever else might be accomplished in the process, all their hardships and sacrifices were aimed at "maintaining by force of arms the supremacy of the Government over the whole country. . . ."[79] For this goal, the men endured.[80]

One of the truly bright features of camp life was Old Abe. The mascot brought flattering notoriety both to the Eighth Wisconsin and the Eagle Brigade as a whole. Old Abe's adventures helped dispel the gloominess of camp. He became the protagonist of amusing stories, as well as a central focus for gossip. Most importantly, Old Abe inspired the men.

WHi(X3)12955

Old Abe in 1865, photographed for a soldiers' aid fair. The bird's size and fierce gaze made him a favorite with photographers and the public.

In camp, Old Abe's every mood became a topic for conversation. The men attributed human qualities to their mascot, and genuinely felt a sense of affection for him. "All the brigade adore him," wrote Private Burdette of the Forty-Seventh Illinois.[81] "Our eagle is the pet of the whole regiment . . . all think as much of him as we do of our Colonel and that is saying a great deal," explained Corporal Brown.[82]

In Missouri and at Cairo, Old Abe enjoyed the companionship of a nondescript mongrel dog named Frank who had attached himself to the regiment in Madison. Frank always shared fresh-killed rabbits with Old Abe. The pair became the center of attention during the dull months before the Eighth Wisconsin exchanged their Wisconsin gray uniforms for Federal blue. The men taught both animals tricks.[83] The boredom of inactivity eventually had its debilitating effects, and predictably, the men began passing the time teasing Old Abe, causing a "draft on his patience."[84] When Frank unsuspectingly came within range of the frustrated Old Abe, the eagle ran forward and pounced on the dog, digging his talons into Frank's fur.[85]

At Camp Clear Creek, after the capture of Corinth, Old Abe enjoyed himself immensely. While the men suffered from disease in the sweltering heat, Old Abe was at liberty. Eagle-bearer Thomas Hill allowed Old Abe complete freedom.[86] The eagle never strayed far from camp. Hill and others accompanied Old Abe to Clear Creek, enjoying themselves as the eagle swam and frolicked in the stream.[87]

Abe roamed the camp. He tipped over water pails, chased large insects, learned to catch bullets which the men rolled along the ground, visited the sutler's tent, attacked clothes hung out on lines to dry, and raided the provisions of various companies. The sight of cooks chasing Old Abe down a company street while the eagle clutched the main ingredient for an officer's chicken dinner filled the camp with delight.[88]

Old Abe learned to entertain the local citizenry. A Mississippi farmer and his daughter—"a beautiful brunette"—paid to witness Old Abe. "The celebrated Eagle, which the Confederate soldiers say is carried by a Yankee regiment," devoured one of their chickens.[89] So profitable did showing off eventually become that General Mower had Old Abe entertain the leading citizens of Memphis, who then donated funds to keep the feathered mascot well fed.[90]

Old Abe even became involved with alcohol. In one of his liberty periods, the eagle chanced upon an illicit bottle of wine, hidden away in a soldier's belongings. Abe pilfered the bottle, consumed some of its contents, and became drunk. On another occasion, a soldier left unguarded a saucer of peach brandy. Old Abe, "always on the watch for spoils," drank it and suffered the consequences.[91]

The eagle's wanderings led him into soldier's tents and personal gear. After leaving Camp Clear Creek, therefore, the eagle's freedom was curtailed. One officer explained:

   . . . lately he has been generally restrained. The reason for this abatement of his liberty, is not so much fear of losing him, as to prevent his pilfering. When loose, with a gravity peculiar to himself and an independence characteristic of the American Eagle, he would first go into one tent, and then another, helping himself to whatever suited him best. No one presumed to blame him for this, as it only showed him good at imitation.[92]

Old Abe learned how to shake hands with his bearers.[93] Abe, in fact, played a very important role in the life of the regiment. When he would attempt to fly off the whole camp would be thrown into a burst of activity—itself a healthy occurrence. The men would chase their feathered mascot, usually to a not very distant tree, and try to coax him back. Once, when Old Abe proved reluctant to come back, a soldier climbed the tree, grabbed Old Abe and threw him to the ground. Old Abe immediately got back up and flew into another tree. Sticks and stones were thrown to knock the eagle back into the crowd below. Stubbornly, Abe refused to budge. Then, according to witnesses, "they procured a live chicken . . . and thus tempted him to docility. After that stampede, they never forgot the moral . . . the persuasion of appetite is better than brute force."[94]

The men appreciated Old Abe's comical failures as much as his successes. At La Grange, during the winter of 1863, Old Abe's regiment found themselves in an area where fresh meat was unavailable. The men decided to show Old Abe off to a local farmer in exchange for food. The "half and half unionist" promised that if Old Abe could kill one of his guinea hens, he could eat it. The incident became known as "the battle of the birds," and dozens of men cheered when Old Abe failed to kill the hen. The Tennessee farmer enjoyed himself so greatly that he donated a chicken to the vanquished eagle.[95]

In another incident Old Abe made a fool of himself after becoming agitated. The eagle disliked steamships and mules intensely. After an uncomfortable boat ride down the Mississippi at the beginning of the Vicksburg campaign, Old Abe was secured to a tree limb while the command unpacked the *Ben Franklin* across from the Yazoo Pass. A rain storm broke out and the peals of thunder, the confusion of the landing area, the mules, and the steamer noises threw the eagle into a panic. He entangled himself in his leash and ended up hanging upside down from the tree by his leg. He limped for several weeks afterwards.[96]

Old Abe never failed to add a touch of inspiring symbolism to local events, however. In his role as a symbol, Old Abe made his greatest contributions to regimental morale. In mid-1862, for example, Lorenzo Thomas, Adjutant General of the United States, addressed Union troops stationed in northern Mississippi. Thomas explained how President Lincoln's Emancipation Proclamation had freed the slaves in the Confederacy. Thomas then went on to describe Lincoln's policy of enlisting blacks in the army to help fight the Southern rebels. Thomas was seeking idealistic soldiers who were willing to volunteer to serve with black units. The Eighth Wisconsin heard General Thomas' call at Corinth. Thomas interrupted his speech at one point and remarked to the uniformed crowd that he thought he was addressing strangers, "but I see one familiar personage at least, that majestic Bird of the Eighth Wisconsin—the emblem of American freedom!" Cheers broke out, Old Abe flapped his wings, and several troopers from the Eagle Regiment subsequently transferred to black units.[97]

Wherever the men camped, important general officers were sure to make an appearance sooner or later. As a mark of respect, the men often formed their lines or put on a drill for the various generals. Old Abe always participated in these events. Eagle-bearer Dave McLain recalled: "I have frequently seen Generals Grant, Sherman, McPherson, Rosecrans, Blair, Logan, and others when they were passing our regiment, raise their hats as they passed Old Abe; this always brought a cheer from the regiment, and the eagle would spread his wings as he always did when the regiment cheered. . . ."[98]

On Christmas Day, 1862, at Germantown, Tennessee, the Eagle Regiment celebrated by hoisting "an immense flag" over a stockaded fort made of cotton bales. The men cheered as the flag was raised. Old Abe stood alongside the flag staff, and, sensing the symbolic importance of the moment, let out a trilling "war scream."[99]

It is not difficult to appreciate the esteem which Old Abe generated. Camp life never became enjoyable, but the presence of a genuine celebrity helped the men to overcome some of the more debilitating aspects of soldiering. He gave the men of the Eagle Brigade a symbol of what they were fighting for, a measure of amusement, and a great deal of publicity and fame.

12

On the Move

THE Western Theater in the Civil War stretched from Tennessee to Arizona Territory and from the Ohio River to the Gulf of Mexico. The vastness of the region demanded mobile operations. While railroads and steamboats provided the vital transportation mechanisms, marching also played an important role. Indeed, the long-winded, foot-slogging endurance of Union infantrymen from Midwestern states like Wisconsin made the troops famous. The Eagle Brigade set its own war-time speed record in March, 1864, when it marched 114 miles in seventy-two hours.[1]

It was no easy task to cover such great distances while encumbered by the wherewithal to fight battles, provide shelter from the elements, care for the wounded and the inevitable sick, cook meals, supply food to large numbers of men and draft animals, and, above all, retain the ability to move rapidly. Not surprisingly, shortages occurred. Unforseen difficulties had to be overcome. But the ability of the Union armies to remain on the move, and to conduct simultaneous large-scale operations despite all opposition, helped lead to victory.

The men of Old Abe's regiment displayed their usual range of talents and inadequacies while on the march. The non-admirable forms of behavior that had become common by 1863 were, unfortunately, even more pronounced in 1864. Like most combat infantrymen in the West, members of the Eighth Wisconsin actively participated in looting, pillaging, and burning. The reasons behind their anti-social behavior were several.

Sometimes, the Federal supply system simply failed to provide the troops with adequate provisions. Mismanagement and corruption were not unknown in the Union army.[2] Sometimes, on fast-moving campaigns, the infantrymen outdistanced or overtaxed their own supply wagons, as they did during the Vicksburg campaign in 1863 and would do on the Missouri expedition in 1864. Sometimes, Confederate raiders destroyed rail lines or supply depots, causing widespread shortages, and sometimes the men engaged in reprisals against the local populace. Mostly, however, the richness and abundance of Southern farms tempted the men—

beckoning them to supplement standard army rations with fresh local fare.

After their first engagement at Fredericktown, Missouri, in October of 1861, members of the Eighth stole livestock from local citizens. The citizenry had not informed the Union troops of the Confederates hidden nearby, and for their "treachery" (according to Private Weissert) "the boys . . . killed chickens, turkeys, and hogs . . . by the hundreds."[3] Even Captain Lyon felt compelled to justify the looting of farmyards which had erupted so early in the war, writing to the editor of the Racine *Advocate*:

> Our troops respect the right of property, taking comparatively little without compensation. The truth of history compels me to admit, however, that a process which the soldiers call "jerking" has been indulged in . . . when we were in the neighborhood of pigs and chickens. . . .[4]

Colonel Murphy sanctioned foraging when the Eagle Brigade marched to Tuscumbia, Alabama, just prior to the battle of Iuka in mid-1862. "We had tolerable good times on this march," wrote Private Edward Cronon, "as we had priviledges never allowed us before—that is we helped ourselves to everything in the way of eatables that we wanted. . . ."[5] "I tell you," wrote Private Dave McLain of Company C to his sister, "the second brigade did not leave many chickens or pigs on the road."[6] But McLain was most impressed by the voraciousness of the Eleventh Missouri, which "beats anything in this country for jayhawking."[7]

After the boldly successful raids by Van Dorn and Forrest against Grant's depots and supplies during the first Vicksburg campaign, rations became scarce. The ineffectual pursuit of the mounted Confederates by Union infantrymen during the winter of 1862–1863 caused theater-wide shortages and actual hunger.[8] "We were on ¼ and ½ rations at this time and had been for near two weeks," explained Corporal Rogers, concluding with wry humor, "two hardtack crackers a day will not fatten a man."[9] Coffee ran short, as did all types of meat.[10]

Widespread looting and incendiarism occurred during the Vicksburg campaign of 1863. Grant's men pillaged the fine plantations along the Louisiana shore of the Mississippi River opposite the landing zones at Bruinsburg and Grand Gulf. An enlisted man in Company K of the Eighth Wisconsin recalled:

A certain mess in our company was known never to suffer the want of food, if food was in the country. After going into camp four of that mess, as was the custom, while the others were getting wood, water and preparing coffee . . . etc. were looking around for something more delicate. It was not long before they returned. . . . One of the boys had a string of goldfish taken from the fountain on the premises, another had a peacock, and another a part of a fawn, taken from the park near the palatial residence. These with sweet potatoes, lettuce, young onions, radishes etc. made a supper, though a little late, which was certainly sumptuous.[11]

Members of the Eighth Wisconsin helped loot and then burn Jackson, Mississippi, en route to the Grand Assault before Vicksburg. In fact, Grant's Vicksburg campaign was planned around the idea that Federal troops would draw rations from the Southern countryside. "We were out of tobacco and into Jackson," wrote Corporal Rogers, "and so in we went and helped ourselves to tobacco, rum, sugar, meat, and anything we wanted, and we wanted it I tell you. . . . We destroyed everything in the town burning about half of it. . ."[12] Mechanicsburg, Mississippi, and Richmond, Louisiana, became victims of the torch-wielding Wisconsin soldiers soon afterwards. Saulsbury, Tennessee, which changed hands during the raids by Forrest's Confederates and the inevitable Union response, likewise suffered the torch. In late 1863, Dave McLain wrote to his sister: "This had been a pretty town once but it is all burned now. The rebels came in here and burned out the Union families and then we came and burned out all the rebels . . . there is not a house left standing."[13]

In late February, 1864, the Eagle Brigade participated in the Meridian expedition under General Sherman. The expedition helped train Federal troops to carry out long-distance land offensives without heavy supply lines, and subjected Southern railroad lines to systematic destruction. Again, Southern communities suffered from the boys in blue. Private Weissert wrote of the devastation to a friend in Racine: ". . . Everything was destroyed from Meridian to Enterprise, which like Jackson and Meridian was destroyed. From here the expedition took a different road for home, destroying everything, some of the towns through which we passed were completely demolished, not even a fence post left standing. At Canton . . . I counted

the remains of twenty-three locomotives, living on the country through which we passed, without shelter not even a tent. . . ."[14]

In August, 1864, Captain Britton wrote to the editor of the Janesville *Gazette*: ". . . In a few hours the beautiful village of Oxford [Mississippi] was in ruins. During the conflagration the soldiers took the liberty to plunder, and I must say it outdone all acts of the kind that I have witnessed. . . . It was the most wholesale plundering that any army ever participated in. . . ."[15]

Southern livestock suffered tremendous losses during the Civil War. Long after the war ended, Southern farmers continued to experience serious livestock shortages initiated originally by the destructive Union soldiers.[16] Those soldiers were not, as a rule, evil people. In fact, they were arguably somewhat better-than-average citizens who had volunteered to become soldiers in order to save their government from political disintegration. But they turned to pillage after it became apparent that the Confederate armies would not surrender in spite of Northern superiority in equipment, manpower, supplies, and battles won. To subdue the entire Southern people, therefore, Union troops (encouraged by their commanders) lashed out indiscriminately. The boys in blue came to understand that the road to Wisconsin led through the charred and smoking ruins of the Confederacy. Total victory was the surest route back to civilian life, home, and loved ones.

Marching, unlike mere looting, was hard work. Packing and unpacking camp gear required strenuous effort.[17] On fast-moving campaigns, the men sometimes chose not to use their small "dog" (or pup) tents. They slept in the open, placing their rubber ponchos or gum blankets on the ground and their army-issue coarse wool blankets over themselves. On forced marches, such as those spent chasing mounted Confederate raiders, the men virtually collapsed and slept where they fell when the order to halt came. "Rapid marches are frequently made, through rain, mud, dust, and under scorching sun," wrote Augie Weissert in early 1864. "I have seen men, after traveling all day and night, lay down at the first halt, and no sooner down, then they would be fast asleep as you could imagine. . . ."[18]

Sleep became more elusive when it rained. On election day in 1864, for instance, the Eighth Wisconsin and the Eleventh Missouri were camped twenty miles ahead of their division on a slight rise of ground in west-central Missouri. Headquarters had the only tent; the troops had none. "No sooner had we fairly got in camp," wrote an enlisted man, "when the rain commenced to pour down, . . . all who could went to sleep."[19] Next day, the command was totally surrounded by a fast-flowing river over twelve feet deep. "Guns, hardtack, ammunition and all were washed away by the merciless stream . . . the water still rising . . . many of the men were half under water. . . ."[20] The two regiments were rescued from the flood by the remainder of the division, who helped fell trees to bridge the stream.

Cooking techniques were simplified as much as possible while on the move. When available, meat was cooked in the iron mess plate it was eaten from, or roasted on sticks over the camp fire. Sometimes, the men ate their meat ration raw, or between hardtack crackers.[21] If the unit continued to move rapidly, there was no time to forage. On these occasions, the troops had to satisfy their hunger with the salt meat, hardtack, and coffee which comprised the basic Army ration.

Not surprisingly, some infantrymen thought about transferring to the cavalry. Traveling across the South on horseback, rather than by foot, had an undeniable appeal. Robert Rogers of La Crosse wrote, "I am going to try to get transferred to the 2nd Wisconsin Cavalry . . . for actually I am tired of packing." Rogers also noted that his company lieutenant, the thirty-six-year-old La Crosse blacksmith Alonzo D. Hickock, "is getting to be the meanest of the mean," and that perception encouraged thoughts of a transfer.[22]

But most foot soldiers held horse soldiers in disfavor. Whenever possible, the infantrymen made disparaging remarks about cavalrymen. On the march, the Eagle Brigade sometimes had to move aside and allow the faster-moving cavalry to pass. On such occasions, the horses coated the foot soldiers with dust if it was dry, and with mud when it was wet. As the marching columns stretched for miles along the roads, the cavalrymen would be pursued "with volleys of sarcastic and abusive comments on his horsemanship, his horse, his yellow stripes, his clanking saber, his personal worthlessness and his disgraceful pedigree," recollected a veteran of the Eagle Brigade.[23]

The opportunity to tour large portions of the South, observing its scenery and people, was an

unanticipated benefit of wide-ranging, mobile war. The Western Confederacy did not impress many of the members of Old Abe's regiment, however. Aside from the rich plantation areas of eastern Louisiana, the Vicksburg region, and in the Red River Valley, the Confederate states seemed poor when compared to Wisconsin. So did the inhabitants. George Driggs of Dane County observed in 1864:

As far as the country is concerned, I would not give the poorest farm in Wisconsin for the whole country. . . . It is indeed surprising to notice the destitution . . . husbands have left their starving families . . . and gone off to fight. . . . Dupes they are—they do not appear to be more than half civilized: a sneaking puny set of men, . . . un-uniformed and armed with every conceivable weapon from a pitchfork down to a tooth pick.[24]

Sergeant Crandall from Sheboygan County wrote of the enemy shortly before Confederate raiders captured him:

Their private soldiers were rough looking men without uniforms, with ragged clothes, sheepish looking and silly in conversation. Their dress represents every color and style immaginable. I noticed that a good portion of them wear butternut colors or clothes of home manufacture. . . .[25]

The use of tobacco products by Southern women struck some Wisconsin soldiers as unusual. Some Southern women smoked cigarettes and even dipped snuff. Augie Weissert never got over his amazement at this phenomenon, labeling Southern women "queer beings" in 1864, and many years later writing a story which retained his original sense of bemusement and dismay.[26]

The South, it should be remembered, was an invaded territory, a battleground. The South's planter elite could hardly be expected to remain at home to greet the torch-wielding Union army and impress Wisconsin farmers with their cultured sophistication. Most brave, able-bodied Southerners were in arms. As a result, the wartime impressions gained of the Southern population by the boys in blue did not accurately reflect the peacetime South.

What the Wisconsin citizen-soldiers did come away with was a picture of a society in a state of traumatic dislocation. Thousands of slaves had rushed to the Union lines and freedom—diminishing the Southern labor force. The young white men had left home to serve with Confederate military units. Plantation-owning families fled in terror, leaving their homes and belongings to the blue-clad pillagers. Livestock and fences provided the invaders with food and fuel. Railroads, bridges, and public property of all types were consumed by total war. Crops, markets, trade, and patterns of commerce experienced disruption.

Old Abe adjusted as best he could to the demand of these fast-moving Western campaigns, just as the rest of the command did. The war eagle consumed tainted meat if there was no option. Dave McLain taught Old Abe to drink directly from his canteen while on the march. "There was not a soldier in the regiment but would have divided his last drop of water to quench Old Abe's thirst," recalled McLain.[27]

On the march, the men watched for changes in Old Abe's composure as a sign of developments in the weather. It was believed that the eagle could predict rain. If the eagle felt a storm coming on, he became "uneasy" and "very lively." If thunder was imminent, Old Abe uttered his distinctive cry. When rain fell and no thunder or lightning registered on his internal barometer, the eagle became calm, ducked his head under his wing, and waited for the sunshine.[28]

The bird rode on his perch alongside the flags at the head of the regiment. His staff fitted into a leather socket cinched around the eagle-bearer's waist. The eagle-bearer had no other responsibilities than caring for his feathered burden, and carried neither knapsack nor musket. (Abe's sixteen-foot leash was shortened to three feet while on the march, so as to constrain him to his perch.)[29]

In late December, 1862, the Eagles formed in line of battle to honor the presence of the Twelfth Wisconsin Infantry, marching by during the unsuccessful zig-zag campaign against Van Dorn and Forrest. As the members of the Twelfth passed their fellow Wisconsinites near Waterford, Mississippi, Sergeant Major Driggs proudly noted: "The Eighth brought out the Eagle and formed . . . by the roadside. As they caught a glimpse of our old bird, they commenced cheering. . . ."[30]

Old Abe's human comrades gained a measure of fame from their association with the by now famous Wisconsin war eagle. As one veteran of the Forty-Seventh Illinois Infantry explained:

> The immensity of operations, the vast numbers engaged and the wide scope of territory over which the war was fought gave but little opportunity for small commands to gain more than local

fame. Yet the Eagle Brigade, as it came to be called, won fame not only in the Western Armies but over a large part of the civilized world. . . .[31]

13

The Price of Cotton

EIGHTEEN sixty four was the most eventful year of the war for the Eagle Brigade, which participated in the Meridian expedition during February, the Red River campaign from March to the end of May, the drive against Forrest's rebel cavalry during July, Price's Missouri expedition in the fall, and finally, in resisting the Confederate invasion of Tennessee in December. Two major battles and twenty smaller engagements—including one otherwise insignificant encounter that cost the Eighth Wisconsin nearly as many casualties as the Grand Assault on Vicksburg—took place in 1864. The men also returned to Wisconsin for the first time since 1861—most while on a furlough earned at the cost of re-enlisting, the remainder after mustering out at the expiration of their original three-year term. Furthermore, by the time the year ended, Old Abe had achieved national reknown.

The year began with a general reorganization of the Union armies in the West. The Eagle Brigade became the Second Brigade, First Division, XVI Army Corps, Major General Stephen A. Hurlburt commanding. "Fighting Joe" Mower became divisional commander. Colonel Lucius F. Hubbard of the Fifth Minnesota Infantry took command of the Eagle Brigade. The Eagles never actually served under Hurlburt. General Sherman split the XVI Corps into two detachments, Hurlburt's eventually participating in the Atlanta campaign along with the bulk of the Army of the Tennessee; the other became an independent strike force to be used for unanticipated military contingencies and led by Brigadier General Andrew Jackson Smith.[1]

Smith was a professional soldier. He graduated from the U.S. Military Academy in 1834, and had served in the Mexican War and for a dozen years in the West. He received a promotion to brigadier general of volunteers in 1862 when he gave up mounted service for an infantry command. He distinguished himself throughout the war, earning two promotions for meritorious service in 1864.[2] A slender, grizzled, balding man, he had a reputa-

US Army Military History Institute

Andrew Jackson Smith distinguished himself in every campaign he took part in. His tough, fast-marching command earned such nicknames as "the wandering tribes of Israel" and "Smith's Guerillas."

tion for being an appreciator of fine horses and whiskey. A. J. Smith was no military genius, but he was an aggressive, capable, unsentimental leader who pushed his men to their limits.

Under the leadership of people like Smith and Mower, Wisconsin's citizen-soldiers became tempered and hardened, part of a military force with growing capabilities. The Union Army was an experienced, well-supplied, and increasingly well-led organization by 1864. From regimental level upward, the carnage of two years' campaigning left a nucleus of effectives who had the resolve and the ability to continue the struggle against the South.

The Union Army did not win all its battles in 1864. Far from it. But Federal troops had become highly competitive in spite of Confederate skill, courage, daring, and geographical advantage. The conflict showed no sign of abatement in either the East or the West during 1864. Robert E. Lee and

the Army of Northern Virginia remained powerful even after their defeat at Gettysburg. Northern seizure of the Mississippi River did not automatically mean the end of struggle in the West. When President Lincoln ordered U. S. Grant to assume command of all United States armies and take control of the Eastern Theater, the cigar-smoking general vowed to crush the Confederacy in 1864. Grant planned to use the North's superior manpower and material resources in a massive war of annihilation. The North would hammer the South in simultaneous major campaigns in both Virginia and the West. No matter what the cost, Grant intended to press for a conclusion.

The question of re-enlistment occupied the thoughts of most members of the Eighth Wisconsin in early 1864. Army officials made two promises to encourage re-volunteering: an immediate thirty-day furlough and a bonus of $402. All one had to do was sign on for another three years—or until victory.

Some people agonized over the decision. James Mellor of Company I promised his wife that he would never re-enlist, adding, "I think they will get no one in our Company to re-inlist. . . ."[3] By March, however, nearly three-fourths of the regiment had re-enlisted—including James Mellor.

Some of the men sincerely felt a desire to sustain the Union cause. Private Mellor explained to his wife that their friend and neighbor Robert Rogers "is Heart and Soul for the Supression of the Rebels."[4] Augie Weissert wrote to a friend in Racine, "I wish to see the war out, and I will. . . ."[5] Weissert, however, strongly urged his brothers not to enlist. "I would rather not see you at all than to see you in the army," he wrote after an arduous campaign.[6]

The veteran's bounty was alluring. Some believed that the war would be over before the expiration of their second three-year enlistment. Private Weissert felt this way, and he considered the $402 a fair exchange for the short time remaining in the war.[7] Sam Miles of Company E also wanted the money, but he considered the war far from being over and refused to re-enlist as a veteran.[8]

In all, 181 men elected to return to civilian life following expiration of their enlistment. Regimental commander John Jefferson, promoted to a colonelcy after being wounded at Vicksburg, declined to rejoin, as did almost one-half of Company C.[9] Hospital steward James Jackson decided to use his wartime experience to help gain admittance to medical school. The veterans, grateful for his past services, presented Jackson with a "pot of gold" to help defray the costs associated with attending school in New York City.[10] Because he was part of Company C, Old Abe also failed to reenlist when the majority of the company refused to do so.

Three hundred and three members of the Eighth Wisconsin, however, volunteered to serve for another three years.[11] The regiment earned the right to call itself the Eighth Regiment of Wisconsin Veteran Volunteer Infantry. New recruits arrived from the North to replace regimental losses.

The promised immediate furlough proved to be the first casualty among the veterans. On March 6, 1864, General William T. Sherman made a special request. He asked the veterans of Smith's command to delay their furlough for one month. General Smith was being sent on a short expedition against Confederate forces west of the Mississippi, Sherman explained, along with two other corps from the Department of the Gulf. Smith's veterans would be returned to Memphis and sent home on leave as soon as they completed their assignment.[12] In sturdy democratic fashion, the men of the regiment agreed to Sherman's request, but felt somewhat disappointed since promise of immediate furlough had induced some to "veteranize."[13]

The ensuing Red River campaign was a federal attempt to capture Shreveport, Louisiana, the headquarters of the Trans-Mississippi Confederacy. The Red River wound through a particularly fertile cotton-producing area before it reached Shreveport. Representatives of Northern commercial interests influenced the choice of the invasion route. They hoped that cotton seized by Union forces would provide Northern textile manufacturers with extremely valuable raw materials, in short supply since the cotton-producing states had left the Union. In other words, in order to secure Southern cotton for Northern textile manufacturers, the Union sent an expedition into northwestern Louisiana.[14]

Major General Nathaniel P. Banks, an influential Massachusetts politician who had close ties with New England textile interests as well as with the Lincoln administration, was chosen to lead the campaign. As commander of the Department of the Gulf, General Banks ordered large portions of the XIII and XIX Army Corps to rendezvous at

Alexandria, Louisiana, with the detachment of Sherman's army commanded by A. J. Smith. Smith's Corps consisted of nearly 12,000 men and fifteen pieces of artillery. The XIII and XIX Corps, a cavalry division, as well as considerable artillery support brought the grand total of Banks's entire command to 35,847 troops and ninety guns.[15] Rear Admiral David D. Porter accompanied Smith's Corps with a fleet of sixty vessels that included sixteen ironclad gunboats and four light-draft "tinclads." Porter's squadron mounted 210 guns, and in one naval officer's words "comprised the most formidable force that had ever been collected in the western waters."[16]

Smith's Corps departed from Vicksburg on March 9 and headed down the Mississippi. The Eighth Wisconsin rode the steamer *Des Moines*, 411 muskets strong.[17] Smith's Corps reached Simmsport on March 13 and began working at destroying the Confederate forts that blocked navigation of the Red River. Fort Scurry, at the confluence of Yellow Bayou and Bayou de Glasie, was captured without opposition. Smith's men then pushed on thirty-five miles to Fort De Russy, a much stronger bastion located on the Red River near the village of Marksville. While approaching

US Army Military History Institute

Nathaniel P. Banks, a "political" general who proved weak and irresolute during the Red River campaign.

Fort De Russy, the largely Gallic population of the region displayed the tri-color flag of France to indicate their neutrality in the American struggle.[18]

Fort De Russy mounted six heavy guns in a quadrangular, bomb-proof, casemated battery facing the Red River. Iron railroad ties reinforced its sixteen-foot-high ramparts. From the rear, however, the bastion had only several light field guns and a garrison of three hundred men for protection. Union sharpshooters and artillery showered the Confederate defenders while General Mower positioned his division for an assault. The Eagle Brigade lay concealed until Mower ordered the advance. Private Miles remembered the moment when, "as though by magic raised from out of the fertile soil, appeared a solid line of blue."[19] General Mower, Old Abe, and the Eagles, all veterans of the Grand Assault, "immediately invested" Fort De Russy, rushing across the exposed field of fire and over the walls at the center of the fort. Fort De Russy surrendered three minutes later.

Casualties were very light in the division, and non-existent among the Eagles.[20] The entire action had lasted only twenty minutes.[21]

Mower's Division then embarked on Porter's naval vessels, steamed up the Red River, and occupied Alexandria. General Banks and his large force were expected to arrive as scheduled in mid-March. Banks, however, occupied himself with political affairs in New Orleans, and consequently did not arrive until March 25.[22]

While awaiting the arrival of General Banks, members of the Eighth Wisconsin established a newspaper. The men confiscated the press of the Louisiana *Democrat* and began publishing the *Red River Rover* from the mobile office aboard the steamboat *Des Moines*. "It was a very pithy and interesting sheet," recalled Private Miles.[23]

When the "Eau Claire Eagles" drew guard duty at divisional headquarters, Company I became the color company and Old Abe, of course, remained with the flags. It was the first and only time that he was separated from Company C. Eagle-bearer Burkhardt of Company C continued at his post of honor. A new color guard was organized containing men from different companies. Color Sergeant Ephraim Miller came from Sheboygan County's Company B. Corporals Ambrose Armitage of Company D and Lucas B. Lathrop of Company K had been with the flags since Vicksburg, and they remained part of the reorganized guard. Corporals Francis H. Wagner of Company F, Martin Schenck of Company I, and Walter S. Heal of Company H completed the color guard roster.[24]

Shortly before Banks arrived, General Mower led his division on a raid against Confederate cavalry that had been harassing Union troops. After a seven-and-a-half-hour, twenty-five-mile march along Bayou Rapide through a torrential rain in "mud knee deep," Mower captured several Confederate officers who were passing the stormy evening at a plantation house near Henderson's Hill.[25] Mower "showed the Confederates the Eagle," recalled Private Miles, to let the Southerners know they had been captured by the famous Eagle Brigade. He then obtained the password to approach the nearby Confederate cavalry camp. While part of the Union force made a demonstration in front of Henderson's Hill, Mower and several regiments circled the position, taking a "detour" through the swampy area to come upon it from the rear. In pre-dawn light General Mower,

dressed in a gray jacket taken from one of the captured Confederate officers, strolled into the Southern camp after calling out the password. As day broke, the Southerners were surprised to see a now blue-coated Union general bearing the eagle—Old Abe—in their very midst. About 1,000 muskets were leveled at the drowsy horse soldiers, who immediately surrendered. Some 350 Confederates and 400 horses were captured, all without casualties.[26] Union troops shared rides back to Alexandria on March 22.

General Banks and his forces began arriving as Mower returned from Henderson's Hill. Smith's Corps moved to Cotile Landing, one day's march above Alexandria. There, they boarded transports and steamed up the Red River to Grand Encore, eighty miles above Alexandria near Natchitoches, where the entire Union force united on April 2.[27]

Above Alexandria the geography of the Red River country began exerting a decisive influence on the expedition. Just outside Alexandria, the Red River flows over a series of rocky shallows called "the falls." At times of high water the falls did not obstruct navigation, but when the water level dropped, as it did in April, 1864, the passage of vessels became treacherous. Admiral Porter lost the hospital ship *Woodford* on the way up, and the falls at Alexandria became the most significant environmental feature in the events following General Banks's tardy arrival on the Red River.[28]

When the Union troops gathered for the expedition to take Shreveport, they presented a memorable spectacle. The XIII Army Corps led Banks's force. It was followed by the XIX Corps, composed partially of inexperienced eastern regiments. Banks's men were finely uniformed with white paper collars and gloves, however, and they appeared magnificent in comparison to General Smith's well-worn troops. Colonel Hubbard, commander of the Eagle Brigade and a future governor of Minnesota, remembered:

> Their equipment was as elaborate as the regulations allowed, and altogether it was the proudest army . . . in appearance that graced the Valley of the Mississippi during the war. Quite a contrast was the appearance of the XVI Army Corps . . . it was positively shabby in comparison.[29]

As General Banks reviewed Smith's dusty veterans, he naively exclaimed to Admiral Porter, "What in the name of Heaven did Sherman send

Lucius F. Hubbard led the Eagle Brigade at the Battle of Nashville and later became governor of Minnesota.

me these ragged guerillas for?"[30] Thereafter, the detachment of the XVI Corps was known as "Smith's Guerillas."[31] The proper answer to Banks's question would of course be given on the battlefield. Sherman had sent fighting men, and they resented bringing up the rear of Banks's gleaming force. They also resented the snappy Easterners of the XIX Corps, jeering at them and calling them "Band box brigades!"[32]

General Banks moved on Shreveport along an inland road leading to Mansfield, leaving Porter's fleet on the Red River. The further away from the river the troops went, the more dry and desolate became the countryside. The road was a narrow one, surrounded by dense pine woods and a virtual wilderness. Banks's 3,500 cavalry led the Union advance, followed by nearly 200 wagons, the artillery, and infantry of the XIII Corps. Behind them came the XIX Corps. "Smith's Guerrillas" were a day's march further back, bringing up the rear of the strung-out Union forces.[33] For the men of Old Abe's regiment, the campaign had been simply one more in a long series of hard marches and intermittent boat rides, until late in the day on April 8, 1864.

Then the Confederates turned on Banks at Sabine Cross Roads. Confederate General "Dick" Taylor concentrated his forces in a horseshoe-shaped crescent astride the Mansfield road. Taylor was the only son of President Zachary Taylor. A wealthy slave-owning Louisiana sugar planter and a graduate of Yale University, he was one of the few successful Confederate generals who had no military training beyond his extensive reading on the topic. Taylor had distinguished himself while serving under Robert E. Lee and Stonewall Jackson at various Eastern battlefields before coming West. In addition to being courageous, Taylor was brilliant, a gifted writer, and an outspoken critic of those whom he considered to be incompetent— among them his own superior, Major General E. Kirby Smith.[34]

The battle at Sabine Cross Roads, which ultimately saved the Trans-Mississippi Confederacy, had several phases. Texas cavalrymen halted the mounted Federals on the morning of April 8. Infantry from the XIII Corps came up to the front piecemeal, and Taylor's infantry routed them individually, and with heavy casualties, during the afternoon. Banks's huge wagon train, most of the XIII Corps' artillery and other supplies, as well as large numbers of Federals, were captured in the process. Pandemonium and disorderly retreat soon followed. At dusk, the XIX Corps barely managed to halt the Southerners, whose advancing units had become entangled in the congested mass of panic-stricken Unionists.[35] As night fell, the fighting died away.

All realized that the battle would resume on the next day. The XIX Corps fell back to a position slightly west of Pleasant Hill. The Eagle Brigade and the rest of A. J. Smith's men marched quickly to the scene late on April 8, where they augmented the XIX Corps' front as well as forming the Union reserve and left. Food was unavailable because it had been captured with the wagon train. Instead of hardtack and coffee, the Eagles dined on canned fruit and whiskey—they were all that remained. The Confederates, on the other hand, passed a pleasant evening looting General Banks's wagons, which more than generously supplied their wants.[36]

The Confederate attack on Pleasant Hill came during the late afternoon of April 9. Rebel infantry and cavalry stormed across an open field towards the unentrenched Federal lines. The Union forces held the elevated ground, but the Southerners nevertheless broke their center, which was held by the XIX Corps. A. J. Smith opened his lines to let the demoralized XIX Corps pass through on the way to the rear, closing behind them and in front of the exultant, oncoming Rebels. In face of the disciplined Confederate advance, Smith ordered his men to hold their fire until he gave the word. At 5:00 P.M. "Smith's Guerillas" began an aimed volley fire at close range.[37] Seven thousand rifles blasted the Confederate center. Entire Southern regiments disappeared, "literally torn to pieces," according to Sam Miles of the Eighth Wisconsin, who was on the left.[38] The Confederates slowed, halted, and returned the fire, and the battle settled into a "severe musketry" contest at close range. Losses mounted. Colonel Hubbard of the Eagle Brigade remembered that "our troops stood as if rooted in their tracks. They could be killed, but they could not be driven."[39]

As the first line of Southerners evaporated— "mowed down like grass," according to a participant—and the second one wavered, Smith ordered General Mower to lead a counterattack.[40] Mower's division fixed bayonets and performed a "grand right wheel" at the double quick, rolling up the Confederate flank. The Southerners withdrew, stubbornly at first, and then they broke and fled. The Eighth Wisconsin participated in the charge that left the Union in control of the battlefield, driving the Confederates for three miles as darkness fell.[41]

Old Abe witnessed the battle from his shield-shaped perch. Like other experienced soldiers, the eagle had little fear of booming cannon; in fact, he seemed to enjoy it. When the musketry fire became intense, however, Old Abe became anxious. He "pranced up and down" on his perch, remembered a soldier of the Forty-Seventh Illinois positioned alongside the eagle during the eventful day, and "gave forth fierce screams."[42]

General Banks came on the scene at twilight, as

Behringer-Crawford Museum

Unidentified Federal unit, possibly a brigade or division, drawn up in line of battle near Stevenson, Alabama, c. 1864. The veteran troops of the Western Theater "could be killed, but they could not be driven."

the men were establishing a camp on the corpse-littered field.[43] He rode up to A. J. Smith, exclaiming, "God bless you, General, you have saved the army.[44] It had cost 1,369 men to do so. When coupled with the losses at Sabine Cross Roads, Banks had lost nearly 3,600 men, 156 wagons, twenty cannon, tons of small arms with ammunition, and 1,000 horses. Taylor's losses totaled 2,626 men and three cannon.[45] The two-day action at Sabine Cross Roads and Pleasant Hill was the largest battle of the war west of the Mississippi River. The time had come for a decision.

General Banks ordered an immediate retreat back to Grand Encore despite his Pleasant Hill victory. Hundreds of wounded lay on the battlefield awaiting medical attention; hundreds more required burial. Banks proposed to abandon these unfortunates. A. J. Smith protested vigorously, advising a pursuit of the Confederates and a resumption of the drive towards Shreveport. Banks overruled him.[46]

When news of the Union retreat became known, Banks's reputation among his men declined. A veteran of the Eagle Brigade's Forty-Seventh Illinois recalled, "when Banks and his staff appeared they were received in sullen silence."[47] Not only did Banks desert his own wounded; his retreat also allowed the Confederates to reform and swarm towards the Red River, thereby endangering the Union fleet.

Dick Taylor's men made good use of their newly acquired Union artillery when they moved down both sides of the Red River to attack Porter's ships. On April 12 a squadron of transports and gunboats became involved in one of the strangest battles of the Civil War. The gunboats *Osage* and *Lexington* engaged Southern cavalrymen with their heavy naval cannon at point-blank range. The contest was furious-sounding, and vast quantities of ammunition were expended. But little damage and few casualties resulted from the fight at Blair's Landing, although Union vessels began running aground and suffering from accidents caused by low water level in the river.[48] The Southern cavalry in turn encouraged the naval vessels to withdraw downriver, riddling the unarmed steamers with concentrated small-arms fire. "The sides of some of the transports are half shot away," wrote one soldier, "and their smoke stacks look like pepper boxes."[49]

The Union army and fleet, no longer proud and fine-looking, reunited at Grand Encore on April 14.[50] Now began a combined operation in retreat, with neither the army or the navy trying to do more than escape from the Red River country. The giant ironclad gunboat *Eastport* was severely damaged by a mine above Grand Encore and salvage operations somewhat delayed the withdrawal, allowing the Confederates to encircle Banks.[51] Taylor placed troops in front, on the flanks, and in the rear of the Union army's path of retreat. But just as Banks appeared to be trapped, General Taylor's superior ordered him to send three divisions of infantry to Arkansas where they would be used to repel another Union expedition. Thus, Taylor would confront Banks's retreating Union column of 25,000 men with 6,000 troops, mostly cavalry.[52] Taylor's only advantage was his wealth of recently acquired cannon—and his own abilities as a soldier.

The 100-mile Union retreat to Alexandria along the island formed by the Red and Cane rivers took fourteen days. The troops were engaged in continual skirmishing with the Confederates.[53] Captain Greene of the Eighth Wisconsin described a typical day in the field:

> We are really surrounded—attacked in front, in rear, and on the flank. . . . We started forward, but had not got far when we were compelled to form line of battle and face the rear. The enemy appeared and we had a lively fight for twenty minutes when they retreated. We then double quicked to catch up with our column. All day the experience was repeated . . . our communications in front and rear is cut off, and we have no rations . . . no coffee or crackers.[54]

Dick Taylor strongly contested the Union retreat at the crossing of the Cane River at Monett's Ferry. On April 24, the Eagle Brigade, along with Smith's Corps, fought two separate battles, one at Cloutiersville and the other at Monett's Bluff, before finally driving the Southerners out of the way. With the path to Alexandria opened, Smith's men began systematically demolishing farms and plantations along their route of retreat.

They destroyed everything. Livestock was massacred, buildings, towns and cotton gins were put to the torch, crops and planted fields were trampled. Thousands of slaves fled with the retreating Union Army. A naval officer remembered that the smoke from the burning Southern countryside was so thick that "the sun was obscured and appeared as though seen through a smoked glass."[55] Mem-

Union fleet at Alexandria, Louisiana, in May, 1864. The water level in the Red River is so low
that the ships cannot use the docks.

bers of the XIII and XIX Corps refused to participate in the wanton rampage. All accounts, including those by Confederates, place blame for the
destruction squarely on the shoulders of Smith's
command. A horrified Massachusetts cavalryman
noted:

> The country was in flames. Smith's men were
> burning on every hand. Dense clouds of smoke
> could be seen . . . as they fell back. . . . From the
> Cane River to Alexandria the country was in
> ruins. It was a picture, whose equal the men had
> never seen before.[56]

Smith's men were the last to enter Alexandria.
When the general rode down the column to the
head of his veteran troops late in the evening of
April 26, he received a thundering ovation from
the men in the ranks.[57]

The Navy's vessels, meanwhile, had been subjected to frequent bombardment and mass sniping
attacks as they withdrew. The damaged *Eastport*
was blown up when it became apparent that it
could not be floated. Confederates disabled and
captured two transports. Three "tin clads" were
seriously damaged with considerable loss of life.[58]
At Alexandria, it soon became apparent that there
was not enough water in the Red River to float
Porter's ironclads over the falls. The gunboats
were, in fact, trapped.

While Federal forces dug in at Alexandria,
Taylor sent mobile units down the Red River to
close the channel to Union navigation. Again,
Confederate cavalry armed with small arms and
field guns demonstrated that they could check
powerful naval vessels. By May 5 the Confederates
had captured or sunk three more transports and
two small gunboats. Banks was cut off.[59]

Colonel Joseph Bailey of the Fourth Wisconsin
Cavalry happened to be on duty as an engineering
officer with the XIX Corps. Bailey, a resident of
Kilbourn City, was experienced as a builder of
dams in the logging camps of Wisconsin's north
woods. He volunteered to design and oversee the
construction of a large dam across the 750-foot
channel of the Red River near the falls so as to
raise the water level for the benefit of the Navy.

With his supplies running low, his fleet trapped
above the falls, the enemy besieging the surrounded city and blocking the lower Red River,
and after suffering high losses in men, material,
and shipping the bumbling General Banks turned
his full attention to Bailey's dam project. Bailey
had a considerable selection of talented workmen
to help him; Maine regiments from the XIX Corps
provided experienced woodsmen for the felling of
trees and other construction activities.[60] Work on
the dam continued day and night. Workmen la-

WHi(W6)21063

Joseph Bailey of Kilbourn City (Wisconsin Dells) won a Congressional Medal of Honor for his brilliant improvisational engineering on the Red River expedition in 1864.

bored in neck-deep water, and all seemed ready on May 8. Several ironclads made it over the falls before the pressure of the rising water level burst a section of Bailey's dam. Not all the gunboats escaped, and the Wisconsin engineer went back to his drawing board to come up with a modified plan consisting of a series of smaller dams. While Bailey's men continued their day-and-night efforts, Admiral Porter's crews removed the heavy iron plate and naval guns from the trapped vessels.[61]

Dick Taylor made frequent attacks on Union positions around Alexandria to disrupt work on Bailey's dams. The skirmish line on the outskirts of Alexandria became the scene of heavy fighting. Various commands rotated skirmish-line duty. For ten days the Union infantry fought a constant series of hot engagements, expending large quantities of rifle ammunition.[62] While crossing a sugar field at Bayou La Moore, for example, the Eagle Brigade came under heavy artillery fire. "At every hedge and ditch," reported Lieutenant Colonel Jefferson of the Eighth Wisconsin, "he would come into battery, and open on us with his artillery and musketry."[63]

Finally, on May 13, the fleet succeeded in passing through the channel and below the falls.[64] The retreat of the Union army then resumed towards the safety of the Mississippi. A. J. Smith's men burned Alexandria to the ground after "preparing the place for Hell."[65] General Smith himself rode through the blazing streets, shouting "Hurrah boys, this looks like war!"[66]

Several battles lay between the smoldering Red River country and safety. Southern cavalry snapped after Banks while Taylor prepared for a full-scale engagement at the village of Mansura. Taylor concentrated his entire command across the path of Banks's retreat. With thirty guns, covered by infantry and cavalry, in full view across the strikingly beautiful Avoyelles Prairie, Taylor opened fire on Banks's retreating columns.

An artillery duel continued for several hours during the cloudless morning while the Union infantry readied itself for battle in classic Napoleonic style, completely in the open. With flags waving, bands playing, and messengers galloping across the "bosom of the verdant plain," recalled a veteran of the Eagle Brigade, "it was a glorious scene."[67] Some 18,000 Union soldiers, "resplendent in steel and brass," maneuvered "miles of lines and columns" with "beautiful silken flags" floating above them.[68]

The XIX Corps advanced on the left. The XIII Corps followed immediately behind them. A. J. Smith's men had to forego breakfast and march double quick to the front from their usual position in the rear of Banks's army. They took position on the right, the Eighth Wisconsin being the extreme left regiment of Smith's force.

Smith's XVI Corps now demonstrated that it could out-perform any unit in Banks's army, not only in combat, but also in formal military maneuver. "Smith's Guerillas" moved to the front in speedy columns, four men abreast. Confederate artillery fire caused an evolution in the column after three miles, as General Mower redeployed the Eagle Brigade in the more spread-out echelon pattern. The Eagles then advanced for another half mile before moving into line of battle just outside extreme musket range.[69] At this point, the XIX Corps halted and Smith's command rushed the Confederate position by itself. Without firing, the lines of "Smith's Guerillas" charged, "changing direction from direct to right oblique then left oblique, and front alternately," recalled Sam Miles

View of Joseph Bailey's Red River dam at Alexandria, Louisiana, May, 1864. By raising the water level, the dam enabled the Union fleet to escape downriver.

US Army Military History Institute

of the Eighth Wisconsin.[70] As they moved to within deadly range, the opposing Confederates withdrew. The action at Mansura had not been costly in terms of human life, although the Eighth Wisconsin suffered more than most regiments, taking a loss of eight seriously wounded and twenty-five superficially injured, including the regimental fife major, Andrew Burt.[71]

Ambushes, skirmishes, artillery duels, and hard marching under scorching conditions occupied the Union forces until May 18. While Banks crossed the Atchafalaya River to safety on a bridge of steamboats designed by Wisconsin's ingenious Colonel Bailey, "Fighting Joe" Mower recrossed Yellow Bayou with his division for a final battle with Taylor's Confederates.

The "severe engagement" of Yellow Bayou (or Bayou de Glazie) took place near Simmesport, Louisiana, where the ill-fated Red River Campaign had begun. Taylor's men made repeated and courageous attacks on Mower's position. The Union forces held their own, beating off waves of Southerners and then counterattacking until heavy casualties brought their own advance to a halt. Symbolically, the battle ended when the heavy firing ignited a wooded thicket at the center of combat, and the flaming woods separated two brave, closely matched opponents.[72] Mower withdrew, and the campaign ended.

The Red River campaign had been indecisive. Casualties were insignificant when compared with those suffered in the major battles taking place in Virginia, for example. The Eighth Wisconsin lost sixteen men to serious wounds, and two killed—about the same as they had experienced during the Grand Assault at Vicksburg. Total Union losses amounted to slightly over 5,000; Confederate losses totaled nearly 4,000.[73]

There were several results of the campaign, however. The North's material losses were, in fact, serious. Gunboats, wagons, and cannon could all be replaced in time, but not immediately. Moreover, the assignment of A. J. Smith's Corps to the ill-fated Red River expedition deprived General Sherman of seasoned troops who otherwise would have assisted him in the Atlanta campaign. Smith's absence might have helped prolong the war slightly; it certainly delayed Union plans to capture Mobile. The Navy too lost much by its participation on the campaign. Most significantly for the North, perhaps, was the fact that the price of cotton remained high. Commerce and war seemed incompatible on the Red River.

As for the Confederates, they had missed an opportunity to strike a heavy blow for the Southern cause when General Kirby Smith deprived Dick Taylor of his three infantry divisions after the battles of Sabine Cross Roads and Pleasant

Hill. Sending troops off to Arkansas when Banks had already been trapped on the Red River was a manifestly foolish decision. As a result, Taylor refused to serve any longer under Kirby Smith, and he transferred to another department.

Another less obvious feature of the Red River campaign involved the quality of Sherman's men. Although they may have appeared shabby and indifferently uniformed, "Smith's Guerillas" had proved themselves to be the best troops in Banks's command. Not only could they fight; they could also march, and carry out difficult parade-ground maneuvers under fire. The citizen-soldiers of Andrew Jackson Smith's Corps had been tranformed into professionals.

14

The Battle for Furlough

FOLLOWING the Red River fiasco, the men of the Eagle Brigade received their back pay of nearly $40, and a rest when they returned to Vicksburg. Paymasters also distributed the first $25 installment of the veterans' bounty to those who had reenlisted. Thoughts of furlough and home undoubtedly crossed the minds of the veterans as they took in such local sights as the Stockade Redan, where they had participated in the ill-fated Grand Assault during May of the previous year.[1] Private John Esterling, a twenty-one-year-old English-born "rouster" from the Town of Osceola in Sheboygan County, and one of the most popular men in the regiment because of his good nature, made off with a quantity of beer belonging to a sutler. Sam Miles helped Esterling, and others, consume it.[2] Only a steamboat ride, it seemed, separated Vicksburg and Wisconsin.

One small task remained to be accomplished, however, before departing for home. A band of Confederate cavalry, equipped with several batteries of artillery, had been systematically ambushing Union vessels as they rounded Cypress Bend in the Mississippi River between Columbia and Sunnyside Landing, Arkansas. Using techniques they had perfected on the Red River, the Confederates successfully closed a portion of the river to steamboat traffic. At a convenient assembly point on the outskirts of Lake Village on the shores of Lake Chicot, Arkansas, Colonel Colton Greene and

Major General John Marmaduke's Confederate force shelled twenty-one Union vessels from the banks of the nearby Mississippi. Greene reported that he destroyed three transports, captured two, damaged five others, and drove off five marine-filled gunboats in ten days, with "trifling loss" to himself.[3]

Confederate spies in Vicksburg warned Greene of an impending Union response. Greene was not surprised, therefore, when he learned that A. J. Smith's veteran troops had been ordered to mount an expedition against him.[4] Instead of fleeing, Marmaduke and Greene prepared a defensive position for their 600 men and fourteen guns.[5]

The Eagles disembarked from the steamer *Clara Belle* at Sunnyside Landing on June 5 along with thousands of other infantrymen from the XVI Corps, a large detachment of cavalry, and the Mississippi Marine Brigade. The Union force was supported by seven gunboats. A. J. Smith, now a major general, led the operation, and he confidently expected that his overwhelming force would simply sweep the bothersome Confederate horsemen away.[6]

Union troops began engaging the enemy at 11 A.M. after marching for three hours in a soaking downpour. Federal cavalry drove their gray-clad counterparts back towards the southern edge of Lake Chicot, a thirty-mile-long, crescent-shaped body of water located in a rich cotton-growing region. Fighting began in earnest when General Mower ordered the Eagle Brigade forward. Colonel Hubbard threw out five companies from the Forty-Seventh Illinois to act as skirmishers, while the rest of the brigade moved up to support them in line of battle.[7]

Mower deployed Major George Van Beek's Third Brigade to the left of the Eagles. Together, Mower's division pushed Greene's Confederates back until they withdrew across Ditch Bayou, destroying the bridge and ferry as they went.[8] Greene opened fire with a battery of four guns as the Union forces came to within a half mile of the bayou.[9]

The terrain favored defense. Greene's Confederates were now concentrated in a front three-quarters of a mile long, along a tree line on the west side of Ditch Bayou, their left resting on the shore of Lake Chicot and their right solidly anchored on Bayou Mason's heavily timbered banks. A Confederate battery fired obliquely from its secure position on Lake Chicot down the mile-long front of Mower's Division, thereby enfilading Hubbard's Eagles and Van Beek's Third Brigade.[10] Ditch Bayou, three miles long, 120 feet wide at this point, and quite deep, was fronted on the east by a fallow cotton field which afforded little cover.[11]

Union artillerymen failed to establish a counter battery as their infantry advanced. Confederate cannon fire, in the words of Colonel Hubbard, "became sharp and effective," driving the Union artillery off the field.[12] Colonel Hubbard, therefore, strengthened the Eagle Brigade's skirmishers. Companies B, D, and E of the Eighth Wisconsin moved up to the by now regimental strengthened skirmish line.[13]

General Mower—who, Private Sam Miles later recorded, seemed to be drunk—then dashed up to the front on his horse, waving his sword as he galloped along the line, exclaiming, "Forward Second Brigade, to the charge!"[14] "With a shout," the brigade advanced at the double quick "against a galling fire of musketry, and of grape, and cannister," the skirmishers in front protecting themselves behind occasional stumps, trying desperately to keep their ammunition and rifle locks covered from the heavy rain with their rubber ponchos. The Eagle Brigade halted 100 yards from the moat-like bayou, wavering under the intense Confederate rifle fire. The skirmishers were nearly upon the banks of Ditch Bayou, "at point-blank range of the enemy's muskets," reported Colonel Hubbard, "and wholly without cover."[15]

The exposed skirmishers dropped flat and rapidly fired at the flashes of the Confederate cannon. Private Miles, who was on the skirmish line at Lake Chicot, remembered furiously loading and reloading his Enfield musket while lying on his back.[16] "A severe and prolonged musketry firing took place," laconically reported a Union officer.[17] The Union skirmishers could neither cross Ditch Bayou nor retreat, because they would be easily shot down by the well-protected Confederates in the timberline less than seventy yards away. There seemed to be no alternative but to sustain the volume of rifle fire and shoot it out with the Southerners.

Colonel Hubbard sent forward more ammunition and more skirmishers. Company G of the Eighth Wisconsin reinforced the section of the skirmish line where Sam Miles lay.[18] The skir-

mishers fired so rapidly that their muskets began overheating and fouling. Miles and his comrades, who were now fighting for their lives, poured canteen water down the barrels of their Enfields to cool them off so they would retain their accuracy.[19] When Company G arrived with ammunition and reinforcements, the skirmish line inched forward, the men pouring a continual fire on the enemy gunners, and especially on their horses.[20] (The smoke from their rapid fire also provided a screen which partially hid the skirmishers from the Confederate return fire.)

The skirmishers occupied a desperate position. Men jumped in and out of their own gunsmoke as they aimed, fired, and quickly reloaded—repeating the process throughout the deadly afternoon. Names of comrades struck down by Confederate bullets were called out "for friends to hear."[21] The ugly fight continued with high casualties. Only the constant supply of ammunition saved the Eagle Brigade's skirmishers from destruction.

Mower's other brigade, to the left of the Eagles, fared about the same. High casualties and the impossibility of either crossing Ditch Bayou or of retreating left the Third Brigade shaken.[22] General Smith finally advanced yet another brigade, extending the Union line to the left and stretching the Confederate defense correspondingly. Union cavalry was sent to locate a spot where either Ditch Bayou or Bayou Mason could be forded, while the reinforced Federal infantry massed for an attack on the Confederate right.[23] The new attempt against the Confederate right was repulsed with heavy loss, but A. J. Smith renewed his attack. Finally, at 2:30 in the afternoon, the heavily outnumbered Confederates began running out of ammunition.[24] As their commander explained, "My ammunition was exhausted, my rear not secure and I determined to withdraw."[25] The Confederates retreated, and the Federals did not pursue. The rain kept falling.

Instead of following the enemy, the Union forces occupied Lake Village and licked their wounds.[26] Injured soldiers filled nearly all of the homes in the community, while the dead were buried near the battlefield.[27] The total Federal loss in this unexpectedly fierce engagement at Ditch Bayou was never officially reported, probably in an effort to hush up the entire affair. The Eagle Brigade lost twenty-seven killed and ninety wounded.[28] The Eighth Wisconsin's share of that grim total amounted to three dead and sixteen seriously wounded—about the same loss as experienced during the Grand Assault.[29] Among those killed was John Esterling, transformed by a cannon into an "unrecognizable tangled mass" on the skirmish line alongside his horrified comrade Sam Miles.[30]

The disaster at Lake Chicot understandably left the Federals in what a Southern historian described as an "unamiable mood." Rampaging members of Smith's XVI Corps looted houses in Lake Village, and destroyed the town's newspaper. Several buildings were torched, and all livestock was shot.[31] Smith's Corps then marched to Luna Landing where it embarked on transports and steamed north towards Memphis. Lake Village, Arkansas, recalled a Union officer, "lay trodden in the mud."[32]

Like so many other Civil War engagements, this one should probably never have occurred. Poor reconnaissance on the part of the overly confident and numerically superior Northerners was partially to blame for the unfortunate result. The reek of alcohol, and the number of innuendoes associating several of the more responsible officers with being "indisposed" at various critical moments, did not endear the Union commanders to the soldiers who paid the bill for their overconfidence. The encounter at Lake Chicot is lost in the mists of history, and it probably did not affect the outcome of the war by so much as one hour. But it clearly demonstrated that small, seemingly insignificant actions could be as dangerous as major battles—especially for the common soldier posted on the skirmish lines.

When General Smith's mauled detachment of the XVI Corps reached Memphis, the veterans of the Eighth Wisconsin and the Forty-Seventh Illinois began preparing for their long-overdue furlough. They had been scheduled to return home in early March. It was mid-June, and now many would never see their families again. The veterans of the Eleventh Missouri, who had been sent on furlough prior to the Red River Expedition, rejoined with the Eagles at Memphis.[33] New recruits swelled the rosters of Hubbard's Brigade.[34] All that remained was the posting of the furlough order, and anticipation filled the air.

On June 12, members of Brigadier General Samuel D. Sturgis' combined infantry and cavalry force, which had been chasing Forrest's Confeder-ate horsemen away from the priceless single-track railroad line that brought supplies to General Sherman as his army advanced on Atlanta, staggered into Memphis. Forrest had routed them at the battle of Brice's Cross Roads. Memphis itself was threatened by the doughty Forrest. Alarm spread. General Mower ordered the Eagles to ready themselves for an immediate march against Forrest.

The veterans simply refused. According to Sam Miles, an open "rebellion was threatened by the men if not granted leave."[35] The Wisconsin citizen-soldiers exercised their still-cherished rights as citizens, and come what may, they were going home. No appeals would suffice. On June 16, the order authorizing the return to Wisconsin arrived.[36]

The "Bobtails"—as the non-veterans were called—were consolidated into two companies which remained in the field. They accompanied Generals Smith and Mower on the arduous, costly, and indecisive campaign to catch Forrest which culminated at Tupelo, Mississippi. The veterans boarded the steamer *G. W. Graham* and headed north.[37]

When the veterans arrived in Chicago two days after departing from Memphis, Lieutenant Colonel Jefferson telegramed ahead to Madison to inform Adjutant General Gaylord of the anticipated time of arrival of his regiment.[38] The cooks at Mosher's Railroad House provided the men with an excellent dinner when they arrived in Madison on June 22.[39] After the meal, 240 veterans of the Eighth Wisconsin Infantry marched behind their regimental colors to the park on the Capitol Square for a reception.

Large numbers of people turned out to greet them. Flags waved from housetops, church bells rang, salutes were fired, and prominent citizens made speeches.[40] As part of the color guard, Old Abe naturally attracted much attention. (The eagle mascot had accompanied the veterans northward even though he was scheduled to be mustered out in September. It was hoped that Old Abe's fame would encourage recruits to join the veteran regiment.) Madisonians had not seen Old Abe since 1861, when the young eaglet was barely larger than a healthy rooster. "The Live Eagle, Old Abe, and the tattered and riddled colors of the regiment attracted all eyes," observed the *Wisconsin State*

Journal's editor. "Since we first saw him at Camp Randall," the newspaperman continued, "Old Abe has grown . . . and . . . acquired a dignity and ease of bearing."[41]

Wisconsin's secretary of state, General Lucius Fairchild, one-armed veteran of Gettysburg, one-time member of the Iron Brigade, and on his way to becoming governor, welcomed the Eagle Regiment. Fairchild especially greeted Old Abe, stating, "We welcome your Eagle, that National emblem, whose fame has been widely spread and become historic."[42]

Colonel Jefferson thanked the citizenry of Madison for their cordial hospitality. Jefferson proposed "three cheers and a big Eagle" for the Union, the President, and Wisconsin. "Three cheers were given with great enthusiasm by the boys of the Eighth," noted the *State Journal*, ". . . the Eagle evidently understanding his part, and at the third hurrah, stretching himself to his full height, and expanding his wings to the utmost."[43]

Several days later, the men went off to their respective homes. Old Abe traveled with the re-enlisted portion of Company C back to Eau Claire, where Captain Perkins had formed them up so long ago. Now Perkins was dead, and numerous "Eau Claire Badgers" had either been killed or disabled. Residents of Eau Claire greeted Old Abe and his comrades enthusiastically. Booming cannon, martial music, patriotic songs, and great quantities of food awaited the remnant of Company C and Captain Victor Wolf, who led them.[44] "Well may Eau Claire be proud," wrote the editor of the *Free Press*, ". . . that she has a representative company in the Eagle Regiment—proud that the Eagle, so famous, is a native of the Chippewa Valley."[45]

Old Abe soon departed, traveling to Chippewa Falls to participate in the Fourth of July festivities planned by the Ladies Aid Society of that city. The celebration attracted a large crowd. The Ladies Aid Society members served a meal in a specially constructed wigwam, and, coupled with ice cream and lemonade sales, raised nearly $500 to assist wounded soldiers. It was Old Abe's first venture into fund raising.[46]

The evening culminated in a sermon delivered by Reverend J. O. Barrett, a Universalist minister who resided in Eau Claire. Barrett emphasized the "necessity of Union sentiment, Emancipation, . . .

WHi(X3)15525

Old Abe performs one of his crowd-pleasing stunts: spreading his wings on cue, c. 1879.

and free labor" in his address. Old Abe and veterans of Company C sat with Reverend Barrett at the head of the reviewing stand as the guests of honor. According to local news accounts, Old Abe appeared to understand Barrett's comments, and by his presence seemed to say, "I emblemize your liberty."[47]

Other veterans enjoyed their visits home quite as much as Old Abe did. Augie Weissert, for example, attended a series of picnics and parties in the Racine area. There, he met a "gay girl" named Lucy who became his companion for the remainder of the furlough.[48] The youthful Weissert actually lost weight while at home in spite of frequent home-cooked meals.[49]

The veterans returned to duty as July closed. A new set of flags accompanied the soldiers on the train to Cairo.[50] Old Abe rode alongside eagle-bearer Burkhardt on the trip back to the war. When a railroad conductor asked Burkhardt to buy a ticket for Old Abe—who, after all, occupied a seat—the German immigrant refused. "Pay for that thing, or I'll put you out!" exclaimed the conductor. Burkhardt told the railroad official, in halting English, that Old Abe was a free American eagle and, therefore, should ride for free. "Matters grew squally," as the veterans liked to tell the story, until the carload of soldiers and other passengers came to Burkhardt's defense. The conductor hastily retreated to another car, and Old Abe rode free.[51]

The eagle had changed greatly during his northern vacation. Upon rejoining the regiment in Memphis, the non-veterans immediately observed that the eagle mascot's head feathers had turned white. (The bald eagle attains maturity at about four years of age, complete with the classic white head and tail.)[52]

Reunited with their brigade, the Eighth Regiment of Wisconsin Veteran Volunteers prepared to march after General Forrest's cavalry again in what promised to be another difficult campaign. The Bobtail non-veterans counted the days until their own muster-out, and wondered if they would survive long enough to enjoy their return to civilian life. It was high summer, 1864, and the end of the war seemed nowhere in sight.

15

After the Devil

UPON returning to the field, the Eagle Regiment's veterans joined General Smith's second expedition against the elusive Confederate cavalryman, Nathan Bedford Forrest. Smith's first campaign had been abandoned in mid-July because of supply problems.[1] Forrest's men, however, had been hurt by the no-nonsense Smith in two fierce battles. Both expeditions were undertaken to protect General Sherman's supply route. As the Atlanta Campaign approached its goal, Sherman experienced pangs of anxiety with Forrest at large and in his rear. Describing Forrest as "the very devil," Sherman explained to Secretary of War Edwin Stanton, "there will never be peace in Tennessee till Forest is dead."[2] Sherman expected General Smith to write Forrest's epitaph.

A. J. Smith's expeditionary force consisted of his own battle-scarred detachment of the XVI Corps, some 10,000 strong, a Union cavalry divi-

US Army Military History Institute

Nathan Bedford Forrest, a brilliant Confederate cavalryman who was "the very devil" to those who pursued him.

sion of 4,500 troopers, and sizable artillery reserves. The entire force traveled to Holly Springs, Mississippi, where Smith established a forward supply depot after his infantrymen spent a week rebuilding the railroad line from Memphis. Smith planned to stockpile supplies at Holly Springs and attack Forrest's headquarters at Oxford from another Union base at Abbeville.[3]

Forrest had no intention of becoming involved in a slugging match with the XVI Corps, but he also wanted Smith out of his backyard. He therefore ordered his men to construct a defensive line at Hurricane Creek, between the Union position of Abbeville and the Confederate headquarters at Oxford. Forrest then began planning for the type of operation which best suited his own style: one using maneuver, surprise, and speed.[4]

But "Fighting Joe" Mower did not give the Confederates time to fully prepare their defensive works. On August 13, Mower advanced his division to Hurricane Creek while Union cavalry attacked both flanks of the Confederate position in great strength. At the critical moment, Mower ordered his infantry to storm across the creek and assault the Confederate artillery, which was posted on a high ridge overlooking the stream.[5]

"They had a splendid position on a hill across the creek from where we were," wrote Dave McLain to his sister. The Eagle Regiment had the lead. They rushed across the creek, holding their cartridge boxes and rifle-muskets above their heads "to keep our ammunition dry," after receiving Mower's orders to charge.[6] The Confederates "commenced running," wrote McLain, as soon as the infantry began scaling the ridge above Hurricane Creek. Federal casualties were light.[7]

Old Abe had stormed across Hurricane Creek with the rest of Company C. Shortly thereafter, the Eau Claire company became part of the headquarters guard. As a result, Old Abe did not experience the sharp skirmish at Abbeville on August 25.[8]

General Forrest and 2,000 Confederate cavalrymen, meanwhile, had moved out and around A. J. Smith. The Confederates made a long dash for Memphis in one of the boldest strokes of the war. Entering the unsuspecting city at dawn on a Sunday, Forrest and his cavalrymen captured the downtown area, a military stable which supplied them with fresh horses, and a number of Union officers in their nightshirts. Forrest succeeded in throwing the entire region into a panic—which was the object of the mission. A. J. Smith received orders to return—quickly.[9] Forrest cut Smith's supply lines when he withdrew.[10]

As the Federals recoiled back to Memphis, the Eagles had to subsist on a ration of one ear of green corn per man per day, coffee, and sugar. The hardtack biscuits had all spoiled, and A. J. Smith's expedition had failed.[11] Forrest escaped. Smith's failure highlighted the near-impossibility of using foot soldiers to halt the movements of well-led cavalry, though this folly was repeated again and again.

Smith's Corps glumly marched back to La Grange, where they boarded the railroad, reaching Memphis on August 29. Two weeks remained until the non-veterans were to be mustered out, and the men had to make a decision concerning the future of Old Abe. A number of options existed. The eagle mascot could be presented to the Federal government and sent to Washington. On the other hand, he might be given to the State of Wisconsin. Or, as the property of Company C, Eau Claire seemed an appropriate location for the veteran war eagle. The entire regiment participated in the decision-making process, voting unanimously to present Old Abe to the state authorities in Madison.[12] Hurricane Creek was therefore Old Abe's last battle. Like the eagle-bearers that carried him, Old Abe had never been wounded in any of the thirty-seven engagements he participated in.[13]

Military officials mustered the non-veterans out at Memphis in two groups, twenty-six ex-members of Company C traveling with Captain Wolf to Madison. Eagle-bearer Burkhardt resigned in Chicago and John F. Hill bore Old Abe to Madison. Captain Wolf appeared with John Hill and the eagle at Governor James T. Lewis' office on September 26. When Quartermaster General Nathaniel F. Lund advised Governor Lewis that Old Abe was waiting to see him, Lewis invited the group into the Executive Chamber. In a brief ceremony, Captain Wolf explained how much Old Abe had meant to the members of the Eagle Regiment. Old Abe had "cheered and kept up their spirits . . . during weary marches and the tedium of camp-life," wrote the *State Journal* reporter present at the meeting. "The eagle never looked better than

Victor Wolf, commander of Company C, Eighth Wisconsin, c. 1864. Wolf survived the war and formally presented Old Abe to the governor and people of Wisconsin.

present."[14] Wolf hoped that the State of Wisconsin would accept the eagle mascot "as an honored and inspiring memento of the 8th Regiment, and the times in which it had fought the battles of the nation. . . ."[15] Governor Lewis accepted the eagle on those terms, assuring Wolf that Old Abe would be "well cared for at the Capitol, where it would remain to invoke inspiring memories of the brave boys who had carried it with such honor to themselves and the State.[16] The governor then committed the State of Wisconsin to care for Old Abe "as long as he lived."[17]

How long the remaining members of the Eighth Wisconsin would live, however, was anybody's guess. Only 294 members of the Eighth Wisconsin were present and fit for duty in September of 1864.[18] On September 3, the regiment, now eagleless, boarded the steamer *Silver Wave*, heading south once more.[19] Old Abe and the Eighth Wisconsin Infantry thus parted company. The Eagle Regiment continued to be actively employed in the war, while Old Abe began a new career. In truth, the eagle had become more important than the Eagles, and probably it was a wise decision to send him away from the battle zone.

16

Jackass Cavalry

GENERAL Sterling Price launched the Trans-Mississippi Confederacy's largest offensive of the war during the late summer of 1864. Price aimed at nothing less than the conquest of Missouri. He planned to capture Union supply depots on his way to St. Louis after advancing northward from central Arkansas. About 15,000 Confederate cavalrymen participated in Price's Missouri expedition. Southern guerilla partisans who infested Civil War Missouri also joined the campaign, and Price recruited other Confederate sympathizers as he went.[1]

Union garrisons in southern Missouri lacked the means to resist such a powerful thrust. General Sherman therefore sent A. J. Smith's infantry with cavalry support to follow the invading Confederates.[2] The campaign evolved in two phases. During the first part, Smith's XVI Corps descended the Mississippi from Memphis to the mouth of the

White River, where steamboats carried them northwestward to Du Vall's Bluff, Arkansas, fifty miles east of Little Rock. Smith's Corps then marched northeasterly for twenty days, paralleling the Confederate invasion route.

The eagleless Eagles marched as they never had before. Rain, heat, bad roads, and poor drinking water confronted the struggling Union columns. "I have never been in or seen a place that I so disliked as this miserable portion of the Union," wrote the freshly promoted Sergeant Major, Augie Weissert. "They could not hire me to live here."[3] Weissert described the march: "On, on, we traveled over hills, mountains, valleys, fording large rivers through dense forests where . . . we had to cut roads to get through. Then, over hot plains, dusty roads, and through the immense swamps of Northern Arkansas and Southern Missouri, sometimes marching day and night."[4] At the end of each day's march, the infantrymen collapsed and fell asleep, too exhausted even to set up tents.[5]

Mower's Division led the infantry, and "Fighting Joe" kept his command moving despite all obstacles. Union horse soldiers like William F. Scott of the Fourth Iowa Cavalry were amazed by Mower's troops, who "stopped for nothing." Once a day, Mower's forces actually passed the cavalry, and they were never more than a half-day's march behind.[6]

The infantry's endurance overtaxed both the supply train and the artillery. Rations became scarce, clothing disintegrated, new recuits collapsed, mules and horses died by the scores.[7] The first halt came at Cape Girardeau, Missouri, on October 3, some 347 miles after setting out.[8] The Union troops remained at Cape Girardeau for three days, resting, eating, and delousing themselves.[9] About then, another nickname became associated with the Eighth Wisconsin. They now became part of "Joe Mower's Jackass Cavalry."[10] The "Jackass Cavalry" arrived in St. Louis by steamer on October 9.[11]

The march from Du Vall's Bluff to Cape Girardeau had been an impressive display of endurance and mobility. Price's mounted Confederates never had the free hand that they expected in southeastern Missouri because Smith's Corps kept within striking range. As a result, St. Louis became an impossible goal for the Confederates. Price therefore turned westward across Missouri, towards

Kansas City, the Union infantry and cavalry hot at his heels. The second phase of the Missouri expedition now began.

The Confederate invaders soon became involved in looting. Never well supplied, Price's men began pillaging villages and farms along their line of march. Guerilla bands committed atrocities. As one shocked Confederate Missourian wrote, "It would take a volume to describe the acts of outrage; neither station, age, nor sex was any protection. Southern men and women were as little spared as Unionists; the elegant mansion . . . and

Missouri
Expedition

the cabin of the negro were alike ransacked. . . ."[12] Price's Missouri expedition degenerated into a gigantic raid.

Smith's Corps steamed up the Missouri River to Jefferson City from St. Louis. There they boarded railroad cars and traveled fifty miles further west before resuming the march. Between October 22 and November 15 the "Jackass Cavalry" trudged across Missouri and into Kansas.[13] The infantry never overtook Price's raiders. Instead, Union cavalrymen smashed his Missouri expedition in a series of running battles, forcing Price to retreat back to Arkansas.[14]

General Smith finally ordered the infantry to return to St. Louis, on a march that the Wisconsin troops later called the most severe of the war. The weather turned suddenly cold. Snow and high winds harassed the foot soldiers on their weary march to St. Louis. Four men of the Eighth Wisconsin died, ten more were disabled.[15] The Forty-Seventh Illinois Infantry mustered only 196 men by the end of the campaign.[16] "We could be tracked by the blood of our feet in the snow," wrote William Britton, who was by then a lieutenant colonel and the commanding officer of the Eighth Wisconsin.[17] Four hundred and seventy

William Tecumseh Sherman, commander of the Army of the Tennessee, pictured just after the fall of Atlanta.

more miles had been added to the regiment's total.[18] The men had marched 818 miles in eight weeks. Only 279 members of the Eighth Wisconsin were present and fit for duty when the regiment arrived in St. Louis.[19] Since returning from veteran furlough, the Eighth Wisconsin had traveled 2,029 miles.[20] Repelling Sterling Price's invading army had been a test of physical endurance.

The Missouri expedition was the last important military event west of the Mississippi River in the Civil War. National attention now concentrated on the titanic struggles of General Grant in the East and General Sherman in Georgia. The nation's ordeal was approaching its climax.

Grant had mounted a punishing and costly invasion of northern Virginia in May, 1864. Following a series of bloody encounters with Robert E. Lee at the Wilderness, Spottsylvania, and Cold Harbor, Grant and the Army of the Potomac managed to drive the Confederates into fortified positions around Petersburg, twenty miles from Richmond. A nine-month siege developed around Petersburg, and movement in the Eastern Theater came to a standstill.

In the West, however, after capturing Atlanta in September, General Sherman launched the Army of the Tennessee eastward on its "March to the Sea." Sherman cut himself off from supply lines and fed his 63,000 troops by systematically pillaging central Georgia. His armies cut a fiery swath through the South as they marched towards Savannah and the sea, where Union naval vessels could be of assistance. Sherman then planned to move northward through the Carolinas, placing Robert E. Lee's Army of Northern Virginia between Grant's anvil and his own sledgehammer.

Only one Confederate force retained the strength to hamper Sherman's movements: the 40,000-man Army of Tennessee under General John B. Hood. After the battle of Atlanta, Hood's forces had retreated southwestward. Sherman did not pursue, as he was pre-occupied with his campaign to the sea. Hood planned to move around and behind Sherman, invade Tennessee, capture the Union base at Nashville, threaten Ohio, and march to the relief of Lee in Virginia. Sherman, the Confederates hoped, would drop his own efforts and follow Hood northward. Hood's plan involved great risks. It meant that no significant Confederate force would defend Georgia from

Sherman's troops if the Union commander decided not to follow Hood.[21]

In fact, the Union commander decided not to follow the Confederates as they advanced into Tennessee. Instead, Sherman ordered all troops not then assigned to reinforce Nashville, where Major General George H. Thomas and his Army of the Cumberland were concentrating. If Hood could strike Nashville quickly, before the Union reinforcements arrived, his plan to create a combat zone along the Ohio River and save General Lee might just succeed.

Hood was a fighting general. He had distinguished himself on numerous eastern battlefields and gone on to become one of Lee's bravest lieutenants. Seriously wounded at Gettysburg and again at Chickamauga, he had lost a leg and the use of an arm; at thirty-three years of age Hood had to be tied to his horse because of his physical disabilities.[22] But he lacked patience and administrative talent, and he was aggressive to the point of recklessness.

Thomas was the very antithesis of his fiery Confederate opponent. At fifty-three, Thomas was one of the oldest field commanders in either army. A deliberate planner and a plodder, he had a reputation for carrying out stubborn defenses, earning nicknames such as "Old Safety" and "The Rock of Chickamauga."[23] Thomas carefully entrenched, fortified Nashville, and waited for Union reinforcements.

17

Nashville

THE Eagles expected a rest after returning to St. Louis from the exhausting Missouri expedition. The men of the Eighth Wisconsin looked forward to the generous Thanksgiving dinner that military officials had promised. "Fighting Joe" Mower relinquished command of his division and departed, a Major-General, to join Sherman on the March to the Sea. Brigadier General John A. MacArthur came to lead Mower's troops—the "Jackass Cavalry."[1] Smith's XVI Corps veterans settled down to the relative comforts of garrison life in St. Louis. All seemed peaceful.

Then, just before Thanksgiving, General Sherman ordered A. J. Smith to mobilize his 10,000

WHi(X3)39928

John Bell Hood, the Confederate general whose crushing defeat at Nashville effectively ended the war in the Western Theater.

men immediately and to reinforce General Thomas in Nashville. Turkey dinners were not forthcoming. The Eagles quickly boarded steamboats heading towards Nashville, where they arrived by December 1.[2] Hood's Confederate army made its appearance before the city one day later.[3] The veterans of the Eighth Wisconsin could not know it, but they would soon be involved in their largest and costliest battle.

Hood had allowed himself to be delayed during the invasion of Tennessee. A major battle at Franklin, furthermore, had cost the Confederates more casualties than they could afford to lose. Now, Hood confronted Thomas' 56,000 troops with about 35,000 shoeless, poorly equipped Confederates. The weather had turned bitter cold; muddy roads were slick with ice and snow.[4]

General Grant, in Virginia, directed Thomas to attack Hood immediately. Thomas, however, plodded along in his usual fashion, making careful preparations, inspecting all his positions, organizing everything. His final preparations consumed two weeks.

December 15 dawned foggy. Thomas had, at last, ordered his thoroughly planned attack to

At the Battle of Nashville, George H. Thomas achieved one of the few decisive victories of the Civil War.

commence at 6 A.M. Thomas' left would make a feint. The Union right would then deliver what Thomas expected to be the knockout blow against the Confederates. Smith's Corps occupied a three-mile line on the right of Thomas' outer perimeter, west of Nashville. Union cavalry were posted behind Smith's infantry.[5]

Hood's line was thin compared to Thomas' carefully prepared position. The Confederate left rested on five detached redoubts planted on a series of hills south of Nashville. Infantry and skirmishers helped strengthen the redoubts in front and along the Hillsboro Pike, where a stone wall provided additional defensive protection. Most of Hood's cavalry, under General Forrest, was not present at the crucial hours.[6]

General Smith began his giant wheeling attack against the redoubts on the Confederate left at 8 A.M.[7] The "Jackass Cavalry" encountered the first fort and four twelve-pound guns opened up on them.[8] Colonel Hubbard redeployed the 1,421 men of the Eagle Brigade from column into double line of battle. The Eighth Wisconsin occupied the second line, alongside the veterans of the Eleventh Missouri and directly behind the Fifth Minnesota. While a strong force of advanced skirmishers pinned down the Confederate artillerymen in the redoubt with musket fire, Colonel Hubbard readied the Eagle Brigade for a frontal assault.[9]

The Union charge was irresistible. The Confederate strongpoint fell with little difficulty and few casualties, the Union infantry taking cannon and prisoners.[10] Almost without stopping, the Eagle Brigade continued advancing towards a second redoubt situated some 400 yards to the right. Confederate infantry could be seen advancing in the distance to reinforce the stone wall along the Hillsboro Pike. The second redoubt also fell quickly to a combination of Union infantry and cavalry who struck the detached work seemingly from all sides at 2 P.M. But the Confederate infantry remained for the Eagle Brigade to deal with.[11]

Colonel Hubbard ordered the Eighth Wisconsin to form a right angle with the Eagle Brigade's line of battle on the left, to prevent a Confederate flanking move.[12] At 4 P.M. Hubbard ordered the Eagle Brigade to charge for the second time that day. "It was quite apparent," recalled a veteran of the Eighth Wisconsin, "that the next movement would be a desperate one."[13]

The men advanced on command, "cheer after cheer" filling the air. Augie Weissert never forgot the "shower of shot and shell" they encountered crossing the Hillsboro Pike to attack the Confederate infantry behind the stone wall.[14] Colonel Hubbard described Confederate resistance as "sharp," but the veterans of the Eagle Brigade delivered a "withering fire" which forced the Southerners to retreat. The Confederates fell back as darkness ended the fighting. The Eagle Brigade captured four hundred prisoners, six guns, and the colors of two enemy regiments.[15]

All along the Union right, successive waves of attacks had been victorious. As the Confederate left crumbled, General Thomas poured in fresh divisions to reinforce his successes. Hood finally withdrew his battered forces to a more easily defended position several miles further south.[16]

Both sides prepared as best they could for the next day. Smith's Corps realigned and reformed its line of battle. The Eagle Brigade "slept on their arms" after refilling their cartridge boxes, consuming 65,000 rounds of ammunition. The Southerners entrenched.[17]

On December 16, ever thorough, General Thomas carefully adjusted the Federal lines prior to initiating another attack. (Indeed, his preparations consumed nearly the entire day.) Union and Confederate artillerymen shelled each others' positions until late in the afternoon. At 3 P.M. Thomas

Union defensive line at Nashville on the day of the battle, December 15, 1864.

directed his command to advance, using the same general plan that had proved so successful the day before. The Union left would pin the Confederate right while Hood's left was brought under massive assault.[18] Whereas the battle of December 15 had been characterized by independent rushes, the Union generals planned to deliver a single giant charge in overwhelming strength on the 16th. The Eagle Brigade and Smith's Corps would again be part of the assaulting forces. When the order for the attack came late that afternoon, Smith's Corps had been lying flat, under Confederate artillery fire, the entire day.[19]

On order, the Eagle Brigade rose, dressed their lines, and stormed across an open muddy cornfield in a double line of battle. The Fifth Minnesota led the charge, with the Eighth Wisconsin following twenty paces behind. "Cheers . . . rent the air in great volume," recalled Colonel Hubbard, who led the assault.[20] Volley after volley met the onrushing Eagles. Confederate artillery enfiladed the Eagle Brigade with grape shot and cannister. The battle flags of every regiment in the brigade fell at least once as Confederate fire tore "great gaps" in Hubbard's line.[21] Hundreds of Eagle Brigade members

were hit during the ten minutes it took to cross the cornfield.[22] But they crossed the deadly open ground and shattered the Confederate line.

The Confederate army panicked when it seemed that their retreat would be cut off by dismounted Union cavalry which swept in behind them after the Union infantry crushed their front. A rout developed. "I beheld for the first and only time," recalled General Hood afterward, "a Confederate Army abandon the field in confusion."[23]

The battle of Nashville was one of the very few decisive engagements of the entire Civil War. Total Union casualties amounted to 3,061. Confederate losses were never computed, but about 3,000 prisoners, including a major-general, fell into Union hands, and sixty-five cannon were captured. In the space of a few hours, Hood's army was destroyed.

Despite the generally light Union losses, however, the two-day battle of Nashville cost actively engaged units, like the Eighth Wisconsin, heavy casualties. Of the nine officers present with the Eagle Regiment's eight participating companies, one was killed and five wounded. In addition, seven enlisted men were shot dead and another

Union outer line just after the advance of A. J. Smith's XVI Corps at the Battle of Nashville, December 15, 1864. Note the still-smoldering campfires and wagon trains in the distance.

fifty-six were incapacitated by wounds.[25] The Eagle Brigade as a whole suffered 20 percent losses—the highest casualties of any Union force present at Nashville.[26]

James Mellor was among the mortally wounded. Hit in the shoulder by a Confederate bullet, the thirty-two-year-old La Crosse area man steadily declined until his death two weeks later. Robert Rogers, Mellor's tent-mate, friend, and neighbor from La Crosse, promised to send his worn army blanket home for his wife, Mary, to have as a remembrance. The unpaid balance of the dead private's veteran bounty was forwarded to La Crosse by the regimental authorities after they deducted $5.67 for the uniform ruined by Mellor's blood, and $3.27 for the canteen, knapsack, and haversack he lost on the battlefield.[27]

Augie Weissert fell when a Confederate bullet struck him in the left thigh during the second charge of December 15. Surgeons at the field hospital could not locate the ball, but decided to not amputate the twenty-one-year-old soldier's leg at that time. Weissert received additional treatment at the floating hospital stationed at Nashville before being sent north to New Albany, Indiana, for observation and recuperation. Weissert eventually recovered, although he limped for the rest of his life.[28]

Nashville ended the war in the West. General Thomas' great victory eliminated all hope of a Confederate breakthrough. While other battles remained to be fought, the outcome was more or less inevitable.

The veterans of units like the Eagle Brigade again demonstrated an unbeatable battlefield performance resulting from a combination of high-quality leadership, four years' experience, excellent mobility, superior firepower, high morale, and the polished ability to deploy in classic formation under the most trying circumstances. Napoleon would have been impressed by the fluid ease of movement displayed by the lines and columns of

"Smith's Guerillas" in front of Nashville. And now the end of the war was, at last, in sight.

Replacements helped swell the depleted ranks of Old Abe's regiment as the year 1865 opened. Sadly, the quality of the new soldiers seemed less than the original 973 members or the subsequent volunteer recruits. Deserters, draftees, and substitutes found their way into the ranks of the Eighth Wisconsin, some of whom were little more than children.[29] The regiment, however, had no time to reflect on the diminution of personnel quality. Early in February, the XVI Corps moved to New Orleans and then to Dauphin Island off the coast of Mobile, Alabama, traveling 1,355 miles in eleven days.[30]

At Dauphin Island the XVI Corps enjoyed a six-week rest in a warm climate. An extensive oyster bed surrounded the island and the soldiers carted the "luscious product" to their camps by the wagon load. "Traditional army food," recollected Colonel Hubbard, "was wholly neglected."[31] The stay at Dauphin Island was remembered as a "picnic."[32]

The picnic ended when the forces of the Department of the Gulf advanced on Mobile. Mobile was protected by two Confederate bastions, Spanish Fort and Fort Blakely. Between March 25 and April 9 "Smith's Guerillas" fought their last fights during the siege and assaults on the forts, experiencing moderate casualties in the process.[33] They marched off towards Montgomery, Alabama, 180 miles away, after the fall of Mobile.[34] On the road, while marching in the heat of the day, word came of Lee's surrender in Virginia.

18

Denouement

THE war was over. "The men became simply frantic in their demonstrations of joy," remembered Colonel Hubbard. "The old veterans embraced each other, laughed, cried, shouted, and sang. They threw hats, blouses, canteens, haversacks, and even their muskets in the air. . . ."[1]

Between April and September, the Eighth Wisconsin occupied Uniontown, Alabama, thirty miles west of Selma. On September 5, the regiment assembled at Demopolis for their final muster before boarding railroad cars for Wisconsin.

Eagle Regiment members received their payoff and discharge in Wisconsin's capital city on September 12, 1865. The regiment disbanded the next day.[2] No parades, no demobilization crises, no incidents marred the transition from professional men-of-war to peaceful citizens. Like the vast Union army, the Eighth Wisconsin simply evaporated.

But even after the war ended, it should be noted, sickness continued to kill Eagle Regiment members. Corporal Robert Rogers, the sensitive Irishman who had helped keep his neighbors in La Crosse informed about the activities of their less-well-educated relatives and friends, for instance, died of disease several months after the war ended. Rogers had worked as Surgeon Murta's clerk after accidentally breaking his leg in Tennessee. There Rogers contracted a disease which slowly carried him away.[3]

The Eighth Wisconsin suffered no more than many other Badger State regiments during the Civil War. Indeed, sixteen out of a total of seventy-four Wisconsin units experienced higher losses than the Eagles. But the losses of the Eighth Wisconsin generally illustrate the high rates of loss experienced by all active state regiments. Out of a total strength of 1,342 men, including recruits who arrived after 1861, 280 died. Confederate bullets or shells killed fifty-nine, disease eliminated 208, and fatal accidents accounted for thirteen. Wounds incapacitated another 188. Seventy-one men received discharges for unspecified reasons, most probably associated with the debilitating effects of disease. Coupled with sixty desertions, and three men who suffered unknown fates, the Eighth's losses amounted to 602, or over 44 percent of the total.[4] In other words, nearly half of Old Abe's comrades either died or were incapacitated in some way by their wartime experience.

The men of Old Abe's regiment, their losses notwithstanding, were not all heroes. In fact, in two of the Eagle's three major battles—the first day at Corinth on October 3, 1862, and during the Grand Assault on Vicksburg on May 22, 1863—the Eighth Wisconsin was driven from the field in something approaching disorderly retreat. (They reformed immediately, however.) Although talk of heroism was very much a part of the Civil War era's vocabulary, virtually all soldiers experienced normal fears. The key to maintaining self-esteem and the respect of one's comrades was not to ex-

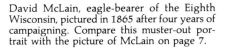

David McLain, eagle-bearer of the Eighth Wisconsin, pictured in 1865 after four years of campaigning. Compare this muster-out portrait with the picture of McLain on page 7.

Edward Homiston of Company C, Eighth Wisconsin, 1865. He was Old Abe's eagle-bearer during the Grand Assault at Vicksburg and is also pictured on page 34.

Frank Barrett, Company C, 1865. By war's end, many Union soldiers looked a bit like Western desperadoes.

press those fears overtly. When Private Pat Lanon of Company E lost control of himself and began hysterically firing his musket at advancing Confederates in spite of orders instructing all to lie flat and wait during the fight before Corinth in May, 1862, he had to be physically constrained by officers and men in his company. All agreed that the circumstances were terrifyingly unnerving, but that Lanon had publicly disgraced himself. Unable to continue under the burden of his shame, Lanon transferred out of the Eighth Wisconsin and joined the Mississippi Marine Brigade.[5]

After the war, when veterans met and talked about their experiences, now safe from the terror of the battlefield, they bragged about the number of casualties their respective units suffered. Members of Old Abe's regiment had to rationalize the fact that while the Eagles had been engaged in the largest number of actions of any Wisconsin infantry unit, other units had suffered higher combat casualties. Old Abe's Regiment did not win a mention in Colonel William F. Fox's "Three Hundred Fighting Regiments," part of the classic Civil War statistical work, *Regimental Losses in the American Civil War*. The Eleventh Missouri did, however, primarily due to its misfortunes at Vicksburg and at Iuka. In the Eagle Brigade, however, only the

Eleventh Missouri suffered a greater total number of deaths from all causes than the Eighth Wisconsin.[6] Sam Miles responded to questioning of the Eagle Regiment's bravery by simply observing, "with no disrespect intended," that "We took care of ourselves."[7]

What had Old Abe's comrades accomplished by their sacrifices? Historians have debated the question since 1865, but several achievements stand out most prominently. The soldiers of the North had won victory—unalloyed, unconditional, and unquestionable. They had preserved the Union—unalterable, indivisible; they had brought an end to slavery—regardless of whether or not that "peculiar institution" had caused the war in the first place. They had won peace.

19

In Tangel's Feature

WHEN Old Abe became the property of the State of Wisconsin, he was classified, along with the battle flags returned by the state regiments, as a "War Relic."[1] No longer a member of the

Adolph Pitsch of Chippewa Falls and Company C, pictured in Madison after mustering out in September, 1865.

Dighton Smith of Lake Pepin and Company C, Madison, 1865.

Burnett Demarest of Eau Claire and Company C, whose rose from sergeant to lieutenant by the time he mustered out in 1865.

Eighth Wisconsin Infantry, the eagle mascot became a Civil War curiosity. As the years passed, Old Abe's fame grew, as did his symbolic political influence. His national role emerged from the peaceful environs of the State Capitol in Madison, and the well-tended park that surrounded it. Under the supervision of the State Adjutant General's Department, Wisconsin's Quartermaster General Nathaniel F. Lund, and State Armorer John H. McFarland, Old Abe occupied a two-room apartment in the basement of the Capitol. He had access to a specially constructed bath tub, was fed fresh rabbits, and had several sawhorses to roost upon. The "Eagle Department" never lacked for visitors.[2]

Old Abe went to the Capitol Park whenever the weather permitted, and in the weeks following his mustering-out, the eagle made several bids for freedom. Unaccustomed to Old Abe's habits, Quartermaster General Lund spent an exciting October afternoon chasing the escaped eagle through Madison's First Ward. Abe eventually landed near the home of Clerk of Court L. F. Kellogg and allowed himself to be coaxed back on to his perch.[3] Not long afterward, the bird broke from his fetters while at the park, this time to make a "raid on a flock of doves."[4] The attend-

ants, now more experienced at eagle-bearing, soon had him retethered.

Wisconsin's War Eagle was not destined to spend the remaining years of his life relaxing at the Capitol, however. In January, 1865, when the Reverend J. O. Barrett of Eau Claire requested permission from Governor Lewis to take Old Abe to Chicago and display him at the Northwest Sanitary Fair, Wisconsin's chief executive approved.[5] (Barrett had been active in the Soldiers Aid Societies of Eau Claire and Chippewa Falls, and had hosted Old Abe's first fund-raising appearance when the eagle attended Fourth of July celebrations during the veterans' furlough.[6])

Barrett, a native of Boston who was active in the Universalist movement, became involved with the reforming work of the Reverend D. P. Livermore and his wife Mary. The Livermores settled in Chicago during the 1850's, and, when the sectional conflict erupted, Mary Livermore spearheaded the drive by Midwestern women to participate in war-related work. Mary Livermore wrote feminist editorials calling upon middle-class women to drop all thoughts of fashion as well as their lives of ease and devote their energies to soldiers' aid. According to Mrs. Livermore and an influential group of female associates, the war

Milwaukee County Historical Society

Lyman J. "Tangel" McCracken (left) with two unidentified friends, Milwaukee, c. 1865. McCracken exhibited Old Abe at the Soldiers Home Fair in the summer of 1865.

could be used to liberate and educate women, transforming them into working contributors to the Union cause.[7]

Women became extremely active in agencies such as the U.S. Sanitary Commission, a forerunner of today's Red Cross. The U.S. Sanitary Commission had several regional headquarters, and Mrs. Livermore, together with Mrs. A. H. Hoge, rose to control the affairs of the Northwest Branch in Chicago.[8] The Wisconsin Soldiers' Aid Society was associated with the Northwest Sanitary Commission. Through its Milwaukee office, Wisconsin women such as Mrs. Joseph S. Colt and Mrs. Lydia Hewitt helped coordinate the activities of Soldiers' Aid Society groups in nearly every village in the Badger State.[9]

Livermore and Hoge originated the sponsoring of "sanitary fairs," which displayed historical artifacts and assorted curios, and sold souvenirs, food, and crafts to visitors. The profits were donated to the Sanitary Commission and supported the organization's charitable work among sick, wounded, and convalescent soldiers. Sanitary fairs became enormously successful, and the

Northwest Branch sponsored two of these events in Chicago.[10]

Old Abe attended the second Northwest Sanitary Fair in Chicago, which opened on May 30, 1865, just after the war ended. Reverend Barrett gathered information for the eagle's first biography. He also arranged for J. F. Bodtker of Madison to photograph the bird and reproduce thousands of small views which would—like the biography—be sold at the fair. When Old Abe posed for the "Sanitary Picture," his attendants took him to the roof of Bodtker's studio, where the sun's light would help the photographer. Thereupon, Old Abe "vaulted into the sky" while still attached to his perch and shield. Attendants barely managed to rescue the dangling eagle from a long fall and certain death.[11]

Governor Lewis authorized State Armorer John McFarland and Eighth Wisconsin veteran John F. Hill to accompany Barrett and Old Abe to Chicago. There, Old Abe became "Wisconsin's emblem of valor," and was displayed along with martial trophies, battle flags, swords, guns, minerals, and artistic works from around the country.[12]

The Northwest Sanitary Fair netted $270,000 in four weeks.[13] Although the blazing sun raised temperatures far above the comfort level and caused "malodorous emanations" from the Chicago River, Old Abe attracted large crowds to the "Alcove of the Eagle."[14] According to a Chicago *Tribune* reporter, Wisconsin's War Eagle became "the grandest contributor to the fair."[15] Barrett's eagle biography and the sale of Old Abe photos raised $16,000, about $400 a day, for the benefit of soldiers' aid projects.[16] P. T. Barnum, the great showman of the last century, offered $20,000 for Old Abe. Another well-to-do visitor offered $10,000 to purchase the eagle.[17] Both offers were refused. Photographer J. Carbutt captured the likenesses of Old Abe and John Hill, in what he called his "Eagle-Bearer Picture."[18]

Nationally important figures found time to visit the Northwest Sanitary Fair. While speaking admiringly of the battle flags and war trophies which underscored the total victory achieved by the Union armies, General William Tecumseh Sherman reached out to pet Old Abe. Even though Old Abe had served under Sherman, the eagle screeched and ruffled his feathers menacingly. Sherman drew back. "I must retreat this time," stammered the blushing general, and the audience roared with laughter.[19] Old Abe had again sparked the public's imagination. "We bare our brow to him," remarked Chicago reporter B. F. Taylor.[20]

Barrett, Hill, and McFarland carried Old Abe to Milwaukee for another charitable fund-raising extravaganza immediately after the Northwest Sanitary Fair closed. The Soldiers' Home Fair was the largest charitable effort undertaken by Wisconsin's citizens in the Civil War era.[21] Women organized, directed, and administered the event. State legislators approved a $5,000 grant towards purchasing the federal hospital in Milwaukee and transforming the West Water Street structure into an asylum for disabled veterans.[22] Additional funds would be raised by contributions and by sales generated at the two-week Soldiers' Home Fair for the construction of a new Wisconsin Soldiers Home. The Home Fair which opened in a specially constructed building at the corner of Huron and Main Street on June 29, 1865.[23]

Old Abe photos and lithographs sold by the thousands. Mrs. H. C. Crocker offered to provide eagle views "in any quantity desired" for charitable sale in support of the Soldier's Home Fair. Distributors were solicited throughout the state to sell Old Abe's photographs. "Who would not want such a souvenir of the war as a likeness of the veteran bird?"[24] Attendance at the Milwaukee fair was compared to a pilgrimage because Old Abe, like Mecca, drew the faithful to his side.[25]

The Soldiers Home Fair opened in a carnival-like atmosphere. Many features and attractions contributed to the success of the event. Ethnic foods, displays of war relics and battle flags, manufactured products offered at discounts, and the presence of Wisconsin's most famous military figure—Old Abe—helped bring in $80,199.69 during the first nine days.[26] Crowds swarmed to the Home Fair. The long war was over and now was the time to celebrate, give thanks, laugh, and contribute to the worthy cause of soldiers' aid.

Milwaukee County Historical Society

Interior view of the Soldiers Home Fair, Milwaukee, 1865. The entryway banner reads: "The Only Debt We Can Never Pay Is the Debt We Owe the Union Soldiers."

Eagle-bearer John Hill with Old Abe in a picture widely distributed during the Centennial of 1876.

"Tangel's Feature" occupied a large tent just outside the main fair building. Showman H. C. "Tangel" McCracken of Milwaukee had gathered "a collection of birds, beasts, and curiosities that would do honor to Barnum" for the benefit of Home Fair visitors. In the center of "Tangel's Feature" roosted Old Abe. A reporter described the scene: "Around this Veteran Bird, on lower perches, are four other eagles . . . Grant, Sheridan, Sherman, and McClellan. There are also some four or five owls, and two or three hawks. . . . Stationed about in different places in the tent are various specimens of the animal kingdom such as a blood hound, brought from Virginia by a Captain of the Second Battery; a bear cub, full of all manner of capers; two sand hill crains [sic]; some

fine sheep; a splended Devon cow; two or three foxes; a coon; two badgers; rabbits and doves of various breeds; New Zealand war clubs; stuffed beavers; otters; and a double headed calf. . . ."[27]

Old Abe attracted many viewers—so many, in fact, that the war eagle became exhausted. Hill, McFarland, and Barrett had to escort their feathered charge away for a rest on at least one occasion. Visitors at "Tangel's Feature" bought eagle pictures by the basket.[28]

In all, the Soldiers Home Fair earned $100,183.88.[29] Additional contributions arrived from donations received from village fairs, local ice cream and lemonade socials, various picnics, the efforts of Wisconsin school children, Punch and Judy shows, and concerts. Total receipts amounted to about $110,000.[30]

Old Abe also helped raise funds for the Soldier's Orphan's Home in Madison during September, 1865. Mrs. Cordelia A. P. Harvey, wife of the late governor of Wisconsin, was instrumental in guiding the work of the Harvey Hospital in Madison. The Harvey Hospital was an impressive octagonal stone building on Spaight Street that had served as a medical facility for wounded soldiers. After the war, Mrs. Harvey felt that the hospital should be transformed into an asylum for children orphaned by the conflict.

Governor Lewis assisted Mrs. Harvey by allowing Old Abe to be sent to the State Fair in Janesville. William J. Jones, a one-armed veteran, accompanied the eagle and helped set up the large tent donated by the state for the charitable event. Old Abe and the raccoon mascot of the Twelfth Wisconsin Artillery went on view to the public for a 10 cent admission. As he had in Chicago and Milwaukee, Old Abe attracted thousands of viewers to his crowded tent at Janesville.[31]

The great sanitary fairs of 1865 cemented Old Abe's reputation as a national symbol. Through the efforts of newspaper reporters and to a lesser extent of Reverend Barrett, Old Abe was transformed from a mascot of a Wisconsin regiment into the eagle hero of the Civil War, flying aloft and cheering his companions to victory. Not even the tawdry setting of "Tangel" McCracken's menagerie tent or the hot, crowded, freak-show atmosphere that prevailed in Chicago and Janesville diminished Old Abe's popular appeal. The public adored the eagle as much for his antics as for his military record in a war that was at long last over.

As one reporter wrote at the time, "There is something grand in his presence. . . . You are looking at an important personage. . . ."[32]

20

Bloody Shirt Politics

IN 1866 Wisconsinites elected Lucius Fairchild to the first of his three terms as governor. The one-armed hero of Gettysburg took a keen interest in the voting behavior of ex-Union soldiers. Veterans, as Governor Fairchild well understood, represented a sizable constituency of great political importance, and he hoped to organize them in support of the Republican party. Loyalty to the Union cause provided the basis for postwar alliances, as Republican politicians reminded voters in every electoral campaign.[1] The so-called Bloody Shirt was waved constantly to remind the citizenry and ex-soldiers of the sacrifices and casualties of the Civil War, and of the perfidy of the rebel South. "Four hundred thousand men," exclaimed Governor Fairchild during a campaign address he delivered in 1868, "lie dead for me and you."[2] Who, by way of contrast, supported the Democratic party? he asked rhetorically at an 1870 political gathering: "Every rebel, every copperhead, every draft sneak, every dirty traitor."[3] Although Fairchild had exaggerated the number of dead by nearly 50,000, Republicans successfully carried the Wisconsin statehouse in every election but two from the onset of the Civil War to 1933.[4]

Welding veterans into a stable, cohesive, national political force, on the other hand, took years to accomplish. Ex-Civil War soldiers faced a number of immediate readjustment problems when they became civilians. Establishing or re-establishing one's self in a trade or an occupation, or returning to farm life after years of military service, seemed more important than becoming a political activist to many ex-soldiers and their families. Thousands of veterans had been crippled or otherwise handicapped by the effects of wounds and disease. To them, fulfilling the basic needs of life was of paramount importance.

Nevertheless, soldiers' clubs and societies formed in cities and hamlets throughout Wisconsin and the nation. Membership in these organizations rose during the 1860's only to fall off precipitously during the 1870's. The Grand Army of the Republic—or G.A.R.—the largest, though decentralized, national veterans' organization, eventually came to dominate the various soldier societies, either by absorbing members or by affiliating with other groups. Although G.A.R. leaders had formed the organization in 1866, rank-and-file membership became truly numerous, and the G.A.R. rose to play a decisive role in electoral politics, only after 1880.

G.A.R. leaders, of course, involved themselves in national, state, and local politics throughout the post-Civil War era. G.A.R. activists included lawyers, judges, postal service employees, governors and prospective governors, as well as aspirants to political offices at all levels, many of whom identified themselves with the Republican party. The "soldier vote" was assiduously cultivated by the G.A.R. leadership, even though the organization was ostensibly a fraternal one and supposedly non-political.

Old Abe played a role in the effort to organize Civil War veterans. The fame and the experience of Wisconsin's war eagle provided him an undeniable appeal to ex-soldiers. When in the service of capable politicians like Governor Fairchild, him-

WHi(X3)20922

Lucius Fairchild lost an arm at Gettysburg, organized the G.A.R. in Wisconsin, and became the state's first three-term governor.

Angus R. McDonald, a veteran of the Eleventh Wisconsin and Old Abe's favorite custodian, c. 1870.

self one of the leading organizers of the G.A.R.,
Old Abe became a perfect symbol of nationalistic
Republicanism, a living version of the Bloody
Shirt.

On warm September days Old Abe often passed
his afternoons in the Capitol Park in the company
of Captain A. R. McDonald, the State Armorer.
The bird developed an affectionate relationship
with McDonald, who served until 1874, throughout the administrations of Governors Fairchild,
C. C. Washburn, and the early part of William R.
Taylor's. The eagle and the armorer played varia-
tions of Old Abe's catch-the-rolling-bullet trick.
McDonald would place a musket part near Old
Abe; the eagle would pick it up with his beak and
dash about with McDonald in hot pursuit.[5] E. B.
Quiner, a newsman and clerk in the governor's
office, occasionally saw Old Abe while on his way
to work at the Capitol and noted that while the
war eagle sometimes managed to break free from
his leash, "he is so far domesticated that he is
easily recovered."[6] Old Abe also continued to enjoy music, as he had since his early days with the
McCanns. He flapped his wings and made noises
whenever instruments were played.[7] Politics, however, regularly intruded on the eagle's continued
appreciation of music.

President Andrew Johnson's policies towards
the defeated South troubled many Republicans,
who thought that the Chief Executive, in Governor Fairchild's words, had adopted "soft reconstruction."[8] Fairchild and others desired that
harsher, more retributive measures be adopted
towards former Confederate states and their wartime leaders. Radical Republicans in Congress led
the fight to establish a rigorously anti-Southern
policy. In September, 1866, a convention sponsored by a veterans' organization called the Boys
in Blue gathered in Pittsburgh to protest President
Johnson's programs and to voice their support of
Radical Congressmen.[9]

Governor Fairchild helped organize and send
the Wisconsin delegation to the gathering.[10] A
number of Wisconsin veterans attended the convention, and chief among them was Old Abe.[11]
After checking in at the St. Charles Hotel, A. R.
McDonald and Old Abe marched in the morning
parade towards the Pittsburgh City Hall where the
mass meeting to support Congressional Radicals
took place. "An immense crowd rushed forward
to get a sight of the royal bird," noted a Milwaukee *Sentinel* reporter.[12]

As McDonald carried Old Abe to the podium
where convention officials and speechmakers sat,
the audience spontaneously rose and cheered. The
band burst into life. Old Abe—ever the music
lover—"flapped his wings on cue."[13] Various soldier—politicians including General Nathaniel P.
Banks of Red River ill-fame—harrangued the veteran delegates for the remainder of the day.

The evening procession capped an eventful day.
Thousands of torch-carrying veterans and thousands of local citizens turned out to watch the
decorated floats of convention officers roll by.
First came the float of the Boys in Blue, followed
by the Pittsburgh fire department's, a local boating
club's, and then Old Abe in a stately carriage surrounded by dignitaries, encircled by red, white,
and blue ribbons, and drawn by four white horses.
Cheering onlookers showered Wisconsin's
feathered veteran with flowers.[14] The Pittsburgh
convention was an important step in familiarizing
Midwestern soldier society members with those of
the East. Old Abe had now been formally intro-
duced to the Eastern veterans.

As fall election time drew near, Old Abe's itinerary picked up. An application to take the Wis-

consin war eagle to Paris, where he would be placed on view at the Wold Exposition, was rejected.[15] But Governor Fairchild needed Old Abe's help with local matters. So instead of Paris, the feathered veteran went to Peoria. There ex-General (now Congressman) John A. Logan, "The Black Eagle of Illinois," one of the founders of the G.A.R., and an ambitious Republican politician, would appear for the dedication of a soldiers' monument on the grounds of the courthouse. Would Governor Fairchild allow Old Abe to attend the dedication of the Peoria monument on October 11, asked S. D. Priterbaugh, last Colonel of the Eagle Brigade's Forty-Seventh Illinois? All expenses would be covered. Governor Fairchild, himself a member of the G.A.R. and ever interested in the good will of veterans' groups, assented. A. R. McDonald and Augie Weissert—still recovering from his Nashville wounds and now a political ally of Fairchild's—accompanied Old Abe.[16]

Forty thousand spectators assembled to watch the dedication of the Peoria monument. Surviving members of the Forty-Seventh Illinois Infantry—who came largely from the Peoria area—provided the war eagle with an honor guard. Clyde Bryner, a veteran of the Forty-Seventh, remembered that day: "The great soldiers and orators were cheered to the echo, but when the eagle came, who can describe the enthusiasm of his reception, the people were wild—handkerchiefs and flags waving, hats tossed high in the air and the eagle moving his head right and left, wings moving ceaselessly, seemed to acknowledge the greeting."[17]

Old Abe had hardly returned from Peoria when he again took to the hustings. He traveled to Elkhorn in Walworth County, where he participated in a veterans' rally just prior to election day.[18] That done, the war eagle attended the National Convention of Soldiers and Sailors in Milwaukee, where he took part in a parade in company with James K. Proudfit, Fairchild's adjutant general, who was also leader of the Wisconsin Chapter of the Soldiers' and Sailors' National Union League and head of the state G.A.R. organization.[19]

Radical Congressmen and President Johnson had reached an impasse in their relations by 1867. Although his enemies narrowly failed to secure Johnson's impeachment "for high crimes and misdemeanors," they virtually dominated the government. As a result, the election of 1868 proved to be

a sounding board over the Reconstruction issue. Republican party officials anxiously expected to attract the soldier vote and hoped to further cement the alliance of veterans' organizations with their own political party.

Governor Fairchild of Wisconsin played a major role in the electoral drama of 1868.[20] The Wisconsin Soldiers' and Sailors' Convention assembled in Milwaukee during mid-May, with the governor presiding. He convinced the representatives that the Republican party was the soldier's true friend, and arranged to have himself named head of the state delegation to the National Soldiers' and Sailors' Convention, scheduled to meet in Chicago one day prior to the Republican National Convention which would nominate a candidate for President of the United States. Fairchild took no chances, for the stakes involved the highest office in the land. Old Abe joined the Wisconsin veterans' delegation.

James R. Stuart painted this oil portrait of Old Abe in 1875. It was displayed at the Wisconsin exhibit at the Centennial in Philadelphia in 1876. Ultimately the portrait was donated to the G.A.R. Memorial Hall by Governor Robert M. La Follette.

The National Soldiers' and Sailors' Convention met in Chicago on May 19, 1868. Fairchild and the Wisconsin delegation led a march of ex-soldiers three-quarters of a mile long to the city's Turner Hall. Old Abe and a number of Wisconsin Civil War battle flags formed the van. Chicago residents turned out en masse to witness the procession. The veterans sang "John Brown's Body" and other Civil War marching songs along their route. Inside the hall—in front, upon, and over the podium, where Governor Fairchild presided—were three exhibits. One was a bust of the martyred Abraham Lincoln. Another was a large portrait of General Grant. The third, Old Abe himself, tethered to his perch, occupied the space in front of the speaker's platform. According to a *Wisconsin State Journal* reporter, the veterans greeted the display with "wildest enthusiasm."[21]

Fairchild handled the convention proceedings skillfully. The National Soldiers' and Sailors' Convention endorsed the Republican party as the official veterans' party. When delegates passed the inevitable resolution proposing General Grant for the presidency of the United States, "the vast multitude rose and cheered."[22] The band played "Hail to the Chief," and Old Abe, wrote a Chicago newsman, "as if understanding it all, stretched . . . and repeatedly flapped his wings in approbation of the nomination."[23]

Fairchild, with a hundred-man delegation of blue-coated veterans, hastened to the Crosby Opera House after the convention meeting disbanded. There, in full uniform, complete with sabre and sash, he marched into the National Republican Convention and mounted the stage. Fairchild's ringing voice filled the theater, his empty sleeve visible to all. He requested that the Republicans nominate "our comrade" General Grant as presidential candidate.[24] A red, white, and blue-painted dove was launched from the top gallery as the delegates cheered Grant's name. On stage, the opera house curtain rose to reveal a huge painting of the Goddess of Liberty alongside the cigar-smoking general.[25] Congressman Logan, a delegate from Illinois and the national commander of the G.A.R., then formally nominated Grant. There were no dissenting votes.[26] Governor Fairchild congratulated General Grant, expressing confidence that he would "again lead the loyal hosts to victory."[27] (Grant did in fact easily defeat the Democratic candidate, Horatio Sey-

mour, in the election of 1868 and became the eighteenth President of the United States.)

By then Wisconsin's war eagle had become a national political figure. Some people even naively believed that Old Abe had carried the day for Grant. Old Abe photographs and colored lithographs were again made available, this time by S. W. Martin, editor of the *Soldiers Record*, a Madison newspaper designed to appeal to veterans. Martin offered a selection of sizes as well as elaborate frames and mounts for his Old Abe views; he solicited distributors for his Old Abe pictures, giving veterans preferential rates.[28]

Politically, Old Abe was firmly perched on Governor Fairchild's bandwagon. For the moment, Fairchild's position seemed happy and unassailable. Indeed, the years 1865–1869 were golden ones for the eagle. Abe's relationship with State Armorer McDonald was a source of comforting stability in a hectic world. McDonald trained the eagle to climb carefully up his outstretched arm without sinking talons into his skin, and Old Abe rubbed his frost-white head against McDonald's face when he wanted to show appreciation for their companionship.[29]

Old Abe was kept busy during Fairchild's first two terms as governor, but he also found time to relax in the park or in his Capitol apartment. Occasionally wartime eagle-bearers such as Ed Homaston visited Old Abe in Madison, and children waited patiently for him to shed a feather that they might take home as a souvenir. While Old Abe's fame had reached national proportions, he yet retained a degree of novelty, and local audiences never seemed to tire of his presence. On July 4, 1869, for example, Old Abe traveled to Whitewater to take part in the community's parade. The war eagle perched upon an old cannon, as he had appeared in the E. R. Curtis photograph of 1865 and in the various sanitary fairs' colored lithographs. The day was hot—and Old Abe whistled for water. When attendant Eugene Bowen brought him a drink, "the populace were pleased to observe the eagle drinking with his bearer from the same glass."[30]

It was too good to last. In 1869, Governor Fairchild ran afoul of the "Madison Regency," a rival clique of Republican organizers and politicians. The Regency blocked Fairchild's hopes to become a United States Senator and further attempted to drive him from the statehouse.[31]

Fairchild responded by running for an unprecedented third term as governor.

Jeremiah M. "Uncle Jerry" Rusk, a leading G.A.R. activist, provided unhesitating support for the embattled Fairchild.[32] G.A.R. members began meeting in the State Capitol. The *Soldiers Record*, solidly G.A.R. in orientation, recommended Governor Fairchild to its readers.[33] Fairchild made the rounds of veterans' reunions and similar gatherings.[34] Old Abe became involved as Fairchild battled for his political life. In fact, the governor used Old Abe up in a seemingly never-ending series of public appearances.

McDonald carried Old Abe to Fond du Lac and Burlington, to Elkhorn, Evansville, and La Crosse.[35] In September Old Abe appeared at the Soldiers' and Sailors' Convention in Milwaukee along with Fairchild and numerous Wisconsin Civil War battle flags.[36] And once more Fairchild carried the gubernatorial elections, winning by a margin of 8,000 votes.[37] Fairchild never doubted the importance of the soldier vote in his victory.

Even after the election, Old Abe appeared at local gatherings. Company K of the Eighth Wisconsin Infantry, for instance, invited the nationally famous regimental mascot to attend their reunion in Racine in August, 1871. Augie Weissert, just finishing law school at the University of Michigan, was the keynote speaker. The battle flags of the Eagle Regiment traveled to the Belle City along with the feathered veteran.[38]

Old Abe participated in the State Fair in Milwaukee during September. There, he became one of the protagonists in "The Union Spy," a drama staged in the Music Hall.[39] McDonald carried the eagle to Neilsville for a veterans reunion several weeks later, where an "immense crowd" watched him with "the greatest interest and curiosity."[40] In February, 1872, Old Abe attended a reunion of the First Wisconsin Infantry held at the Park Hotel in Madison.[41] The war eagle attended the Sixth Annual reunion of the Society of the Army of the Tennessee meeting in Madison during July of 1872.[42]

Lucius Fairchild realized that his third term as governor would be his last. He therefore worked hard to obtain a diplomatic appointment, preferably as ambassador to Russia. Fairchild drove himself mercilessly, campaigning for Republican candidates in neighboring states as well as for the re-election of the scandal-rocked Grant administration.[43] Old Abe continued to attend veterans' rallies, in effect urging ex-soldiers to vote for Governor Fairchild's choice of candidates.[44]

The one-armed Wisconsin governor partially attained his goal. In November, 1872, Secretary of State Hamilton Fish selected Fairchild to be the U.S. Consul at Liverpool, England.[45] Ex-General C. C. Washburn, with the support of the Madison Regency, was elected governor of the Badger State. With Lucius Fairchild out of the country, Old Abe faced a very different set of political circumstances.

21

The Centennial

GOVERNOR Washburn's administration coincided with the financial Panic of 1873 and the onset of a severe national economic depression. Wisconsinites experienced an erosion of the on-again, off-again prosperity that had characterized the state's economy since 1861. For Old Abe the years 1872–1875 were especially sad since they brought physical setbacks as well as personality changes. Although the war eagle regained his strength by 1876, his role in state and national affairs never approached the degree of purposefulness it had under Governor Fairchild. In addition, Republicans could no longer take political victories for granted. The Democrats had made a comeback, both locally and nationally. Even the Bloody Shirt lost some of its appeal, and Old Abe himself developed enemies.

Captain McDonald's duties became increasingly demanding in 1872. As an employee of the Adjutant General's Department, McDonald was forced to devote more and more of his time answering the mountainous correspondence received by the agency concerning Civil War soldiers' records. The requests for such records became greater when bounty equalizations and disability claims, as well as widows' and orphans' benefits, became available. As requests for Civil War records poured in, the original documents upon which the essential information was recorded had begun to deteriorate.[1] The department's staff was overwhelmed, and McDonald could give Old Abe little of the time and affection he so enjoyed.

In addition, Old Abe developed a fierce rivalry

WHi(D31)561

Centennial parade, Madison, July 4, 1876, looking eastward from the Park Hotel near the corner of Carroll and Main streets.

with another eagle. The Forty-Ninth Wisconsin Infantry had spent a total of seven months in service during the Civil War, performing guard and post duties in western Missouri.[2] There, the regiment acquired a golden eagle named Timothy which was presented to Adjutant General James K. Proudfit in March, 1866.[3] (Timothy's name was changed to Phil Sheridan and later to Andy Johnson.) He occupied a roost in the basement of the Capitol, and Old Abe's custodian, Captain McDonald, had charge of his care.[4] The golden eagle was untamed, and he did not attend rallies.[5]

Old Abe and Andy Johnson became bitter enemies. Fights were common, and the golden eagle managed to injure Old Abe on one occasion. In late 1873, Old Abe retaliated. The war eagle ambushed Andy Johnson, attacking his rival from above and from the rear, sinking his talons deep into his neck. Andy Johnson died, apparently from the effects of Old Abe's attack, in the spring of 1874.[6]

But Old Abe also lost his own greatest friend that same year. The election of 1873 left William R. Taylor, a Democrat, in the governor's chair. In a move aimed at retrenchment, Taylor reduced the number of state employees, abolishing "all expenditures not absolutely essential to official business. . . ."[7] Captain McDonald was dismissed.[8] According to Republican commentators, Old Abe's care and feeding were neglected.[9] For whatever reason, Old Abe languished and grew ill. Hugh Lewis, a Capitol employee and an Iron Brigade veteran, became alarmed when he saw Old Abe weakening to the point where the eagle could not even stand. Old Abe lay on his side and "drooped."[10] Lewis wrapped the feathered veteran in blankets and nursed the ailing war eagle. Before too long Old Abe recovered, but his health became a source of concern.[11]

Two veterans' rallies in 1875 left Old Abe physically shaken. In May, the G.A.R. sponsored a three-day reunion in Chicago which drew huge numbers of participants and spectators. Hugh Lewis carried the war eagle in several rain-swept parades, and crowds "loudly cheered" when the feathered veteran passed by in his stately carriage.[12] Shortly thereafter, Old Abe appeared at a veterans' reunion in Milwaukee. Again, cold, driving rains marred the event.[13] Old Abe's feathers were glazed with ice, and he collapsed after becoming chilled.[14]

A change now developed in Old Abe's personality, revealing itself slowly but inexorably between 1875 and 1881. He became more cantankerous, and his health remained uncertain. When the Republicans recaptured the statehouse in the election of 1875, they subjected Old Abe to a grueling series of public appearances which further weakened his health while serving little purpose other than entertainment.

Indeed, entertainment had become an important feature of veterans' rallies during the late 1870's. As the G.A.R. struggled to organize and maintain itself during a period of internal division and Democratic resurgence, the concept of fraternal reunions, or "campfires," gained favor.[15] The social aspect of veterans' gatherings popularized soldier societies like the G.A.R. and helped them sustain both ogranizational apparatus, and political potential.

Old Abe's career as an entertainer, moreover, was not solely restricted to appearances before veterans' groups. In fact, Wisconsin's war eagle par-

GAR Memorial Hall

One of Old Abe's "autograph" photos from the Centennial, 1876. The triangular mark in front of his breast was made by the eagle's beak.

ticipated in a variety of public programs ranging in scale from events with purely a local focus to those having a nationwide appeal. He participated in celebrations associated with the centennial of America's independence, which took place over a two-year period from 1875 to 1876. The Women's State Centennial Executive Committee of Wisconsin, for example, sponsored a living history extravaganza in the Assembly Chamber of the State Capitol on July 5, 1875. Short dramatic performances—or tableaux—were presented before a very select audience. Mrs. Ole Bull, wife of the famous Norwegian violinist, decorated the legislative hall for the occasion:

> Our Assembly Chamber was a pillared Shade, high over arched, and dotted with vine and moss baskets of fairy shapes and velvet hues. Glittering amid this temple which appeared a grove, were banners and bruised arms hung up for monuments . . . the Speaker's desk had been transformed by artistic hands into a niche with state insignia, and before which hung a mysterious curtain. On the opposite side of the hall a mossy grotto, enshrining flower nymphs, added its own charm to the scene. . . .[16]

The spectators dressed in Colonial-era costumes, some wearing powdered wigs, others dressing as members of the English royal court during the 1770's. Refinement abounded, and the dramas took place without "that rudeness of behavior which sometimes characterizes Madison entertainments," according to the official publication of the Women's Centennial Committee.[17]

Vignettes focusing on the lives of George and Martha Washington, General LaFayette, and King George III took place. The final tableau featured the aging Major Charles G. Mayers, who was dressed to resemble the youthful John Paul Jones. Mayers recited a poem entitled "The Eagle of Freedom," by Lizzie Doten. At the appropriate moment, the "mysterious" curtain on the Speaker of the Assembly's desk was drawn back, revealing Old Abe to the audience. Instead of spreading his wings and uttering his famous cry, however, Old Abe "drooped his head," from modesty as some people assumed.[18] The war eagle in fact was unwell, and none of his 1875 appearances should have taken place.

For the next seven months Wisconsin's winged veteran rested in his Capitol apartment. This recuperative period improved his health, but not his personality. When W. W. Barrett, the brother of

Reverend Barrett, visited the "Eagle Department" at the Capitol, Old Abe attacked him. Barrett and the eagle's attendant drove off the menacing bird with a broom.[19] Other such incidents were reported as well.[20]

Governor Taylor established the State Board of Centennial Managers in 1875. The Board joined forces with the Women's State Centennial Committee to organize Wisconsin exhibits for the International Exposition scheduled to take place in Philadelphia in 1876.[21] While prominent committee members encouraged Wisconsin's citizens to support the Philadelphia Exposition, the wives of state legislators organized a party.[22] The Leap Year Legislative Party on February 9, 1876, popularized centennial activities. Again the Assembly Chamber hosted an elaborate gathering and historical costumes once more graced the Capitol. A dramatic presentation of the French Revolution began with the singing of the "Marseillaise," followed by Ms. H. M. Page's solo performance as the "Daughter of the Regiment." Old Abe sat atop the new Centennial Perch, flapping his wings to the dance music. The war eagle returned to his apartment in the basement before the gala affair ended.[23]

When Republican Harrison Ludington took office as governor in January, 1876, he called for an increased appropriation to support the State Board of Centennial Managers. A joint resolution of the Legislature, furthermore, authorized the expenditure of $500 to send Old Abe to the Philadelphia gathering. Madison's famous artist, James Reeve Stuart, himself a Confederate veteran, painted an oil portrait of the war eagle to be hung in the Wisconsin home exhibit at Philadelphia.[24] Reverend Barrett updated and enlarged his 1865 eagle biography for sale at the Centennial Exposition.[25] Old Abe photographs and lithographs were again produced in great quantities, and the eagle's former bearer, John Hill, agreed to accompany and care for Old Abe at the Centennial.[26]

Indeed, so extravagant did the preparations concerning Old Abe appear that newspapers such as the Milwaukee *Sentinel*, recently converted to the Democratic viewpoint, questioned the necessity of some of the expenses. The fact that Hill would receive $90 per month for his work (only a bit less than the governor), angered the *Sentinel's* editor, who recommended that instead of placing Old Abe on display in Philadelphia, "we could have forwarded a batch of our politicians or a bevy of our orators." But he finally conceded that "these things all appear stale . . . when compared with our invincible eagle."[27]

President Grant strolled down the aisle of Machinery Hall in company with the Emperor Dom Pedro of Brazil in May, 1876. There, America's most famous Civil War veteran paused to flick the switch starting the great Corliss engine which supplied power to the miles of galleries and displays of the International Exposition. The gigantic dynamo hummed, working flawlessly, and the Centennial was officially opened.[28]

The exposition displayed many of the contrasts that characterized American society in 1876. The mechanical wonders of Machinery Hall attracted as many visitors as the display featuring "wild men" from Borneo. Charles Hire's root beer exhibit vied for public attention with Queen Victoria's handwoven furnishings. Shooting galleries were as attractive to visitors as Benjamin Franklin's hand-operated printing press.[29]

America, peaceful and reunited, congratulated itself on its material and mechanical progress, wondering what effects these might have on the rural values most citizens clung to. Transcontinental railroads were no longer dreams; indeed, competing lines existed. Jay Gould and his associates had completed New York's first elevated railroad. Immigrants from exotic homelands had begun trickling into America, soon to become a flood. The National League enjoyed its first no-hit baseball game. Scandals continued to rock the Grant administration during the President's last year in office, and Federal bayonets were yet needed to control affairs in several Southern states. Ex-cavalryman Nathan B. Forrest organized and led an association of Confederate veterans under the outlandish name Ku Klux Klan. The Sioux and Cheyenne still dominated vast areas of the western frontier after defeating Civil War hero George Armstrong Custer on the Little Big Horn.[30]

The weather seemed determined to not cooperate. Three months of intense heat kept attendance low. The sun beat down mercilessly on the asphalt pavements at the Exposition grounds, producing what one witness described as a "sickening odor."[31] A G.A.R. parade, however, drew a large crowd. Hundreds of veterans marched under their Civil War regimental banners, and despite the heat, onlookers cheered "the glorious raggedness"

of the battle flags.[32] August brought a break in the weather, and after that crowds began flocking to the Centennial Exposition. Between May and October, 8,181,080 individuals paid the 50 cent admission fee. On September 28, some 257,000 people viewed the Centennial's many attractions, setting the record for a single day. The 160-day Philadelphia International Exposition proved to be a grand success.[33]

Wisconsin's war eagle occupied a place of honor in Agricultural Hall, amid displays of different varieties of wheat, corn, grains, and farm implements.[34] Old Abe, reported Philadelphia journalist, Helen Austin, drew "a larger crowd than any other exhibit in the building."[35] John Hill and Reverend Barrett sold eagle photos and biographies as fast as they could ring them up.[36] "There was always a crowd around him," explained a Centennial souvenir guide book, "the services of this celebrated Eagle having gained him a national reputation."[37] Old Abe spread his pinions and screamed in reply to the cheers of old veterans who passed by.[38] John Hill tossed the eagle and its new standard up and down when he wanted Old Abe to flap his wings.[39] Spectators asked numerous questions about the war eagle and Hill "softly turned his tobacco from one cheek to the other while he discoursed about the bird."[40] Sometimes he even allowed children to touch Old Abe, but on at least one occasion the bird scratched a viewer who ventured too near.[41]

Old Abe's great coup at the Centennial involved the sale of "Eagle Autographs." Hill trained Old Abe to peck carte-de-visite-sized photos of himself, thereby "autographing" them, while customers watched in amazement. Autographed portraits of the war eagle sold for $1.00 each.[42]

Old Abe returned to Madison after his extended visit to the East Coast. In May, 1877, the Soldiers and Sailors of the Chippewa Valley invited the winged veteran to attend their July 4 reunion. R. C. Brice, district attorney of Dunn County, helped organize the veterans' gathering, explaining to the adjutant general of Wisconsin: "As Old Abe is a native of this valley it is eminently proper, not only on the part of the soldiers, but of the whole community, that the eagle should be here on that occasion."[43] Brice's point was irrefutable, and Old Abe went to Menomonie. There, local schoolchildren spent some of their free time trapping birds and small mammals to feed Old Abe. Captain Victor Wolf of Company C, Eighth Wisconsin Infantry, helped popularize the reunion; eagle-bearer Dave McLain and several other members of the Eau Claire Eagles were also present.[44] Old Abe's attendant, I. E. Troan, accompanied the war eagle on this trip, and cared for him during the festivities. "Old Abe had a glorious reception," reported Troan to his superiors.[45]

Soon other invitations flooded in. Ohio-born Rufus R. Dawes, the ex-colonel of the Sixth Wisconsin Infantry—a part of the Iron Brigade—gave his "urgent endorsement" to the request of the Soldiers and Sailors of Ohio that Governor Ludington permit Old Abe to attend their encampment in Marietta during September.[46]

So popular did Old Abe become with Ohio's veterans that they asked him back year after year. In 1878, for example, the Society of the Soldiers and Sailors of Licking County invited Old Abe to attend the Veterans of Ohio Reunion at Newark on July 22.[47] Peter B. Field carried Wisconsin's war eagle to the affair. A band met Field and his feathered companion at the Newark depot and escorted Old Abe to his quarters in the shade of a walnut tree.[48] The following year, more Ohio veterans' organizations requested Old Abe's presence.[49] Old Abe attended other reunions as well, including those at Lake Geneva, Wisconsin, and a large veterans' gathering at the Minnesota State Fair in St. Paul.[50]

Perhaps the most satisfying, and certainly the most purposeful trip, made by Old Abe in the post-Fairchild era was the war eagle's extended visit to Boston during the winter of 1878–1879. Reverend Barrett had passed through Boston with Old Abe on the return to Madison after the Centennial. In Boston, Old Abe appeared at the Old South Church, which was then threatened by commercial development and urban renewal. Citizens' action groups had formed to preserve the historic Colonial structure. Old Abe helped raise money for the preservation effort by luring Bostonians to Old South, where the famous eagle could be viewed for a small price. According to Governor Alexander Rice of Massachusetts, Old Abe proved to be a "strong attraction."[51]

Two years later, Old Abe returned for a longer and more decisive effort in behalf of historic preservation. Mrs. Augustus Hemenway, a wealthy

Bostonian, donated $100,000 for the preservation of the Old South Church and enlisted the aid of C. Alice Baker, a local schoolteacher, to begin a movement whose purpose would be "to prevent the destruction of old landmarks of New England patriotism."[52] Together, Baker and Hemenway helped establish the Old South Historical Society. Periodic fairs were held at Old South Church to raise additional funds, while Miss Baker held Saturday morning story sessions for schoolchildren and displayed artifacts of the Revolutionary War.[53] Governor William E. Smith of Wisconsin dispatched Old Abe to Boston in December, 1878, with his attendant Peter Field, and together they helped assure the success of the Old South Church Fair.[54]

Bostonians treated the war eagle and his veteran attendant like princes during this second visit. Field purchased fresh fish, pigeons, pheasants, chickens, and "other delicacies" for Old Abe.[55] The eagle rested in a spacious cage housed in the church proper and entertained the crowds of visitors drawn to the varied programs of Hemenway and Baker. Field had the bird perch on his outstretched arm, chase around the floor with his wings flapping, and glide majestically back to his perch.[56]

The Old South Fair culminated on Washington's birthday, 1879. Miss Baker presented her poetical story "Old Abe, the War Eagle of Wisconsin" before a packed house comprised largely of school groups. (Her account was quite fanciful, incorporating several of the famous Old Abe legends.)[57] The feathered veteran flapped his wings when the audience clapped.[58] Blind children were allowed to touch the eagle, and a choir sang an ode to Old Abe.[59]

Thus, more than a dozen years after the end of the Civil War, the eagle had once again demonstrated his ability to excite interest and enthusiasm, this time among elements of Boston's ruling elite. The cause Old Abe served had benefitted from the war eagle's presence, and his altruistic efforts reflected well upon the Badger State. Even spokesmen for Wisconsin's Democrats admitted that the Boston trip had generated good will. The Milwaukee *Sentinel* had lambasted Old Abe and the Republicans during 1878, claiming that the eagle had died of his 1875 illnesses and that his numerous appearances were faked.[60] After the Old South affair, however, the *Sentinel*'s editor, began mellowing his critical tone. The old war eagle had, in fact, won the respect of the opposition party.[61]

22

Old Abe at Peace

OLD Abe resumed his everyday life at the State Capitol after returning from Boston. He obviously enjoyed his apartment with its large custom-built bath tub and dining table, and according to Frank A. Flower, a state employee and historical writer who closely observed Old Abe's antics, would rush happily down the corridor leading to his rooms, without being tethered, after each trip.[1]

Visitors at the Wisconsin State Capitol continually asked to see the war eagle. One such visit was undertaken by the young Jane Addams and her family, who lived near Freeport, Illinois, only sixty-five miles from Madison. One of the significant experiences of her girlhood, she later wrote, was "a visit made to the war eagle Old Abe, who, as we children well knew, lived in the State Capitol of Wisconsin. . . ."[2]

The Addams family reached Madison after an all-day buggy ride. At the Capitol, they headed directly to the Eagle Department. There, "sitting sedately upon his high perch," was Old Abe. His keeper, dressed in an old blue army coat, answered questions concerning the feathered veteran for the awe-struck girls. Years later, when Jane Addams had become one of the most famous social workers of her day, she fondly recollected that the "journey to the veteran war eagle had itself symbolized that search for the heroic and perfect which so persistently haunts the young."[3] For Jane Addams, and perhaps for others, Old Abe symbolized "all that was great and good."[4]

Old Abe made a number of appearances during the fall of 1879. In early September Old Abe and his one-legged keeper, Mark Smith, went to Aurora, Illinois, to attend what was called "the largest gathering of veterans since the war."[5] The Chicago Union Veterans Club organized the event which they titled the Soldiers Reunion of the Northwest; the G.A.R. wholeheartedly supported the program.[6] The three-day reunion drew 150,000 people. Smith was worn out from answering thousands of questions concerning Old Abe, and by the end of the event he had lost his voice.[7]

Immediately after the Aurora gathering, Smith rushed Old Abe to Oshkosh. There, the war eagle went on public view in a tent on the grounds of the Northern State Fair. The proceeds (at 10 cents per person) supported the charitable work of the Ladies Aid Society of the First Methodist-Episcopal Church of Oshkosh.[8] Old Abe spent several weeks at the Oshkosh Fair where, as usual, he attracted "considerable attention."[9]

Smith and the eagle then traveled to Menomonie for a soldiers' reunion after the Northern State Fair ended. It was Old Abe's second postwar visit to his Chippewa Valley home region. Governor Smith also sent a number of Civil War battle flags to the two-day gathering.[10]

After that, Mark Smith and Old Abe attended the reception for former President Grant hosted by the Society of the Army of the Tennessee in Chicago.[11] Grant and his wife had returned to the United States from their world tour after the close of his second term. Some believed that Grant was developing plans to seek the nomination for the presidency in 1880. A parade drew a crowd, but Old Abe and Smith were so worn out by their travels that they could not attend. Rather, the pair showed up for a lavish banquet at the Palmer House on the evening of November 13. At first hotel officials would not let the modestly dressed Smith in, but the one-legged veteran explained that if he were excluded, Old Abe would not participate. Both veterans were seated. After a long night of speeches and toasts, William F. Vilas, a Democratic politician from Madison, delivered an oratorical tribute to Ulysses S. Grant, at the end of which Old Abe flapped his wings and screeched.[12]

George Gilles became Old Abe's attendant in 1880.[13] Traveling kept the pair occupied. Old Abe attended the Citizens and Soldiers of Portage County rally in Plover in May.[14] The war eagle joined other veterans of the Eighth Wisconsin for a regimental reunion organized by Augie Weissert in June.[15] An immense week-long rally took place in Milwaukee during the same month, and both Old Abe and General Grant appeared in a parade.[16] Gilles and the war eagle later that year traveled to Columbus and to Canton, Ohio, where they were extremely well treated.[17] In late August, Old Abe joined the First Battalion of the Wisconsin National Guard at Janesville. The First Battalion's commander was none other than William Britton, who had led the Eighth Wisconsin during

The Grand Reunion parade in Milwaukee, June, 1880, which marked the resurgence of the
Grand Army of the Republic in Wisconsin. According to press accounts, more than 250,000
people turned out for the event.

the last year of the Civil War.[18] The Wisconsin Guardsmen, along with Old Abe, traveled to Rockford, Illinois, where they rendezvoused with several other units from the neighboring state and set up a camp.[19]

These were Old Abe's last public appearances. The bitter cold winter of 1880–1881 proved disastrous. In February, 1881, a small fire erupted in the basement of the State Capitol in a storage area containing paints and oils. Although Capitol staff members quickly brought the blaze under control, the fire produced "an enormous volume of black and offensive smoke," which filled the war eagle's quarters. Old Abe, wrote the historian Frank Flower, was grievously affected by the incident.[20]

On March 20, 1881, Old Abe refused to eat. During the following week he visibly lost strength. Governor Smith and Superintendent of Public Property George E. Bryant employed doctors to attend the ailing bird, but to no avail. Old Abe declined steadily. On Friday, March 25, the bird went into spasms and appeared to be suffering from "serious lung difficulties." Old Abe died in George Gilles' arms the following afternoon.[21]

Thus passed Old Abe the Wisconsin War Eagle, veteran of thirty-seven battles and skirmishes, Bloody Shirt politician, fund raiser, entertainer, historic preservationist, and rallying point for the Boys in Blue. Old Abe, observed the Milwaukee *Sentinel*, "belongs to the number of those who have had greatness thrust upon them. . . . It has rarely been given to a member of the feathered species to attract as much attention in the world as Old Abe. . . . The whole country has heard of him."[22]

Discussion immediately arose as to what should be done with the eagle's remains. Veterans volunteered to act as pallbearers at Old Abe's funeral. Union Rest at Madison's Forest Hill Cemetary was suggested as an appropriate grave and monument site. Taxidermy, however, won out over burial. Major C. G. Mayers stuffed the war eagle in order to preserve Old Abe for future generations.[23] The taxidermist's rendition was not completely successful; Old Abe's body was saved, but it did not look especially life-like.

It did not matter. Old Abe's stuffed remains seemed to command as much attention as the feathered veteran himself had in life. The secretary of the Soldiers' and Sailors' Association of Bellair, Ohio, for example, requested the presence of the

WHi(D485)6254

The taxidermist's treatment of Old Abe was stiff and unnatural, but the eagle remained a proud relic of the Civil War between his death in 1881 and the destruction of the State Capitol in 1904.

stuffed Old Abe for the regimental reunion of the Forty-Third Ohio Infantry and promised to pay "any amount of security for the safe return" of the war eagle's remains.[24] Wisconsin's adjutant general refused.[25]

By May a dispute arose over where and how the stuffed war eagle would be displayed.[26] Pressure from state veterans convinced the governor to place Old Abe in a glass case mounted on a pedestal in the rotunda of the Capitol. (A suggestion that the glass-enclosed eagle be suspended "by chains hanging down from the dome" was rejected.[27]) On September 17, 1881, Old Abe went on display in the rotunda of the State Capitol.[28] Four years later, the eagle had been moved to the War Museum, part of the State Historical Society of Wisconsin's rooms in the Capitol.[29] The eagle and his octagonal black walnut and glass case stood near the rows of tattered battle flags brought back from the war by Wisconsin's soldiers.

Legends concerning Old Abe, which had abounded during the eagle's lifetime, began taking on fantastical qualities after 1881. The Milwaukee

Sentinel reported, for example, a series of "yarns" by "an old soldier" which described Old Abe's divebombing attacks on Confederate "leading generals," the war eagle's aerial reconaissance missions, his ability to direct the artillery fire of his comrades, and, best of all, his capture of rebel battle maps—on the wing.[30] Some dispute arose as to Old Abe's early life at Jim Falls, and especially about who had cared for the eagle prior to his volunteering to join the "Eau Claire Badgers." (Dan McCann's brother, Stephan S. McCann, received credit for being the original owner.[31])

The first discussion involving the question of Old Abe's gender arose in an 1889 issue of the *Milwaukee Sentinel*. The feature carried the assertion by Lillie Deveraux Blake that Old Abe had laid eggs and was therefore a female eagle. (Blake, the *Sentinel* explained, "is a woman's rights woman.") Although Blake offered no evidence to

GAR Memorial Hall

George W. Sutherland of Clintonville, a G.A.R. activist, poses c. 1900 with a replica of Old Abe. Note the stuffed badger at right.

back up her claim, that did not settle the matter.[32] Three years later, Edward H. Ranney, editor of the Madison *Democrat*, revitalized the issue in his article "Did Old Abe Lay Eggs?" Ranney wrote that the war eagle was a fitting symbol for the woman's rights movement of the day.[33] Lafayette Bunnell, formerly surgeon of the Thirty-Sixth Wisconsin Infantry, continued the theme in his 1897 book on the natural history of the Winona, Minnesota, area. After describing the habits and coloration of bald eagles, Bunnell wrote, "Whether true or not, it has been reported that Old Abe . . . while at Madison in charge of the warden appointed to its care, was proved to be a female by laying eggs."[34] Others hotly refuted these assertions.[35] Perhaps the most that can be said about the question of Old Abe's gender is that we lack sufficient data to prove the case.

What *is* known is that Old Abe continued to attract public attention even after being stuffed. He even traveled. In September of 1887, for instance, the glass-encased eagle appeared in Milwaukee at the Wisconsin State Fair along with other displays at the Exposition Building. A wooden tablet bore the inscription, "Hatched February 1861; died March 26, 1881."[36] The bird attended the Twenty-Fifth National Encampment of the G.A.R. at Detroit in 1891 where members of the Wisconsin delegation carried him. In 1893, Old Abe went on display at the World's Columbian Exposition in Chicago.[37] Hosea W. Rood, a veteran of the Twelfth Wisconsin Infantry and an active G.A.R. member, noted in 1903, "Interest in him seems all the time to be growing stronger."[38]

When the State Historical Society moved into its new building on the University of Wisconsin campus in 1900, Old Abe went along.[39] Pressure from veterans, however, convinced Governor Robert M. La Follette to have Old Abe and Wisconsin's Civil War flags returned to the State Capitol. In April of 1903, therefore, the encased Old Abe became part of the exhibits at the G.A.R. Memorial Hall in the Capitol. There, President Theodore Roosevelt viewed the state's most famous Civil War veteran while passing through Madison. "By George!" exclaimed T. R., "I'm glad to see him! I read about him in my reader when I was a boy at school." He said to Hosea Rood that he had "always felt a lively interest" in Old Abe.[40]

But Old Abe did not even spend an entire year

Old Abe held pride of place in this gallery of the State Historical Society of Wisconsin, c. 1902, along with other artifacts of the Civil War and Spanish-American War. Colonel Joseph Bailey's presentation sword and a silver punch bowl awarded him by the U.S. Navy are displayed in the case at right.

in the G.A.R. Memorial Hall. In February, 1904, a fire broke out in the State Capitol. Despite all efforts, the conflagration spread relentlessly and consumed the building. Old Abe and his glass case were destroyed. Letters of sympathy streamed in to the G.A.R. Memorial Hall expressing grief at the loss of Old Abe's remains. Citizens of Boston, school children from Michigan, and state educators wrote of their sadness and feelings of "irreparable loss of our most treasured emblem of liberty."[41]

Replicas of Old Abe attempted to fill the void left by the loss of the original. George Sutherland, a G.A.R. man from Clintonville, Wisconsin, traveled to local encampments with such an eagle.[42] Members of the G.A.R. from Eau Claire began calling their unit "The Eagle Post," and they had a "good representation" of Old Abe on hand during reunions.[43] The Wisconsin Assembly received a replica Old Abe in 1915 which legislators had

mounted over the Speaker's desk in the new State Capitol.[44] The G.A.R. Memorial Hall received three eagles after the new Capitol opened, and the Smithsonian Institution has a replica Old Abe in its collection.[45]

Old Abe statues were perhaps more important than the replica stuffed eagles. Between 1901 and 1907 the State of Wisconsin appropriated $131,000 to support the activities of the Wisconsin Vicksburg National Military Park Commission. The commission designed and sited the monuments honoring the nearly 10,000 Wisconsin citizen-soldiers who had participated in the Vicksburg campaign of 1863. In addition to regimental markers, the commission helped create the state marker at the Vicksburg National Military Park. The Wisconsin monument was a granite column fifty-seven and a half feet tall, topped by a six-foot bronze likeness of Old Abe.[46] Governor Francis E. McGovern dedicated the commemorative statue on

GAR Memorial Hall

One of the most spectacular commemorations of Old Abe remains the Wisconsin monument at Vicksburg, Mississippi, pictured here on the day it was dedicated, May 22, 1911 (anniversary of the ill-fated Grand Assault in 1863). When the eagle was struck by lightning in the 1940's, another likeness replaced him atop the column.

May 22, 1911, exactly forty-eight years after Old Abe and his regiment particpated in the ill-fated Grand Assault.[47] When a lightning bolt damaged the bronze eagle in 1944, another likeness was fashioned for the monument.[48]

Eagle-oriented stone work can be seen in Madison, Eau Claire, and Racine. The Camp Randall Memorial Arch has Old Abe carved in its facade. Memorial High School in Eau Claire has a large statue of Old Abe on its entryway roof. The Chippewa Valley Museum in Eau Claire has a colonnaded Old Abe in front of its entrance.[49] Jerome I. Case, founder of the agricultural machinery firm which bears his name, had been a member of the State Board of Centennial Managers. Impressed by the figure of Old Abe, Case adopted the war eagle's likeness for his company's trademark. In later years, Old Abe statues both large and small appeared at and were distributed by the Racine-based corporation.[50]

The large and impressive cyclorama painting produced by Milwaukee artists for the Atlanta Exposition in the latter part of the nineteenth century included Old Abe in their rendition of the "Battle of Atlanta." Of course, Old Abe and part of the Eighth Wisconsin had already mustered out of service during the period of the Atlanta campaign, and the eagle had become a peaceful citizen when Sherman's men took the city. But Old Abe had become so synonomous with Civil War matters that the artists felt compelled to include Wisconsin's feathered hero in their work.

On June 6, 1944, when the Allies launched their invasion of France, it was somehow fitting that Old Abe should symbolically take part in the greatest airborne assault in history. The likeness of Old Abe still appears on the uniform of the 18,000 troopers of America's elite 101st Airborne Division, "The Screaming Eagles," whose left shoulder patch depicts an eagle's head on a black shield.[51]

Notes to the Text

Preface

[1]Such imaginative Old Abe stories include: Charlotte A. Baker, *Old Abe the War Eagle of Wisconsin* (Deerfield, Mass., 1904); Norman Carlisle, "Yankee Bird of Battle," in *True Magazine* (February, 1961), 27; Gerald Carson, "The Glorious Bird," in *Natural History* (October, 1979), 30–34; Earl Chappin, *Tales of Wisconsin* (River Falls, 1973); B. B. Crofutt, "Old Abe the Battle Eagle," in *Boy's Life Magazine* (July, 1923), 10; Margarite C. Dodge, *Old Abe the Wisconsin War Eagle* (n.p., 1930); Kenneth Gilbert, "The Bird that Led an Army," in *Western Story Magazine* (January 18, 1930), 100–107; Fred L. Holmes, "Old Abe the Warrior Eagle," in *Eagle* (June, 1944), 11; Robert E. Gard, *This Is Wisconsin* (Madison, 1969); Madeline F. King, *The Story of Old Abe* (King, Wisconsin, 1976); Russell R. Miller, "Some New Notes on 'Old Abe' the Battle Eagle," in *Military Collector and Historian*, Vol. 15 (Winter, 1963), 109–113; C. P. Nelson, *Abe, the War Eagle* (Lynn, Mass., 1903); Lorraine Sherwood, *Old Abe: American Eagle* (New York, 1946); Beatrice S. Smith, "Old Abe," in *Vista for Adults*, Vol. 64 (July 5, 1970); Maria P. Todd, "Old Abe War Eagle of the 8th Wisconsin," in *Military Collector and Historian*, Vol. 4 (Spring, 1952), 72–73; John Rauschenberger, "Old Abe: Wings of Victory," in *Exclusively Yours*, October 6, 1981; Leroy Gore, "Old Abe, Bird of Battle," in *Yarns of Wisconsin* (Madison, 1978), 157–160; Edmund Lindop, *War Eagle: The Story of a Civil War Mascot* (Boston, 1966); "The Soldier Bird," in C. W. Sanders (ed.), *Union Fifth Reader* (New York, 1867), 69–73; Sarah P. Bradish, "Old Abe," in *Little People of the Air* (Boston, 1884), 11–13.

[2]See "Old Abe" Papers, G.A.R. Memorial Hall Museum, Madison, and especially Lee Hill, "Old Abe, Bird of Battle," *Wisconsin Week-End*, April 30, 1975. This story originated with a Vicksburg newspaper editor.

[3]Among the more balanced accounts are: Joseph O. Barrett, *The Soldier Bird: History of "Old Abe" the Live War Eagle* (Chicago, 1865), and his updated version *The Soldier Bird Old Abe: The Live War Eagle of Wisconsin That Served a Three Year Campaign in the Great Rebellion* (Madison, 1876); J. Stanley Dietz, *The Story of Old Abe the War Eagle* (Madison, 1946); Frank A. Flower, *Old Abe the Eighth Wisconsin War Eagle* (Madison, 1885); Charles H. Henry, *The History of Old Abe the War Eagle* (Madison, 1933); David McLain, "The Story of Old Abe," in *Wisconsin Magazine of History*, Vol. 8 (June, 1925), 407–414; Frederick Merk, "The Story of Old Abe," in *Wisconsin Magazine of History*, Vol. 2 (1918–1919), 82–84; C. S. Selim [S. C. Miles], "The Eagle of the Regiment, An Epic on Old Abe, the War Eagle," unpublished manuscript, c. 1892, G.A.R. Memorial Hall Museum Archives, in the Augustus Weissert Papers, box 7; Bruce Catton, "Old Abe the War Eagle," in *American Heritage* (October, 1963), 32–33.

[4]For instance, Bette J. Davis, *Freedom Eagle* (New York, 1972); Patrick Young, *Old Abe the Eagle Hero* (Englewood Cliffs, N.J., 1965); and Madison Public Schools, "Old Abe, the Civil War Eagle," in *Instructional Materials About Our Community* (n.p., n.d.).

[5]Joseph O. Barrett, *Soldier Bird: History of "Old Abe" the Live War Eagle* (Chicago, 1865), 35. Cited hereinafter as Barrett, *Soldier Bird* (1865), to distinguish it from Barrett's updated version of 1876.

[6]Robert J. Burdette, *The Drums of the 47th* (Indianapolis, 1914), 67.

1: Old Abe and the Coming of the War

[1]Henry McCann to J. Stanley Dietz, September 25, 1937, Dietz Papers, G.A.R. Memorial Hall Archives, box 1, reprinted in Dietz, *The Story of Old Abe the War Eagle* (Madison, 1946), 1–4.

[2]*Ibid.*; also see Barrett, *Soldier Bird* (1865), 19–20. The "bushel of corn" might well have been a euphemism for liquor.

[3]*Ibid.*, 16. In 1937 Henry McCann, son of Dan and Margaret, stated that he believed Old Abe's original nest was located "at the mouth of the Jump River" at Surveyor's Point. See McCann in Dietz, *The Story of Old Abe*, 1. Others have stated that the Indians captured Old Abe at Island Lake near Chippewa Falls and that S. S. McCann rather than Dan and Margaret first obtained the bird. See James P. Welsh to W. B. Stoddard, March 6, 1925, in the John E. Perkins Papers, Chippewa Valley Historical Museum Archives; Chippewa Falls *Herald Telegram*, June 17, 1969.

[4]Henry McCann in Dietz, *The Story of Old Abe*, 2.

[5]Barrett, *Soldier Bird* (1865), 19–20; also see E. D. Rounds, "Old Abe the War Eagle," manuscript presented to Chippewa Valley Historical Society, May 5, 1926, on behalf of Sol Fuller, Co. C, 8th Wisconsin Infantry, Chippewa Valley Historical Museum Archives.

[6]Henry McCann in Dietz, *The Story of Old Abe*, 2.

[7]Frank Klement, "Wisconsin in the Civil War," in the *Wisconsin Blue Book, 1962*, p. 81; Augustus Gaylord, "In and Out of the Wisconsin Adjutant General's Office, 1862–66," *War Papers, Wisconsin MOLLUS* [Military Order of the Loyal Legion of the United States], Vol. III (1896), 310.

[8]Wisconsin Adjutant General, Descriptive Roll and Roster of the 8th Wisconsin Infantry, State Archives. Hereinafter cited as Descriptive Roll and Roster.

[9]Barrett, *Soldier Bird* (1865), 20; Chippewa Falls *Herald Telegram*, June 17, 1969; Flower, *Old Abe*, 10.

[10]Rounds, "Old Abe the War Eagle," 4; Barrett, *Soldier Bird* (1865), 25.

[11]Carolyn Mattern, *Soldiers When They Go: The Story of Camp Randall, 1861–1865* (Madison, 1981), 1–24.

[12]Barrett, *Soldier Bird* (1865), 24; *Wisconsin State Journal*, September 10, 1861; a Non Vet of Co. "H" [John M. Williams], *The Eagle Regiment, the 8th Wisconsin Infantry Volunteers: A Sketch of its Marches, Battles, and Campaigns From 1861–1865* (Belleville, Wisconsin, 1890), 40. Cited hereinafter as Williams, *Eagle Regiment*.

[13]Rounds, "Old Abe the War Eagle," 4; Williams, *Eagle Regiment*, 41; Descriptive Roll and Roster; Charles D. Stewart, "Old Abe's Shield," in *Wisconsin Magazine of History*, Vol. 36 (Spring, 1953), 203–204. Cited hereinafter as *WMH*.

2: Meet the Eighth Wisconsin

[1]Williams, *Eagle Regiment*, 1; William P. Lyon, *Reminiscences of the Civil War* (San Jose, Cal., 1907), 1; Parker M. C. Reed *The Bench and Bar of Wisconsin* (Milwaukee, 1882), 72–73; State Bar Association of Wisconsin, *Proceedings*, Vol. 10 (Madison, 1912–14), 37–38.

[2]Descriptive Roll and Roster.

[3]*Ibid.*

[4]Philip H. Gould, Letters, 1860–1862, in N.C. Gould Papers, State Archives; Edward Cronon, Civil War Letters, 1861–1865, in the Cronon Papers, State Archives.

[5]Edward C. Dwight, December 12, 1861, Civil War Diary, State Archives; Descriptive Roll and Roster.

[6]Descriptive Roll and Roster; John M. Williams, Civil War Diaries, 1861–1864, State Archives; A Non-Commissioned Officer [George W. Driggs], *Opening the Mississippi or Two Years Campaigning in the South West: A Record of the Campaigns, Sieges, Actions, and Marches in Which the Eighth Wisconsin Volunteers Have Participated* (Madison, 1864); James H. Greene, *Reminiscences of the War, Bivouacs, Marches, Skirmishes and Battles* (Medina, Ohio, 1886); John Woodworth, *Reminiscences of 1861–1865* (Eau Claire, 1887); Edwin Farley, *Experiences of A Soldier 1861–1865* (Paducah, 1918); A Staff Officer of the 8th Regiment Wisconsin Volunteers, *Army Life and Stray Shots by A Staff Officer of the 8th Regiment Wisconsin Volunteers, 15th Army Corps 3rd Division* (Memphis, 1863); Lyon, *Reminiscences.* See also E. B. Quiner, Correspondence of Wisconsin Volunteers, Quiner Papers, State Archives. Hereinafter cited as Quiner, Cor. Wis. Vols.

[7]Miles, "Eagle of the Regiment," chap. XI, 2; Descriptive Roll and Roster.

[8]See discussion of ethnic backgrounds in Richard N. Current, *The History of Wisconsin. Volume II: The Civil War Era, 1848–1873* (Madison, 1976), 306–309.

[9]Descriptive Roll and Roster; Mattern, *Soldiers When They Go,* 30–31; Quiner, Cor. Wis. Vols., vol. 2, p. 7.

[10]*Ibid.*; Williams, *Eagle Regiment,* 138.

[11]*Ibid.*

[12]Descriptive Roll and Roster.

[13]J. H. Greene to wife, September 14, 1861 in *Reminiscences,* 3; Lyon, *Reminiscences of the Civil War,* 2–3.

[14]Descriptive Roll and Roster.

[15]*Ibid.*; McLain, "The Story of Old Abe," *WMH,* 7:407–414; David McLain, Papers, 1860–1976, State Archives.

3: The Making of Soldiers

[1]James H. Greene to wife, September 10, 1861, in *Reminiscences,* 2.

[2]J. Baker to Dear Brother, September 20, 1861, in the Jeremiah Baker Papers, 1856–1874, State Archives; Mattern, *Soldiers When They Go,* 29. For pay scales, see *The Legislative Manual of the State of Wisconsin, 1863* (Madison, 1863), 217–218.

[3]Bell I. Wiley, *The Life of Billy Yank* (Indianapolis, 1951), 22.

[4]Edward C. Dwight, Diary, January 12, 1862; Descriptive Roll and Roster.

[5]Williams, Diary, January 27, 1862, February 7, 1863; Descriptive Roll and Roster.

[6]Clothing and Equipment Records Diary, September 2, 1862–April 19, 1864, in the Burnett Demarest Papers, 1862–1874, State Archives; "G" to unidentified newspaper, January 8, 1862 in Quiner, Cor. Wis. Vols., vol. 4, p. 36.

[7]James E. Brown to Dear Mother, August 12, 1862, in the James E. Brown Papers, Chippewa Valley Historical Museum Archives.

[8]Burdette, *Drums of the 47th,* 15–16.

[9]Williams, Diary, September 14, 1861; Table of Regiments, *Annual Report of the Adjutant General of the State of Wisconsin for the Year 1862* (Madison, 1863), 228. Cited hereinafter as *Rpt. Adj. Gen. Wis.*

[10]Unidentified news article, September 6, 1861, in Quiner, Cor. Wis. Vols., vol. 2, p. 6; see also Thomas Priestly to Dear Father, October 9, 1861, in the Thomas Priestly Papers, 1865–1891, State Archives.

[11]Dwight, Diary, March 22, 1862.

[12]Miles, "Eagle of the Regiment," chap. XXI, 2; "M" to *Wisconsin State Journal,* November 24, 1862, in Quiner, Cor. Wis. Vols., vol. 4, p. 135.

[13]Return of the 8th Wisconsin, March 1864, "numbers of arms," Wisconsin National Guard, Office of the Adjutant General, Records of Volunteer Regiments, State Archives, box 75. Cited hereinafter as Records of Vol. Regts.

[14]Williams, *Eagle Regiment,* 120.

[15]*Ibid.*

[16]General Order No. 1, September 3, 1861, Quiner, Cor. Wis. Vols., vol. 2, p. 6.

[17]Miles, "Eagle of the Regiment," chap. II, 3.

[18]Quiner, Cor. Wis. Vols., vol. 2, p. 6.

[19]*Ibid.*, vol. 2, p. 7.

[20]Greene to wife, September 5, 1861, in *Reminiscences,* 2.

[21]Williams, *Eagle Regiment,* 2.

[22]W. P. Lyon to unidentified newspaper [Racine *Advocate*], October 15, 1861, in Quiner, Cor. Wis. Vols., vol. 2, pp. 12–13.

[23]Williams, *Eagle Regiment,* 2.

[24]Jeremiah Baker to Dear Brother, September 20, 1861, Baker Papers.

[25]Greene to wife, September 5, 1861, in *Reminiscences,* 2.

[26]Unidentified news article, September 13, 1861, in Quiner, Cor. Wis. Vols., vol. 2, p. 6.

[27]Unidentified news article, September 3, 1861, *ibid.*

[28]Miles, "Eagle of the Regiment," chap. II, 3.

[29]Greene to wife, September 10, 1861, in *Reminiscences,* 2; Mattern, *Soldiers When They Go,* 29.

[30]*Ibid.*

[31]Priestly, Diary, September 25, 1861, Priestly Papers; Mattern, *Soldiers When They Go,* 32–33.

4: To the Front

[1]Williams, *Eagle Regiment,* 43.

[2]*Ibid.*

[3]Lyon to Racine *Advocate,* October 15, 1861, in *Reminiscences,* 3.

[4]William B. Britton to Augustus Gaylord, Adjutant General of Wisconsin, October 1, 1863, Records of Vol. Regts., box 72; also see "Record of Engagements of Wisconsin Troops in Civil War" in J. Stanley Dietz (comp.), *The Battle Flags and Wisconsin Troops in the Civil War and War with Spain* (Madison, 1943), 4–62.

[5]R. C. Murphy to Governor Alexander Randall, December 6, 1861, Records of Vol. Regts., box 72.

[6]Williams, *Eagle Regiment,* 3.

[7]Wiley, *Billy Yank,* 64.

[8]Williams, *Eagle Regiment,* 3; Dwight, Diary, October 14, 1861.

[9]Barrett, *Soldier Bird* (1865), 28.

[10]*Ibid.*; also see Williams, *Eagle Regiment,* 4.

[11]W. B. Britton to August Gaylord, October 1, 1863, Records of Vol. Regts., box 72; Driggs, *Opening the Mississippi,* 11–12.

[12]R. C. Murphy to Governor Alexander Randall, December 6, 1861, Records of Vol. Regts., box 72.

[13]Williams, *Eagle Regiment,* 5; Williams, Diary, October 21, 1861.

[14]Jeremiah Baker to Dear Brother, October 26, 1861, Baker Papers; also see unsigned news article, Racine *Advocate,* October 30, 1861, in Quiner, Cor. Wis. Vols., vol. 2, p. 13.

[15]A. G. Weissert to Dear George, November 16, 1861, Civil War Correspondence, Weissert Papers, G.A.R. Memorial Hall Archives.

[16]Williams, Diary, October 22, 1861.

[17]A. G. Weissert to Dear George, November 16, 1861, Weissert Papers.

[18]R. C. Murphy to Alexander Randall, December 6, 1861, Records of Vol. Regts., box 72; Williams, Diary, October 21, 1861; Jeremiah Baker to Dear Brother, October 26, 1861,

Baker Papers; Driggs, *Opening the Mississippi*, 13; *Rpt. Wis. Adj. Gen., 1861*, p. 54.

[19]Murphy to Randall, December 6, 1861, Records of Vol. Regts., box 72; Britton to Gaylord, October 1, 1863, *ibid.*; J. H. Greene to wife, November 22, 1861, in *Reminiscences*, 5; William P. Lyon to Racine *Advocate*, November 12, 1861, in *Reminiscences*, 7–10.

[20]Williams, Diary, December 30, 1861, Miles, "Eagle of the Regiment," chap. 2, 5.

[21]Williams, Diary, January 1, 1862.

5: The Valley of the Mississippi

[1]John D. Milligan, *Gunboats Down the Mississippi* (Annapolis, 1965), xxii; William S. McFeely, *Grant: A Biography* (New York, 1981), 91; A. T. Mahan, *The Navy in the Civil War. Volume III, The Gulf and Inland Waters* (New York, 1883), 11.

[2]Milligan, *Gunboats*; Mahan, *Gulf and Inland Waters*; William T. Sherman, *Memoirs of William T. Sherman Written by Himself* (2 vols., New York, 1875), 1:332.

[3]Britton to Gaylord, October 1, 1865, Reports Vol. Regts., box 72. Also see Descriptive Roll and Roster; and Edward Cronon to A. G. Weissert, May 13, 1905, Weissert Papers. The Eighth traveled 3,645 miles by rail and 4,000 by marching. Some 2,000 rail miles were spent in travel to and from Cairo and Madison, which left 1,645 miles of rail travel in the war zone.

[4]Greene to wife, January 19, 1862, in *Reminiscences*, 9.

[5]"M" to *Wisconsin State Journal*, January 25, 1862, in Quiner, Cor. Wis. Vols., vol. 4, p. 40.

[6]*Ibid.*

[7]Greene to wife, January 26, 1862, in *Reminiscences*, 10.

[8]Williams, *Eagle Regiment*, 6–7; Driggs, *Opening the Mississippi*, 12–13.

[9]Milligan, *Gunboats*, 53.

[10]Williams, *Eagle Regiment*, 7; *Report of the Adjutant General of the State of Illinois*, revised by Brig. Gen. J. N. Reece (Springfield, 1900), Vol. II, 386. Cited hereinafter as *Rpt. Adj. Gen. Ill.*

[11]Milligan, *Gunboats*, 56.

[12]*Rpt. Adj. Gen. Wis., 1862*, p. 116; W. B. Britton to Augustus Gaylord, October 1, 1863, Records of Vol. Regts., box 72; "G" to *Wisconsin State Journal*, March 19, 1862, in Quiner, Cor. Wis. Vols., vol. 4, p. 59; "H" to *Wisconsin State Journal*, April 10, 1862, *ibid.*, 67; Byron C. Byrner, *Bugle Echoes, The Story of the Illinois 47th* (Springfield, 1905), 39; Driggs, *Opening the Mississippi*, 14–15; Edward Cronon to Dear Mother, April 10, 1862, Cronon Papers; Henry Walke, *Naval Scenes and Reminiscences of the Civil War* (New Haven, Conn., 1877), 193–195. Some of the Confederates were incarcerated at Madison, Wisconsin; see Edward Y. McMorries, *History of the First Regiment Alabama Volunteer Infantry C.S.A.* (Montgomery, 1904); and Gaylord, "In and Out of the Wis. Adj. General's Office," *MOLLUS*, 312.

[13]U. S. Grant, *Personal Memoirs of U. S. Grant* (2 vols., New York, 1885), 1:371–372.

[14]Field Return, Confederate Forces, May 28, 1862, in *The War of the Rebellion: A Compilation of the Official Records of the Union and Confederate Armies* (128 vols., Washington, 1880–1902), Vol. X, Series I, Pt. 1, p. 791. Cited hereinafter as *OR* with volume and part. Unless otherwise noted, all are Series I.

[15]Grant, *Memoirs*, 1:371–372.

[16]Miles, "Eagle of the Regiment," chap. X, 15.

[17]E. B. Quiner, *Military History of Wisconsin: A Record of the Civil and Military Patriotism of the State in the War for the Union* (Chicago, 1866), 520.

6: The Eagle Regiment

[1]Miles, "Eagle of the Regiment," chap. X, 19.

[2]Albert E. Castel, *General Sterling Price and the Confederate Defeat in the West* (Miami, Florida, 1980), 86; Report, Brig. General D. S. Stanley, June 14, 1862, *OR*, Vol. X, Pt. 1, pp. 720–729.

[3]Quiner, *Military History of Wisconsin*, 528; Report, Maj. Gen. John Pope, May 9, 1862, *OR*, Vol. X, Pt. 1, p. 804; Report, Col. J. M. Loomis, May 11, 1862, *ibid.*, 805–806.

[4]Greene to wife, May 10, 1862, in *Reminiscences*, 18–19; Report, John Loomis, May 11, 1862, *OR*, Vol. X, Pt. 1, pp. 805–806.

[5]Greene to wife, May 10, 1862, in *Reminiscences*, 18–19; Report, John Loomis, May 11, 1862, *OR*, Vol. X, Pt. 1, pp. 805–806; also see Dave McLain to Dear Sister, June 9, 1862, McLain Papers.

[6]*Ibid.*; W. B. Britton to *Wisconsin State Journal*, May 10, 1862, in Quiner, Cor. Wis. Vols., vol. 4, pp. 74–75.

[7]*Ibid.*; Williams, *Eagle Regiment*, 9; Britton to Gaylord, October 1, 1863, Records of Vol. Regts., box 72; Monthly Return, May, 1862, *ibid.*, box 75.

[8]*Ibid.*

[9]Miles, "Eagle of the Regiment," chap. VII, 42.

[10]Williams, *Eagle Regiment*, 47; interview with Dighton Smith, Private, Co. C, 8th Wis. Inf., by Theodore Coleman, Eau Claire *Leader*, July 12, 1914.

[11]A Staff Officer, *Army Life and Stray Shots*, 11; McLain, "The Story of Old Abe," *WMH*, 3:411; Barrett, *Soldier Bird* (1865), 31.

[12]Williams, *Eagle Regiment*, 47; *Rpt. Adj. Gen. Wis., 1862*, p. 117; William P. Lyon to Mrs. Lyon, May 31, 1863, in *Reminiscences*, 44.

[13]Report, General P. G. T. Beauregard, June 13, 1862, *OR*, Vol. X, Pt. 1, pp. 762–765; Col. William P. Johnston to Jefferson Davis, July 15, 1862, *ibid.*, 780–785.

[14]Report, Col. R. C. Murphy, June 1, 1862, to Adj. Gen. Wis., Records of Vol. Regts., box 75.

7: The Battle of Corinth

[1]Britton to Gaylord, October 1, 1863, Records Vol. Regts., box 72.

[2]Report, Col. R. C. Murphy, September 13, 1862, *OR*, Vol. XVII, Pt. 1, p. 60; Report, Maj. Gen. Sterling Price, September 26, 1862, *ibid.*, 119–120; "M" to *Wisconsin State Journal*, September 23, 1862, in Quiner, Cor. Wis. Vols., vol. 4, p. 116.

[3]Britton to Gaylord, October 1, 1863, Records of Vol. Regts., box 72.

[4]"M" to *Wisconsin State Journal*, September 23, 1862, in Quiner, Cor. Wis. Vols., vol. 4, p. 115.

[5]Britton to Gaylord, October 1, 1863, Records of Vol. Regts., box 72; Miles, "Eagle of the Regiment," chap. XI, 4. Prior to 1864, prisoners were returned or paroled to their own lines on promise not to return to combat operations until formally exchanged for prisoners captured by the opposing side. The system eventually was discontinued.

[6]Williams, *Eagle Regiment*, 11; Britton to Gaylord, October 1, 1863, Records of Vol. Regts., box 72; Report, Capt. A. W. Dees, September 22, 1862, *OR*, Vol. XVII, Pt. 1, p. 61.

[7]Capt. W. B. Britton to *Wisconsin State Journal*, January 17, 1863, in Quiner, Cor. Wis. Vols., vol. 8, p. 423. See Francis B. Heitman, *Historical Register and Dictionary of the United States Army, 1789–1903* (2 vols., Washington, D.C., 1903), 1:733; D. McCall, *Three Years in the Service: A Record of the Doings of the 11th Missouri Vols.* (Springfield, Ill., 1864).

[8]Capt. A. E. Smith, "Few Days with the Eighth Regiment, Wisconsin Volunteers at Iuka & Corinth," *War Papers, Wisconsin MOLLUS*, Vol. IV (1914), 61; Britton to Gaylord, October 1, 1863, Records of Vol. Regts., box 72.

[9]Report, Maj. Gen. E. O. C. Ord, October 15, 1862, *OR*, Vol. XVII, Pt. 1, pp. 117–119; Report, Maj. Gen. C. S. Hamilton, September 23, 1862, *ibid.*, 89–93; C. S. Hamilton, "The Battle of Iuka," in *Battles and Leaders of the Civil War*, Vol. II, (New York, 1885), 735; Williams, *Eagle Regiment*, 11–12. See also Smith, "Iuka and Corinth," 61.

[10]Report, Lt. Col. G. W. Robbins, September 22, 1862, *OR*, Vol. XVII, Pt. 1, p. 89. General Rosecrans commended the Eleventh Missouri for its bravery. See William F. Fox, *Regimental Losses in the American Civil War, 1861–1865* (New York, 1898), 413; Report, Gen. Sterling Price, September 26, 1862, *OR, ibid.*, 123; Brig. Gen. Louis Hebert, September 25, 1862, *OR, ibid.*, 124–126. Confederate casualties amounted to 530.

[11]Report, Maj. Gen. Earl Van Dorn, October 22, 1862, *OR*, Vol. XVII, Pt. 1, p. 377; Castel, *Price*, 106, 125.

[12]Driggs, *Opening the Mississippi*, 19; Smith, "Iuka and Corinth," 62; Report, Maj. Gen. W. S. Rosecrans, October 25, 1862, *OR*, Vol. XVII, Pt. 1, p. 166.

[13]Report, Gen. Earl Van Dorn, October 20, 1862, *OR*, Vol. XVII, Pt. 1, pp. 378–379; Report, Gen. W. S. Rosecrans, October 25, 1862, *ibid.*, 166–168.

[14]*Ibid.*; William S. Rosecrans, "The Battle of Corinth," *Battles and Leaders*, Vol. II, 746.

[15]*Ibid.*

[16]Report, Col. J. A. Mower, October 15, 1862, *OR*, Vol. XVII, Pt. 1, p. 197.

[17]Report, Maj. A. J. Weber, 11th Mo., October 9, 1862, *ibid.*, 201.

[18]Report, Capt. Samuel R. Baker, 47th Ill., October 9, 1862, *ibid.*, 199–200; *Rpt. Adj. Gen. Ill.*, 1861–1866, p. 430; Lt. John H. McClay, "Defense of Robinett," *War Papers, Nebraska MOLLUS*, Vol. I (1895), 168; Bryner, *Bugle Echoes*, 60. Fox, *Regimental Losses in the American Civil War*, 443, differs with the Illinois Adjutant General.

[19]Report, Maj. J. W. Jefferson, October 13, 1862, *OR*, Vol. XVII, Pt. 1, pp. 202–203.

[20]Smith, "Iuka and Corinth," 63; Descriptive Roll and Roster.

[21]W. J. Dawes to William D. Love, in William De Loss Love, *Wisconsin in the War of the Rebellion: A History of All Regiments and Batteries the State Has Sent to the Field* (Chicago, 1866), 519.

[22]McLain, "The Story of Old Abe," *WMH*, 3:410–411.

[23]Greene to wife, October 8, 1862, in *Reminiscences*, 31.

[24]Report, J. W. Jefferson, October 13, 1862, *OR*, Vol. XVII, Pt. 1, p. 203; Smith, "Iuka and Corinth," 64–65; Britton to Gaylord, October 1, 1863, Records of Vol. Regts., box 72.

[25]Smith, "Iuka and Corinth," 64–65; Britton to Gaylord, October 1, 1863, Records of Vol. Regts.; Monthly Return, October, 1862, *ibid.*, box 75.

[26]Report, Gen. Earl Van Dorn, October 20, 1862, *OR*, Vol. XVII, Pt. 1, p. 379.

[27]Rosecrans, "The Battle of Corinth," 744; Report, Capt. George A. Williams, October 6, 1862, *OR*, Vol. XVII, Pt. 1, pp. 247–248.

[28]Report, Gen. D. S. Stanley, October 13, 1862, *OR*, Vol. XVII, Pt. 1, p. 180; Charles H. Smith, *The History of Fuller's Ohio Brigade, 1861–1865* (Cleveland, 1909), 85–86.

[29]Report, Gen. Earl Van Dorn, October 20, 1862, *OR*, Vol. XVII, Pt. 1, p. 379.

[30]Lucius F. Hubbard, "Minnesota in the Battle of Corinth," *War Papers, Minnesota MOLLUS*, Vol. VI (1907), 492.

[31]Report, Brig. Gen. John C. Moore, October 13, 1862, *OR*, Vol. XVII, Pt. 1, pp. 307–308. Rogers was in Moore's Brigade of Maury's Division; see Dwight to Dear Mother, October 9, 1862, Dwight Papers.

[32]Burdette, *Drums of the 47th*, 125–126.

[33]McClay, "Defense of Robinette," 170–171.

[34]Report, Gen. Earl Van Dorn, October 20, 1862, *OR*, Vol. XVII, Pt. 1, p. 381; Report, Capt. George A. Williams, October 16, 1862, *ibid.*, 247–248; Return of Casualties—Union, October 13, 1862, *ibid.*, 166–176; Return of Casualties—Confederate, *ibid.*, 382–383; Castel, *Price*, 117.

[35]Britton to Gaylord, October 1, 1863, Records of Vol. Regts., box 72; Monthly Return, October, 1862, *ibid.*, box 75.

[36]Return of Casualties, October 13, 1862, *OR*, Vol. XVII, Pt. 1, pp. 166–176.

[37]"M" to *Wisconsin State Journal*, October 6, 1862, in Quiner, Cor. Wis. Vols., vol. 4, p. 122; McClay "Defense of Robinette," 171; Capt. Britton, "In Pursuit of Price and Van Dorn," in *Wisconsin State Journal*, October 9, 1862, in Quiner, Cor. Wis. Vols., vol. 4, p. 126.

[38]Dwight to Dear Mother, October 9, 1862, Dwight Papers.

[39]Smith, "Corinth and Iuka," 65; Descriptive Roll and Roster.

[40]McLain, "The Story of Old Abe," *WMH*, 3:411; "G" to *Wisconsin State Journal*, November 24, 1862, in Quiner, Cor. Wis. Vols., vol. 4, p. 135.

[41]*Ibid.*; see also Ephraim Wilcox, "Corinth, Oct. 3 and 4, 1862," in the Eau Claire *Free Press*, October 9, 1862.

[42]Williams, *Eagle Regiment*, 52.

[43]Monthly Return, October, 1862, Records Vol. Regts., box 75; Capt. Britton to *Wisconsin State Journal*, January 17, 1863, in Quiner, Cor. Wis. Vols., vol. 8, p. 423.

[44]Report, D. S. Stanley, October 13, 1862, *OR*, Vol. XVII, Pt. 1, p. 179; Klement, "Wisconsin in the Civil War," in the *Wisconsin Blue Book, 1962*, p. 138, reprinted with exactly the same text by the State Historical Society of Wisconsin (1963).

[45]Sherman, *Memoirs*, 1:304; Quiner, *Military History of Wisconsin*, 527; Britton to *Wisconsin State Journal*, January 17, 1863, in Quiner, Cor. Wis. Vols., vol. 8, p. 423; Frederick Phisterer, *Statistical Record of the Armies of the United States* (New York, 1883), 54.

8: Opening the Mississippi

[1]On the Vicksburg campaign, see Samuel Carter III, *The Final Fortress: The Campaign for Vicksburg, 1862–1863* (New York, 1980); Mahan, *Gulf and Inland Waters*; Admiral D. D. Porter, *The Naval History of the Civil War* (New York, 1886); William F. Vilas, *A View of the Vicksburg Campaign*, Wisconsin History Commission, Original Papers, No. 1 (Madison, 1908); S. H. Lockett "The Defense of Vicksburg," in *Battles and Leaders*, Vol. III, 482–492; and Hosea W. Rood (comp.), *Wisconsin at Vicksburg: Report of the Wisconsin-Vicksburg Monument Commission: Including the Story of the Campaign and Siege of Vicksburg in 1863* (Madison, 1904).

[2]Sherman, *Memoirs*, 1:232.

[3]Mahan, *Gulf and Inland Waters*, 99–106; Lockett, "Defense of Vicksburg," 484–485; Milligan, *Gunboats*, 84–91.

[4]Lockett, "Defense of Vicksburg," 484; Carter, *Final Fortress*, 209.

[5]Rowena Reed, *Combined Operations in the Civil War* (Annapolis, 1978), 254–255; W. B. Britton to Janesville *Gazette*, December 2, 1862, in Quiner, Cor. Wis. Vols., vol. 4, pp. 136–137; Chicago *Tribune*, December 25, 1862, *ibid.*, 140–141.

[6]Britton to Gaylord, October 1, 1863, Records of Vol. Regts., box 72; Grant, *Memoirs*, 1:428; Williams, *Eagle Regiment*, 14–15.

[7]Barrett, *Soldier Bird* (1876), 44–46; Lockett, "Defense of Vicksburg," 484; A. F. Brown, "Van Dorn's Operations in Northern Mississippi—Recollections of a Cavalryman," in *Southern Historical Society Papers*, Vol. 6 (1878), 159–161; Williams, *Eagle Regiment*, 14–15.

[8]McLain to Dear Sister, January 19, 1863, McLain Papers; Bryner, *Bugle Echoes*, 43; Barrett, *Soldier Bird* (1876), 44–46; Robert Rogers to Edward Cronon, February 8, 1863, Cronon Papers.

[9]George W. Morgan, "The Assault on Chickasaw Bluffs," in *Battles and Leaders*, Vol. III, 462–470.

[10]Williams, *Eagle Regiment*, 99; General Orders No. 4, January 8, 1863, Records of Vol. Regts., box 75.

9: The Vicksburg Campaign

[1]Carter, *Final Fortress, passim.*

[2]Barrett, *Soldier Bird* (1876), 46; Williams, *Eagle Regiment*, 56; Driggs, *Opening the Mississippi*, 26–27.

[3]Charles Palmetier to Dear Brother and Sister, January 28, 1863, in the Charles Palmetier Papers, State Archives.

[4]A Staff Officer, *Army Life and Stray Shots*, 14.

[5]*Ibid.*, 19–20.

[6]Robert Rogers to Edward Cronon, April 3, 1863, Cronon Papers.

[7]*Ibid.*; Williams, *Eagle Regiment*, 16.

[8]Bryner, *Bugle Echoes*, 75–76.

[9]Grant, *Memoirs*, 1:525–530; Sherman, *Memoirs*, 1:332; Report, Capt. W. B. Britton to Augustus Gaylord, October 1, 1863, Records of Vol. Regts., box 72; Miles, "Eagle of the Regiment," chap. XVI, 5–7.

[10]Robert Rogers to Edward Cronon, April 3, 1863, Cronon Papers.

[11]Charles Palmetier to Dear Brother and Sister, April 14, 1863, Palmetier Papers; Robert Rogers to Edward Cronon, April 18, 1863, Cronon Papers; Williams, Diary, April 1, 1863.

[12]Sherman, *Memoirs*, 1:314.

[13]Mahan, *Gulf and Inland Waters*, 155.

[14]Porter, *Naval History of Civil War*, 310–318.

[15]Mahan, *Gulf and Inland Waters*, 160.

[16]*Ibid.*, 162.

[17]U. S. Grant, "The Vicksburg Campaign," in *Battles and Leaders*, Vol. III, 495.

[18]Mahan, *Gulf and Inland Waters*, 495.

[19]Grant, "The Vicksburg Campaign," 499.

[20]Williams, Diary, May 7, 1863.

[21]Grant, *Memoirs*, 1:480–481.

[22]Grant, "The Vicksburg Campaign," 501–502.

[23]Grant, *Memoirs*, 1:532–533.

[24]Miles, "Eagle of the Regiment," chap. XVIII, 11.

[25]Williams, Diary, May 14, 1863; William F. Scott, *History of a Cavalry Regiment: The Career of the Fourth Iowa Veteran Volunteers from Kansas to Georgia, 1861–1865* (New York, 1893), 83.

[26]Miles, "Eagle of the Regiment," chap. XVIII, 3.

[27]Burnett Demarest, Diary, May 14, 1863, Demarest Papers; also see A. G. Weissert, "Battles Preceding the Siege of Vicksburg," Weissert Papers, box 10.

[28]Scott, *Fourth Iowa Cavalry*, 84.

[29]Burdette, *Drums of the 47th*, 56–58.

[30]Report, Maj. Gen. W. T. Sherman, May 24, 1863, *OR*, Vol. XXIV, Pt. 1, p. 754.

[31]*Rpt. Adj. Gen. Ill., 1861–1866*, p. 430.

[32]Grant, "The Vicksburg Campaign," 509.

[33]*Ibid.*, 511–513.

[34]*Ibid.*, 513–517.

[35]Scott, *Fourth Iowa Cavalry*, 94.

[36]Carter, *Final Fortress*, 251.

[37]Grant, "The Vicksburg Campaign," 517.

[38]Grant, *Memoirs*, 1:530–531.

[39]*Ibid.*, 531.

[40]Miles, "Eagle of the Regiment," chap. XX, 3.

[41]Report, Maj. Gen. W. T. Sherman, May 24, 1863, *OR*, Vol. XXIV, Pt. 1, p. 757.

[42]Lockett, "The Defense of Vicksburg," 489.

[43]Grant, *Memoirs*, 1:521; Report, W. T. Sherman, May 24, 1863, *OR*, Vol. XXIV, Pt. 1, p. 757.

[44]Report, Brig. Gen. J. M. Tuttle, May 23, 1863, *ibid.*, 760.

[45]Report, Col. Lucius F. Hubbard, May 25, 1863, *ibid.*, 762; A. G. Weissert, "The Eighth Infantry," in Rood (comp.), *Wisconsin at Vicksburg*, 241.

[46]Burdette, *Drums of the 47th*, 80; J. H. Greene to wife, May 26, 1863, in *Reminiscences*, 56.

[47]Report, Col. L. F. Hubbard, May 23, 1863, *OR*, Vol. XXIV, Pt. 1, p. 762.

[48]*Ibid.*; Report, Britton to Gaylord, October 1, 1863, Records of Vol. Regts., box 72; Britton to Janesville *Gazette*, May 23, 1863, in Quiner, Cor. Wis. Vols., vol. 8, p. 460.

[49]Britton to Janesville *Gazette*, May 23, 1863, *ibid.*

[50]Greene to wife, May 26, 1863, in *Reminiscences*, 56.

[51]Report, Col. L. F. Hubbard, May 23, 1863, *OR*, Vol. XXIV, Pt. 1, p. 762.

[52]Report, W. T. Sherman, May 24, 1863, *ibid.*, 575.

[53]Fox, *Regimental Losses*, 413.

[54]Report, J. M. Tuttle, May 23, 1863, *OR*, Vol. XXIV, Pt. 1, p. 760; *Rpt. Adj. Gen. Ill., 1861–1866*, p. 430; Col. William L. Barnum, 11th Missouri Infantry, to John B. Gray, Adj. Gen. Mo., December 21, 1863, in *Report of the Adjutant General of Missouri, 1865* (St. Louis, 1865), Vol. I, 144–145; Report, Col. L. F. Hubbard, May 23, 1863, *OR*, *ibid.*

[55]Britton to Janesville *Gazette*, May 23, 1863, in Quiner, Cor. Wis. Vols. Vol. 8, p. 460; Greene to wife, May 26, 1863, in *Reminiscences*, 56; Miles, "Eagle of the Regiment," chap. XX, 3; George W. Robbins to A. G. Weissert, December 31, 1901, Weissert Papers, box 10.

[56]John Woodworth to A. G. Weissert, March 21, 1904, Weissert Papers, box 10.

[57]J. H. Greene [?] to A. G. Weissert, December 5, 1904, Weissert Papers, box 10, *ibid.*; W. B. Britton to A. G. Weissert, November 30, 1901, and Britton to Weissert, May 18, 1906, *ibid.*, box 12.

[58]Descriptive Roll and Roster; Monthly Return, June, 1863, in Records of Vol. Regts., box 75.

[59]Barrett, *Soldier Bird* (1876), 62–65; Williams, *Eagle Regiment*, 62.

[60]*Ibid.*

[61]Monthly Return, May, 1863, in Records of Vol. Regts., box 75; Report, Col. L. F. Hubbard, May 23, 1863, *OR*, Vol. XXIV, Pt. 1, p. 762; Report, W. T. Sherman, May 24, 1863, *ibid.*, 757.

[62]Grant, *Memoirs*, 1:531.

[63]Grant, "The Vicksburg Campaign," 519; Monthly Return, May, 1863, in Records of Vol. Regts., box 75.

[64]Carter, *Final Fortress*, 251.

10: Used Up: The Siege of Vicksburg

[1]Robert Rogers to Edward Cronon, June 12, 1863, Cronon Papers.

[2]Britton to Gaylord, October 1, 1863, Records of Vol. Regts., box 72; Williams, *Eagle Regiment*, 18.

[3]*Rpt. Adj. Gen. Wis., 1865*, p. 114; Williams, *Eagle Regiment*, 18; Bryner, *Bugle Echoes*, 88; Greene to wife, June 8, 1863, in *Reminiscences*, 58.

[4]Rogers to Cronon, June 12, 1863, Cronon Papers.

[5]*Ibid.*

[6]Miles, "Eagle of the Regiment," chap. XIX, 6.

[7]Williams, *Eagle Regiment*, 19.

[8]Monthly Return, March, 1863; Records of Vol. Regts., box 75; Monthly Return, June, 1863, *ibid.*

[9]Williams, Diary, July 31, 1863; Miles, "Eagle of the Regiment," chap. XXII, 5; Wisconsin National Guard Organization Records, Surgeon's Records, Eighth Wisconsin Volunteers, 1862–1865, State Archives; Alice F. and Bettina Jackson (eds.), *Autobiography of James A. Jackson, Sr., M.D.* (Madison, 1945), 21–23.

[10]Greene to wife, July 14, 1863, in *Reminiscences*, 63–64.

[11]*Battles and Leaders*, Vol. III, 549.

[12]William T. Sherman to the Governor of Wisconsin, September 21, 1863, Records of Vol. Regts., box 72.

[13]"Thomper" to Milwaukee *Sentinel*, October 15, 1863, in Quiner, Cor. Wis. Vols., vol. 8, p. 27.

[14]Britton to Gaylord, October 1, 1863, Records of Vol. Regts., box 72.

[15]*Rpt. Adj. Gen. Wis., 1863*, p. 300.

11: Camped Among the Pines

[1]Greene, August 26, 1863, in *Reminiscences*, 65.

[2]JWD to Madison *Patriot*, June 27, 1862, in Quiner, Cor. Wis. Vols., vol. 4, p. 99.

[3]A. G. Weissert to Dear Friend, January 22, 1864, Weissert Papers.

[4]James E. Brown to Dear Mother and Sisters, August 12, 1862, Brown Papers.

[5]"Thomper" to Milwaukee *Sentinel*, December 8, 1862, in Quiner, Cor. Wis. Vols., vol. 4, p. 139.

[6]Hubbard, "Minnesota in the Battle of Corinth," 481.

[7]*Ibid.*; James Mellor to Dear Wife, March 9, 1863, Cronon Papers.

[8]Surgeon's Records, Eighth Wisconsin Volunteers, 1862–1865.

[9]Robert Rogers to Friend Edward, March 4, 1864, Cronon Papers.

[10]"Record of Engagements," in Dietz (comp.), *Roster of Wisconsin Volunteers*, 1:577–603.

[11]"Thomper" to Milwaukee *Sentinel*, December 8, 1862, in Quiner, Cor. Wis. Vols., vol. 4, p. 139; Miles, "Eagle of the Regiment," Chap. XXIV, 1.

[12]James E. Brown to Dear Mother and Sisters, August 12, 1862, Brown Papers.

[13]"G" to *Wisconsin State Journal*, December 3, 1861, in Quiner, Cor. Wis. Vols., vol. 2, p. 26.

[14]Captain J. E. Perkins, December 17, 1861, Perkins Papers.

[15]Charles Palmetier to Dear Brother and Sister, January 28, 1863, Palmetier Papers.

[16]James Mellor to Dear Wife, February 6, 1863, Cronon Papers; see also James Mellor to Dear Wife, January 16, 1864, *ibid.*

[17]Army Regulations, 1863, Article 43, Paragraph 1190, cited in Wiley, *Billy Yank*, 224.

[18]Augustus Weissert to Dear Friend, November 14, 1863, Weissert Papers.

[19]Wiley, *Billy Yank*, 237–238.

[20]Weissert to Dear Friend, November 14, 1863, Weissert Papers.

[21]Wiley, *Billy Yank*, 238.

[22]*Ibid.*, 242.

[23]Captain Lyon to Racine *Advocate*, November 12, 1861, in *Reminiscences*, 10; "JWD" to Madison *Patriot*, June 27, 1862, in Quiner, Cor. Wis. Vols., vol. 4, p. 89.

[24]*Ibid.*, 244.

[25]"Incidents in the War of the Rebellion," by an unknown enlisted man, Company "K," Eighth Wisconsin Infantry, in Weissert Papers, box 7. Cited hereinafter as "Incidents in the War."

[26]*Ibid.*

[27]A. G. Weissert to Dear George, February 24, 1862, Weissert Papers.

[28]Robert Rogers to Edward Cronon, October 22, 1863, Cronon Papers. See also Robert Rogers to Friend, April 3, 1863, *ibid.*

[29]"JWD" to Madison *Patriot*, June 27, 1863, in Quiner, Cor. Wis. Vols., vol. 4, p. 99.

[30]James Mellor to Dear Wife, April 18, 1863, Cronon Papers.

[31]One of the Boys [Hosea Rood], *The Story of the Service of Company E and the Twelfth Wisconsin Regiment of Veteran Volunteer Infantry in the War of the Rebellion* (n.p., 1893), 194.

[32]Robert Rogers to Mr. Edward Cronon, February 17, 1863, Cronon Papers.

[33]Miles, "Eagle of the Regiment," chap. XVI, 212.

[34]"Incidents in the War," Weissert Papers, box 7.

[35]Miles, "Eagle of the Regiment," chap. X, 2.

[36]Robert Rogers to Edward Cronon, February 17, 1863, Cronon Papers.

[37]*Ibid.*

[38]Robert Rogers to Friend Edward, March 4, 1864, *ibid.*

[39]"Incidents in the War," Weissert Papers, box 7.

[40]*Ibid.*

[41]*Ibid.*

[42]Augie Weissert to Dear Friend, January 22, 1864, Weissert Papers.

[43]Wiley, *Billy Yank*, 250.

[44]Burdette, *Drums of the 47th*, 71.

[45]Bryner, *Bugle Echoes*, 19.

[46]James E. Brown to Dear Mother, August 12, 1862, Brown Papers.

[47]Robert Rogers to Edward Cronon, August 18, 1863, Cronon Papers.

[48]Weissert to Dear Friend, January 22, 1864, Weissert Papers.

[49]Williams, Diary, May 27, 1864.

[50]"Quad" [T. B. Coon] to Eau Claire *Free Press*, February 2, 1862, in Quiner, Cor. Wis. Vols., vol. 4, p. 41.

[51]Weissert to Dear Friend, August 30, 1864, Weissert Papers.

[52]Charles Palmetier to Dear Brother and Sister, January 28, 1863, Palmetier Papers.

[53]Augustus Root to Dear Wife, February 14, 1863, Augustus Root Papers, G.A.R. Memorial Hall Archives.

[54]Descriptive Roll and Roster.

[55]James Mellor to Dear Wife, March 31, 1863, Cronon Papers.

[56]James Mellor to Dear Wife, [1862], *ibid.*; Mellor to Wife, June 21, 1862, *ibid.*; Mellor to Mrs. Mellor, February 12, 1862, *ibid.*; Mellor to Dear Wife, April 28, 1862, *ibid.*; A. G. Weissert to Dear Charles, March 16, 1863, Weissert Papers.

[57]Jeremiah Baker to Dear Brother, October 11, 1862, Baker Papers.

[58]"M" to *Wisconsin State Journal*, December 12, 1861, in Quiner, Cor. Wis. Vols., vol. 2, p. 27.

[59]Greene to wife, April 19, 1922, in *Reminiscences*, 15.

[60]James E. Brown to Dear Mother, August 12, 1862, Brown Papers.

[61]A. J. Weissert to Dear Friend, August 30, 1864, Weissert Papers.

[62]James Mellor to Dear Wife, 1862, *passim*, Cronon Papers.

63James Mellor to Dear Wife, June 21, 1862, *ibid.*

64James Mellor to Dear Wife, no date, *ibid.* Captain Greene became involved in distributing military supplies, and, according to the charges brought against him at his court martial, "appropriating the proceeds to his own use and selling government stores to disloyal persons." Greene was ultimately exonerated. See Descriptive Roll and Roster; Court Martial Records, National Archives and Records Service.

65Wiley, *Billy Yank*, 260.

66Robert Rogers to Friends, April 3, 1863, Cronon Papers.

67James Mellor to Dear Wife, January 16, 1864, *ibid.*

68Greene to Dear Wife, November 22, 1861, in *Reminiscences*, 6; Greene to wife, December 15, 1861, *ibid.*; J. H. Greene to W. B. Britton and A. G. Weissert, June 5, 1880, in *Proceedings of the Reunion of the Eighth Regiment Wisconsin Veteran Volunteer Infantry* (Milwaukee, 1880), 8.

69Lyon, *Reminiscences*, 14.

70"JWD" to *Wisconsin State Journal*, January 5, 1862, in Quiner, Cor. Wis. Vols., vol. 4, p. 4.

71Robert Rogers to Friend, April 3, 1863, Cronon Papers.

72Charles Palmetier to Dear Brothers and Sister, January 28, 1863, Palmetier Papers.

73Miles, "Eagle of the Regiment," chap. XXV, 5.

74A Staff Officer, *Army Life and Stray Shots*, 5.

75J. M. Flint to *Wisconsin State Journal*, April 8, 1863, in Quiner, Cor. Wis. Vols., vol. 8, p. 453.

76Greene to wife, April 28, 1862, in *Reminiscences*, 16.

77Britton to Janesville *Gazette*, September 11, 1862, in Quiner, Cor. Wis. Vols., vol. 4, pp. 114–115.

78Driggs, *Opening the Mississippi*, 58.

79A Staff Officer, *Army Life and Stray Shots*, 6.

80"C. Mc D." to Janesville *Gazette*, November 18, 1861, in Quiner, Cor. Wis. Vols., vol. 1, p. 24; "M" to *Wisconsin State Journal*, January 6, 1862, *ibid.*, vol. 4, p. 36; Bryner, *Bugle Echoes*, 18.

81Burdette, *Drums of the 47th*, 67.

82James E. Brown to Dear Mother, August 12, 1862, Brown Papers.

83Barrett, *Soldier Bird* (1876), 31.

84*Ibid.*

85Williams, *Eagle Regiment*, 46. Frank was not present when the regiment moved on to Island Number 10, and apparently Old Abe came to dislike dogs.

86McLain, "The Story of Old Abe," *WMH*, 8:409–410.

87James E. Brown to Dear Mother, August 12, 1862, Brown Papers.

88Barrett, *Soldier Bird* (1876), 35–36.

89*Ibid.*

90Barrett, *Soldier Bird* (1865), 43.

91*Ibid.* (1876), 38.

92A Staff Officer, *Army Life and Stray Shots*, 11.

93Barrett, *Soldier Bird* (1876), 38.

94*Ibid.*, 38.

95*Ibid.*, 45.

96*Ibid.*, 50.

97*Ibid.* (1865), 43; also see Descriptive Roll and Roster, and Farley, *Experiences of a Soldier, passim.*

98McLain, "The Story of Old Abe," *WMH*, 8:414.

99Barrett, *Soldier Bird* (1876), 51.

12: On the Move

1Bryner, *Bugle Echoes*, 43.

2Wiley, *Billy Yank*, 225.

3A. G. Weissert to Dear George, February 24, 1862, Weissert Papers.

4Captain Lyon to Racine *Advocate*, November 12, 1861, in *Reminiscences*, 7.

5Edward Cronon to Dear Bro., August 29, 1862, Cronon Papers.

6Dave McLain to Dear Sister, August 29, 1862, McLain Papers.

7*Ibid.*

8Wiley, *Billy Yank*, 226.

9Robert Rogers to Friend Edward, February 8, 1863, Cronon Papers.

10*Ibid.*

11"Incidents in the War," Weissert Papers, box 7.

12Robert Rogers to Friend Edward, June 12, 1863, Cronon Papers.

13Dave McLain to Dear Sister, December 22, 1863, McLain Papers.

14A. G. Weissert to Dear Friend, March 5, 1864, Weissert Papers.

15W. B. Britton to Janesville *Gazette*, August 27, 1864, in Quiner, Cor. Wis. Vols., vol. 10, p. 126.

16Gavin Wright, *The Political Economy of the Cotton South: Households, Markets and Wealth in the Nineteenth Century* (New York, 1978), 160–164.

17Miles, "Eagle of the Regiment," 4.

18Augie Weissert to Dear Friend, January 22, 1864, Weissert Papers.

19Augie Weissert to Dear Friend, December 1, 1864, *ibid.*

20*Ibid.*

21Augie Weissert to Dear Friend, January 22, 1864, *ibid.*

22Robert Rogers to Mr. Edward Cronon, February 17, 1863, Cronon Papers; Descriptive Roll and Roster.

23Burdette, *Drums of the 47th*, 44–45.

24Driggs, *Opening the Mississippi*, 51–52.

25H. E. Crandell to Evergreen City *Times*, February 18, 1862, in Quiner, Cor. Wis. Vols., vol. 4, p. 49.

26Augie Weissert to Dear Friend, August 26, 1864, Weissert Papers. See also story on back of "Incidents in the War," Weissert Papers, box 7.

27Dave McLain, "The Story of Old Abe," *WMH*, 8:412.

28Barrett, *Old Abe* (1876), 37.

29*Ibid.*, 49.

30Driggs, *Opening the Mississippi*, 119.

31Bryner, *Bugle Echoes*, 43.

13: The Price of Cotton

1Bryner, *Bugle Echoes*, 97; Army of the Tennessee, Roster, March 31, 1864, *OR*, Vol. XXXIV, Pt. 1, p. 171.

2Francis B. Heitman, *Historical Register and Dictionary of the United States Army, 1789–1903* (Washington, 1903), 1:891.

3James Mellor to Dear Wife, October 23, 1863, Cronon Papers; General Order #15, Aug. 18, 1863, *Rpt. Adj. Gen. Wis., 1863*, pp. 164–165.

4*Ibid.*

5Augie to Dear Friend, January 22, 1864, Weissert Papers.

6Augie to My Dear Brothers, December 1, 1864, *ibid.*

7Augie to Dear Brothers, August 28, 1864, *ibid.*

8Miles, "Eagle of the Regiment," chap. XXV, 4.

9Williams, *Eagle Regiment*, 111.

10*Ibid.*, 147; Jackson, *Autobiography*, 31–33.

11Re-enlistment, 1864, March 3, 1864, in Records of Vol. Regts., box 75.

12Lt. Col. John W. Jefferson to Governor James T. Lewis, May 22, 1864, *ibid.*

13Miles, "Eagle of the Regiment," chap. XXV, 4.

14Bryner, *Bugle Echoes*, 99; Ludwell A. Johnson, *Red River Campaign: Politics and Cotton in the Civil War* (Baltimore, 1958), 101.

[15]Abstract and Returns Grand Total, Red River Expedition, March 31–April 30, 1864, *OR*, Vol. XXXIV, Pt. 1, p. 168.

[16]Porter, *Naval History of the Civil War*, 494; Johnson, *Red River Campaign*, 99–100; Thomas O. Selfridge, "The Navy in the Red River," in *Battles and Leaders*, Vol. IV, 362; Richard B. Irwin, "The Red River Campaign," *ibid.*, Vol. V, 347.

[17]Greene, *Reminiscences*, 72; Monthly Return, March 1864, in Records of Vol. Regts., box 75 (308 Enfields; 103 Springfields).

[18]Johnson, *Red River Campaign*, 92.

[19]Miles, "Eagle of the Regiment," chap. XXV, 7.

[20]Lt. Col. Jefferson to Governor J. T. Lewis, May 22, 1864, Report of Red River Expedition, in Records of Vol. Regts., box 75.

[21]Bryner, *Bugle Echoes*, 99; Report, Gen. A. J. Smith to W. T. Sherman, September 26, 1864, *OR*, Vol. XXIV, Pt. 1, pp. 304–312; N. P. Banks to H. W. Halleck, March 18, 1864, *ibid.*, 177; Barrett, *Soldier Bird* (1876), 71–72.

[22]Johnson, *Red River Campaign*, 98; Report, A. J. Smith, September 26, 1864, *OR*, Vol. XXXIV, Pt. 1; J. W. Jefferson to Governor J. T. Lewis, May 22, 1864, Report of Red River Expedition, in Records of Vol. Regts., box 75.

[23]Miles, "Eagle of the Regiment," chap. XXV, 8.

[24]Monthly Return, May 1864, in Records of Vol. Regts., box 75.

[25]J. W. Jefferson to Governor J. T. Lewis, May 22, 1864, Report of Red River Expedition, *ibid.*; Report, A. J. Smith, September 26, 1864, *OR*, Vol. XXXIV, Pt. 1, pp. 304–312.

[26]Miles, "Eagle of the Regiment," chap. XXVI, 1–2; J. W. Jefferson to Governor J. T. Lewis, May 22, 1864, Report of Red River Expedition, in Records of Vol. Regts., box 75; *Rpt. Wis. Adj. Gen., 1865*, p. 117; Johnson, *Red River Campaign*, 96–97; Barrett, *Soldier Bird* (1876), 72–73.

[27]J. W. Jefferson to Governor J. T. Lewis, May 22, 1864, in Records of Vol. Regts., box 75.

[28]Johnson, *Red River*, 108.

[29]Lucius F. Hubbard, *Minnesota in the Civil and Indian Wars* (St. Paul, 1890), 269; Greene, *Reminiscences*, 75.

[30]Porter, *Naval History of Civil War*, 501.

[31]Hubbard, *Minnesota in Civil War*, 269.

[32]Miles, "Eagle of the Regiment," chap. XXVI, 3.

[33]Report, A. J. Smith, September 26, 1864, *OR*, Vol. XXXIV, Pt. 1, pp. 304–312; J. W. Jefferson to Governor Lewis, Report of Red River Expedition, in Records of Vol. Regts., box 75; Bryner, *Bugle Echoes*, 101; Porter, *Naval History of Civil War*, 503; McCall, *11th Missouri*, 32.

[34]Ezra J. Warner, *Generals in Gray* (Baton Rouge, 1959), 299; Douglas Southall Freeman, *Lee's Lieutenants: A Study in Command* (3 vols., New York, 1942), Volume I, introd.; Richard Taylor, *Destruction and Reconstruction* (New York, 1879), 153.

[35]Report, A. J. Smith, September 26, 1864, *OR*, Vol. XXXIV, Pt. 1, pp. 304–312; McCall, *11th Missouri*, 32; Report E. Kirby Smith to Jefferson Davis, May 4, 1864, *OR*, *ibid.*, 448; Johnson, *Red River Campaign*, 139–140.

[36]McCall, *11th Missouri*, 33; Miles, "Eagle of the Regiment," chap. XXVII, 1; Report, A. J. Smith, September 26, 1864, *OR*, Vol. XXXIV, Pt. 1, pp. 304–312.

[37]Report, A. J. Smith, *ibid.*

[38]Miles, "Eagle of the Regiment," chap. XXVII, 1.

[39]Hubbard, *Minnesota in Civil War*, 270.

[40]McCall, *11th Missouri*, 32–33.

[41]J. W. Jefferson to Augustus Gaylord, July 31, 1864, in Records of Vol. Regts., box 75.

[42]Bryner, *Bugle Echoes*, 102–103.

[43]Miles, "Eagle of the Regiment," chap. XXVII, 1.

[44]Report, A. J. Smith, September 26, 1864, *OR*, Vol. XXXIV, Pt. 1, p. 309.

[45]Report, Brig. Gen. A. F. Lee, April 5, 1864, *ibid.*, 452; Taylor, *Destruction and Reconstruction*, 171.

[46]Johnson, *Red River Campaign*, 168–169; Report, A. J. Smith, September 26, 1864, *OR*, Vol. XXXIV, Pt. 1, p. 309.

[47]Bryner, *Bugle Echoes*, 107.

[48]Taylor, *Destruction and Reconstruction*, 178; Captain Thomas O. Selfridge, "The Navy in the Red River," in *Battles and Leaders*, Vol. IV, 363; Porter, *Naval History of Civil War*, 512–515.

[49]Johnson, *Red River Campaign*, 214.

[50]Bryner, *Bugle Echoes*, 107.

[51]Johnson, *Red River Campaign*, 218.

[52]*Ibid.*, 220; E. Kirby Smith, "The Defense of the Red River," in *Battles and Leaders*, Vol. IV, p. 372; E. Kirby Smith to Jefferson Davis, May 4, 1864, *OR*, Vol. XXXIV, Pt. 1, p. 448.

[53]Bryner, *Bugle Echoes*, 107; J. W. Jefferson to Governor J. T. Lewis, May 22, 1864, Records of Vol. Regts., box 75.

[54]Greene, *Reminiscences*, 76–77.

[55]Selfridge, "Navy on the Red River," 363; Taylor, *Destruction and Reconstruction*, 194; Johnson, *Red River Campaign*, 224–225.

[56]Quoted in Johnson, *Red River Campaign*, 234.

[57]*Ibid.*, 235.

[58]Taylor, *Destruction and Reconstruction*, 183–185; Porter, *Naval History of Civil War*, 527–528.

[59]Taylor, *Destruction and Reconstruction*, 186; Johnson, *Red River Campaign*, 257; Porter *Naval History of Civil War*, 528.

[60]Henry Fairbanks, "The Red River Expedition of 1864," in *War Papers, Maine MOLLUS*, Volume 1 (1898), 181–190.

[61]Porter, *Naval History of Civil War*, 527; Bryner, *Bugle Echoes*, 112; Johnson, *Red River Campaign*, 263–265.

[62]Bryner, *Bugle Echoes*, 112.

[63]J. W. Jefferson to Governor J. T. Lewis, May 22, 1864, Report of the Red River Expedition, in Records of Vol. Regts., box 75.

[64]Porter, *Naval History of Civil War*, 521.

[65]Quoted in Johnson, *Red River Campaign*, 270.

[66]*Ibid.*

[67]Bryner, *Bugle Echoes*, 114.

[68]Quoted in Johnson, *Red River Campaign*, 273.

[69]Bryner, *Bugle Echoes*, 114; J. W. Jefferson to Augustus Gaylord, July 31, 1864, Records of Vol. Regts., box 72.

[70]Miles, "Eagle of the Regiment," chap. XXVII, 3.

[71]Williams, *Eagle Regiment*, 25–26; Jefferson to Gaylord, July 31, 1864, Records of Vol. Regts., box 72; Bryner, *Bugle Echoes*, 114.

[72]Jefferson to Gaylord, July 31, 1864, Records of Vol. Regts., box 72; Report, A. J. Smith, September 26, 1864, *OR*, Vol. XXXIV, Pt. 1, p. 312; Bryner, *Bugle Echoes*, 115; Taylor, *Destruction and Reconstruction*, 191–192.

[73]List of Killed and Wounded in Action in Red River Expedition, June 2, 1864, Records of Vol. Regts., box 75; Report, E. Kirby Smith, May 4, 1864, *OR*, Vol. XXXIV, Pt. 1, p. 477; Report, N. P. Banks, April 30, 1864, *ibid.*, 192; Taylor, *Destruction and Reconstruction*, 191–192.

14: The Battle for Furlough

[1]Greene to wife, August 18, 1863, in *Reminiscences*, 65.

[2]Miles, "Eagle of the Regiment," chap. XXIX, 1; Descriptive Roll and Roster; Jackson, *Autobiography*, 28.

[3]Reports, Colonel Colton Greene, May 26, 1864, *OR*, Vol. XXXIV, Pt. 1, pp. 948–949, and June 8, 1864, *ibid.*, 952–953.

[4]Report, Col. Colton Greene, May 30, 1864, *ibid.*, 949–950.

[5]Report, Col. Colton Greene, June 9, 1864, *ibid.*, 984–985. See also John N. Edwards, *Shelby and His Men: or, The War in the West* (Kansas City, 1897), 372.

[6]Report, Col. Colton Greene, June 9, 1864, *OR*, Vol. XXXIV, Pt. 1, pp. 984–985; Report, Brig. Gen. J. A. Mower, June 8, 1864, *ibid.*, 971; Emmet C. West, *History and Reminiscences of the Second Wisconsin Cavalry Regiment* (Portage, 1904), 11–12; Williams, *Eagle Regiment*, 26; Miles, "Eagle of the Regiment," chap. XXIX, 1; George E. Currie, *Warfare Along the Mississippi: The Letters of Lt. Col George E. Currie* (Mt. Pleasant, Mich., 1961), 103; Warren D. Crandall and Isaac D. Newall, *History of the Ram Fleet and the Mississippi Marine Brigade in the War for the Union* (St. Louis, 1907), 413; William Shea, "Battle at Ditch Bayou," in *Arkansas Historical Quarterly*, Volume 39 (Autumn, 1980), 195–207; Edwards, *Shelby and His Men*, 370.

[7]Report, Col. L. F. Hubbard, June 11, 1864, *OR*, Vol. XXXIV, Pt. 1, pp. 973–974.

[8]Report, J. A. Mower, June 18, 1864, *ibid.*, 971–972; Report, L. F. Hubbard, June 11, 1864, *ibid.*, 973–974; Report, Major George W. Van Beek, June 7, 1864, *ibid.*, 976.

[9]Report, Col. Colton Greene, June 9, 1864, *ibid.*, 984–985.

[10]Report, Captain Alexander J. Campbell, June 9, 1864, *ibid.*, 979.

[11]*Ibid.*; Shea, "Battle at Ditch Bayou," *Arkansas Historical Quarterly*, 39:199; Edwards, *Shelby and His Men*, 372; Miles, "Eagle of the Regiment," chap. XXIX, 21.

[12]Report, L. F. Hubbard, June 11, 1864, *OR*, Vol. XXXIX, Pt. 1, pp. 973–974.

[13]*Ibid.*; List of Killed and Wounded of 8th Regt. W.V.I. in Engagement at Lake City, Ark. on June 6, 1864, in Records of Vol. Regts., box 75; Miles, "Eagle of the Regiment," chap. XXIX, 4.

[14]Miles, *ibid.*, 2, 4.

[15]*Ibid.*; Report, L. F. Hubbard, June 11, 1864, *OR*, Vol. XXXIV, Pt. 1, pp. 973–974; Report, Major John C. Brecht, June 10, 1864, *ibid.*, 975–976; Edwards, *Shelby and His Men*, 373.

[16]Miles, "Eagle of the Regiment," chap. XXIX, 2, 4.

[17]Report, Major John C. Brecht, June 10, 1864, *OR*, Vol. XXXIV, Pt. 1, pp. 975–976.

[18]Miles, "Eagle of the Regiment," chap. XXIX, 41; Report, Lucius Hubbard, June 11, 1864, *OR*, Vol. XXXIV, Pt. 1, pp. 973–974.

[19]Miles, "Eagle of the Regiment," chap. XXIX, 4.

[20]Report, Major John C. Brecht, June 10, 1864, *OR*, Vol. XXXIV, Pt. 1, pp. 975–976; Col. L. F. Hubbard, June 11, 1864, *ibid.*, 973–974; Edwards, *Shelby and His Men*, 373.

[21]Miles, "Eagle of the Regiment," chap. XXIX, 1–5.

[22]Report, Major George W. Van Beek, June 7, 1864, *OR*, Vol. XXIV, Pt. 1, p. 976.

[23]Report, Colonel Colton Greene, June 9, 1864, *ibid.*, 984–985.

[24]Col. Colton Greene to Maj. Gen. John S. Marmaduke, June 10, 1864, *ibid.*, Pt. 4, p. 665.

[25]Report, Col. Colton Greene, June 9, 1864, *ibid.*, Pt. 1, pp. 984–985.

[26]Report, Col. Colton Green, June 9, 864, *ibid.*, Pt. 1, pp. 984–985.

[27]"Battle of Ditch Bayou," General Henry Lee Chapter of the Daughters of the American Revolution of Lake Village, Arkansas, (no date), Chicot County Historical Society.

[28]Williams, Diary, June 6, 1864.

[29]Monthly Return, June, 1864, in Records of Vol. Regts., box 75; see also List of Killed and Wounded of 8 Regiment Wis. Veteran Infantry at Engagement at Lake City, Ark. on 6th of June 1864, *ibid.*

[30]Miles, "Eagle of the Regiment," chap. XXIX, 1; Descriptive Roll and Roster; Jackson, *Autobiography*, 28.

[31]"Lake Village Looted," *Chicot County*, Susquecentennial Issue, Chicot County Historical Society (no date); Edwards, *Shelby and His Men*, 375.

[32]George Currie, "The Fight at Lake Village Against Rebel General Marmaduke's Forces," in *Warfare Along the Mississippi*, 8.

[33]*Rpt. Adjutant General of Missouri, 1865*, pp. 147–148.

[34]Williams, *Eagle Regiment*, 27.

[35]Miles, "Eagle of the Regiment," chap. XXIX, 6; C. F. MacDonald, "The Battle of Brice's Crossroads," in *War Papers, Minnesota MOLLUS*, Volume VII (1906); Edwin C. Bearss, *Forrest at Brice's Cross Roads and in North Mississippi in 1864* (Dayton, Ohio, 1979), 231.

[36]Printed in Williams, *Eagle Regiment*, 27.

[37]*Ibid.*, 28.

[38]J. W. Jefferson to Augustus Gaylord, June. 21, 1864, Records of Vol. Regts., box 72.

[39]*Wisconsin State Journal*, June 23, 1864.

[40]*Ibid.*

[41]*Ibid.*

[42]*Ibid.*

[43]*Ibid.*

[44]Barrett, *Soldier Bird* (1876), 81; Eau Claire *Free Press*, July 14, 1864.

[45]*Ibid.*, June 28, 1864.

[46]*Ibid.*, July 7, July 21, 1864.

[47]*Ibid.*

[48]Augie to Dear Brothers, August 28, 1864, Weissert Papers.

[49]Augie to Dear Friend, August 30, 1864, *ibid.*

[50]J. W. Jefferson to Governor James T. Lewis, June 29, 1864, Records of Vol. Regts., box 72.

[51]Barrett, *Soldier Bird* (1876), 82.

[52]*Ibid.*, 62–63.

15: After the Devil

[1]Bearss, *Forrest*, 231; Miles, "Eagle of the Regiment," chap. XXX, 8.

[2]Quoted in Bearss, *Forrest*, 137.

[3]*Ibid.*, 239; Report, C. C. Washburn, August 21, 1864, *OR*, Vol. XXXVII, Pt. 1, p. 468.

[4]*Ibid.*, 271–273, 281.

[5]*Ibid.*, 275.

[6]McLain to Dear Sister, August 15, 1864, McLain Papers.

[7]*Ibid.*; Burnett Demarest to Mr. A. E. Blake, September 17, 1864, Demarest Papers.

[8]*Ibid.*; Barrett, *Soldier Bird* (1865), 70.

[9]C. C. Washburn to A. J. Smith, August 21, 1864, *OR*, Vol. XXXVII, Pt. 1, p. 469.

[10]A. J. Smith to C. C. Washburn, August 24, 1864, *ibid.*, 470; Report, C. C. Washburn, September 2, 1864, *ibid.*, 471; Report, Gen. R. P. Buckland, August 24, 1864, *ibid.*, 472–475; Report, Gen. N. B. Forrest, August 22, 1864, *ibid.*, 484.

[11]Williams, *Eagle Regiment*, 29.

[12]Barrett, *Soldier Bird* (1865), 80.

[13]Dietz (comp.), *Wisconsin Battle Flags*, 28–29.

[14]*Wisconsin State Journal*, September 27, 1864.

[15]*Ibid.*

[16]*Ibid.*

[17]*Ibid.*; Receipt for Old Abe, James T. Lewis to N. F. Lund, September 26, 1864, in Williams, *Eagle Regiment*, 75–76; *Annual Report of the Quartermaster General of the State of Wisconsin, October 1, 1864* (Madison, 1864), 422. Hereinafter cited as *Rpt. Wis. Q. M.*

[18]Monthly Returns, September, 1864, in Records of Vol. Regts., box 75.

[19]Williams, *Eagle Regiment*, 30.

16: Jackass Cavalry

[1]Report, Maj. Gen. Sterling Price, December 28, 1864, *OR*, Vol. XLI, Pt. 1, p. 625; Castel, *Price*, 204.

[2]Report, Maj. Gen. W. S. Rosecrans, December 7, 1864, *OR*, Vol. XLI, Pt. 1, p. 307.

[3]Augie to Dear Friend, September 13, 1864, and Augie to Dear Mother, September 13, 1864, Weissert Papers.

[4]Augie to Dear Friend, October 11, 1864, *ibid.*

[5]Augie to Dear Friend, September 13, 1864, *ibid.*

[6]Scott, *Fourth Iowa Cavalry*, 312–313.

[7]Augie to Dear Friend, October 11, 1864, Weissert Papers.

[8]Monthly Return, September, 1864, in Records of Vol. Regts., box 75.

[9]Williams, *Eagle Regiment*, 93.

[10]*Ibid.*, 37.

[11]*Ibid.*, 93.

[12]Governor Reynolds to Jefferson Davis, quoted in Castel, *Price*, 222.

[13]Monthly Return, October 1864, in Records of Vol. Regts., box 75; Williams, *Eagle Regiment*, 93; Burnett Demarest to A. E. Blake, December 3, 1864, Demarest Papers.

[14]Scott, *Fourth Iowa Cavalry*, 302, 319.

[15]Monthly Return, October, 1864, in Records of Vol. Regts., box 75; Augie to Dear Brothers, November 15, 1864, Weissert Papers.

[16]*Rpt. Adj. Gen. Ill., 1865*, p. 431.

[17]W. B. Britton to J. M. Williams, in *Eagle Regiment*, 144.

[18]*Rpt. Adj. Gen. Missouri, 1865*, p. 149; Williams, *Eagle Regiment*, 32, 94.

[19]Monthly Return, November 17, 1864, in Records of Vol. Regts., box 75.

[20]Burnett Demarest to A. E. Blake, December 3, 1864, Demarest Papers.

[21]John B. Hood, "The Invasion of Tennessee," in *Battles and Leaders*, Vol. IV, 425–439. See also Thomas R. Hay, *Hood's Tennessee Campaign* (New York, 1929); Thomas L. Connelly, *Autumn of Glory: The Army of Tennessee, 1862–1865* (New York, 1970); and James D. Cox, *The March to the Sea: Franklin and Nashville* (New York, 1882).

[22]Freeman, *Lee's Lieutenants*, II:xviii; Warner, *Generals in Gray*, 142–143.

[23]Warner, *Generals in Blue*, 500–502; Augie Weissert to My Dear Friend, December 7, 1864, Weissert Papers.

17: Nashville

[1]Report, Brig. Gen. J. A. MacArthur, November 30, 1864, *OR*, Vol. XLI, Pt. 1, p. 903; Report, A. J. Smith, June 10, 1865, *ibid.*, 433.

[2]*Ibid.*

[3]Augie Weissert to My Dear Friend, December 7, 1864, Weissert Papers.

[4]Hood, "Invasion of Tennessee," 437; Hay, *Hood's Tennessee Campaign*, 136; Grant, *Memoirs*, 2:383.

[5]Report, Maj. Gen. A. J. Smith, January 10, 1865, *OR*, Vol. XLV, Pt. 1, p. 432.

[6]Report, Col. Lucius Hubbard, December 27, 1864, *OR*, *ibid.*, 444; Lucius F. Hubbard, "Minnesota in the Battle of Nashville, Dec. 15–16, 1864," in *War Papers, Minnesota MOLLUS*, Volume VI (1905), 273.

[7]Report, A. J. Smith, January 10, 1865, *OR*, Vol. XLV, Pt. 1, pp. 432–433; C. S. Mergell, *Battlefield in Front of Nashville...*, Top. Engr. Office, Dept. of the Cumberland (Chattanooga,

[1865]); Hay, *Hood's Tennessee Campaign*, 152–153.

[8]Report, Brig. Gen. J. A. McArthur, December 28, 1864, *OR*, Vol. XLV, Pt. 1, p. 437.

[9]Report, Lt. Col. W. B. Britton, December 21, 1864, *ibid.*, 457; Report, Col. L. F. Hubbard, December 27, 1864, *ibid.*, 445.

[10]W. B. Britton to Gov. J. T. Lewis, December 21, 1864, in Records of Vol. Regts., box 75; Hubbard, "Minnesota in the Battle of Nashville," 273.

[11]Report, A. J. Smith, January 10, 1865, *OR*, Vol. XLV, Pt. 1, p. 433; Report, J. A. McArthur, December 28, 1864, *ibid.*, 437; Report, L. F. Hubbard, December 27, 1864, *ibid.*, 445; Report, W. B. Britton, December 21, 1864, *ibid.*, 457.

[12]Report, W. B. Britton, December 21, 1864, *ibid.*

[13]"Incidents in the War," Weissert Papers.

[14]Augie Weissert to My Dear Friend, December 17, 1864, *ibid.*

[15]Report, L. F. Hubbard, December 27, 1864, *OR*, Vol. XLV, Pt. 1, p. 446; W. B. Britton to Gov. J. T. Lewis, December 21, 1864, Records of Vol. Regts., box 75.

[16]Hubbard, "Minnesota in the Battle of Nashville," 273; Hay, *Hood's Tennessee Campaign*, 156–157; Mergell, *Battlefields in Front of Nashville*.

[17]Hubbard, "Minnesota in the Battle of Nashville," 273.

[18]Hay, *Hood's Tennessee Campaign*, 159.

[19]Hubbard, "Minnesota in the Battle of Nashville," 276.

[20]*Ibid.*

[21]Hubbard, *Minnesota in Civil War*, 275; Hubbard, "Minnesota in the Battle of Nashville," 276.

[22]*Ibid.*; Return of Casualties of U.S. Forces...at Nashville..., *OR*, Vol. XLV, Pt. 1, p. 101.

[23]Hood, "Invasion of Tennessee," 437.

[24]Hay, *Hood's Tennessee Campaign*, 169.

[25]Monthly Return, December, 1864, in Records of Vol. Regts., box 75; W. B. Britton to Gov. J. T. Lewis, December 21, 1864, *ibid.*

[26]Return of Casualties of U.S. Forces...at Nashville, *OR*, Vol. XLV, Pt. 1, pp. 97–105.

[27]Susan Grissell to Mrs. Mellor, February 5, 1865, Cronon Papers; Robert Rogers to Mrs. M. A. Mellor, March 18, 1865, *ibid.*; Hollister Phillips to Mrs. James Mellor, February 21, 1865, *ibid.*; Final Statement, James Mellor, in Records of Vol. Regts., box 72.

[28]Augie Weissert to Dear Friend, December 17, 1864, Weissert Papers.

[29]Muster Rolls, February, 1865–July, 1865, in Records of Vol. Regts., box 72; Monthly Return, December, 1864–February, 1865, *ibid.*, box 75.

[30]Hubbard, *Minnesota in Civil War*, 278; C. C. Andrews, *History of the Campaign of Mobile: Including the Cooperative Operations of General Wilson's Cavalry in Alabama* (New York, 1867), 26.

[31]Hubbard, *Minnesota in Civil War*, 278.

[32]*Ibid.*

[33]Andrews, *Campaign of Mobile*, 51.

[34]Hubbard, *Minnesota in Civil War*, 279.

18: Denouement

[1]Hubbard, *Minnesota in Civil War*, 278.

[2]Williams, *Eagle Regiment*, 37; *Wisconsin State Journal*, September 13, 1865.

[3]Descriptive Roll and Roster.

[4]Author's compilation, based on Charles E. Esterbrook (ed.), *Wisconsin Losses in the Civil War* (Madison, 1915); *Roster of Wisconsin Volunteers*, vol. 1, pp. 577–603; Weissert, "The Eighth Infantry," in Rood (ed.), *Wisconsin at Vicksburg*, 131–139.

[5]Descriptive Roll and Roster.

[6]Fox, *Regimental Losses in the Civil War*, 413, 506 f.

[7]Miles, "Eagle of the Regiment," chap. II, 5.

19: In Tangel's Feature

[1]*Rpt. Adj. Gen. Wis., 1864*, pp. 156, 422.

[2]Barrett, *Soldier Bird* (1876), 91; Charles R. Tuttle, *Illustrated History of the State of Wisconsin* (Boston, 1875), 458.

[3]*Wisconsin State Journal*, October 3, 1864; Federal Manuscript Census, 1870, Dane County, vol. 2, p. 502.

[4]*Wisconsin State Journal*, October 10, 1864.

[5]J. O. Barrett to Gov. J. T. Lewis, January 17, 1865, Department of the Executive, Administration, Civil War Memorials, Correspondence. Cited hereinafter as Exec. Cor. Civil War Mem. See also F. Firmin to J. O. Barrett, January 24, 1865, *ibid.*; Barrett, *Soldier Bird* (1876), 94.

[6]See Chapter 15, "After the Devil."

[7]L. P. Brockett and Mrs. M. C. Vaughn, *Women's Work in the Civil War* (Philadelphia, 1867), 577; Mary Livermore "Women and the War," quoted in Brockett and Vaughn, *ibid.*, 578–579; see also "Useless Young Ladies," in *Home Fair Journal* (Milwaukee), June 28, 1865.

[8]Mrs. A. H. Hoge, *Boys in Blue, or Heroes of the Rank and File* (New York, 1867) *passim*; Frank Moore, *Women of the War: Their Heroism and Self Sacrifice* (Hartford, Conn., 1866), 580.

[9]Moore, *Women of the War*, 581; Klement, "Wisconsin in the Civil War," *Wisconsin Blue Book, 1962*, p. 177; Ethel A. Hurn, *Wisconsin Women in the War* (Madison, 1911), 167–173.

[10]Moore, *Women of the War*, 351; Brockett and Vaughn, *Women's Work*, 561.

[11]Barrett, *Soldier Bird* (1876), 100.

[12]*Ibid.*, 94–95; J. O. Barrett to Gov. Lewis, January 17, 1865, Exec. Cor. Civil War Mem.; J. O. Barrett to Gov. J. T. Lewis, April 17, 1865, *ibid.*; J. M. Lynch to William Allen, June 16, 1865, Wisconsin National Guard Records, Quartermaster Corps, Outgoing Correspondence, Letter Books, 1861–1873 State Archives. Cited hereinafter as Wis. Q. M.

[13]*Wisconsin State Journal*, June 22, 1865.

[14]*Ibid.*, June 3, 1864, June 5, 1865; *Chicago Tribune*, June 2, 1865.

[15]*Chicago Tribune*, June 2, 1865.

[16]*Wisconsin State Journal*, May 10, 1865; Flower, *Old Abe*, 61; Barrett, *Soldier Bird* (1876), 95.

[17]*Ibid.*

[18]Barrett, *Soldier Bird* (1876), 101.

[19]*Ibid.*, 96; Flower, *Old Abe*, 62.

[20]*Chicago Tribune*, June 2, 1865.

[21]Hurn, *Wisconsin Women in the War*, 167–173; Klement, "Wisconsin in the Civil War," *Wisconsin Blue Book, 1962*, p. 177; J. M. Lynch to William Allen, June 16, 1865, Wis. Q. M., Outgoing Correspondence, Letter Books, 1861–1873.

[22]Klement, "Wisconsin in the Civil War," *Wisconsin Blue Book, 1962*, p. 177; Proclamation of Governor James T. Lewis, in *Home Fair Journal*, May 20, 1865.

[23]Hurn, *Wisconsin Women in the War*, 167–173.

[24]*Home Fair Journal*, May 20, 1865.

[25]*Ibid.*, June 28, 1865.

[26]*Ibid.*, July 8, 1865; Milwaukee *Sentinel, June 30, 1865*.

[27]*Home Fair Journal*, June 29, 1865; Frank A. Flower, *History of Milwaukee* (2 vols., Milwaukee, 1881), 2:782.

[28]Hurn, *Wisconsin Women in the War*, 173.

[29]*Wisconsin State Journal*, September 8, July 13, 1865.

[30]*Ibid.*; Klement, "Wisconsin in the Civil War," *Wisconsin Blue Book, 1962*, p. 177.

[31]Flower, *Old Abe*, 66–67; Hurn, *Wisconsin Women in the War*, 144–148; Milwaukee *Sentinel*, September 25, 1865.

[32]*Home Fair Journal*, June 29, 1865.

20: Bloody Shirt Politics

[1]Sam Ross, *The Empty Sleeve: A Biography of Lucius Fairchild* (Madison, 1964), 94–97; see also Mary R. Dearing, *Veterans in Politics: The Story of the G.A.R.* (Baton Rouge, 1954), *passim*, esp. 72.

[2]Lucius Fairchild, Campaign Scrap-Book, 1868, Fairchild Papers, State Archives.

[3]Fairchild, "Campaign Scrap Books," 1870, *ibid.*

[4]*Wisconsin Blue Book, 1981–1982*, p. 697.

[5]Barrett, *Soldier Bird* (1876), 93.

[6]Quiner, *Military History of Wisconsin*, 539.

[7]*Ibid.*

[8]Gov. Hacheld to Lucius Fairchild, September 12, 1866, Fairchild Papers; Lucius Fairchild to President and Soldiers' and Sailors' Convention, September 22, 1866, Fairchild Papers.

[9]*Ibid.*; also Dearing, *Veterans in Politics*, 99.

[10]*Ibid.*; Ross, *Empty Sleeve*, 82–93; Barrett, *Soldier Bird* (1876), 104.

[11]Milwaukee *Sentinel*, September 20, 1866.

[12]*Ibid.*, October 2, 1866; Lucius Fairchild to John Gibbon, October 1, 1866, Fairchild Papers.

[13]*Wisconsin State Journal*, September 27, 1866.

[14]*Ibid.*; Milwaukee *Sentinel*, October 2, 1866; Barrett, *Soldier Bird* (1876), 108; Dearing, *Veterans in Politics*, 99.

[15]*Wisconsin State Journal*, October 2, 1866; Milwaukee *Sentinel*, October 3, October 10, 1866.

[16]S. D. Priterbaugh to Governor Lucius Fairchild, September 29, 1866, Exec. Cor. Civil War Mem.; Bryner, *Bugle Echoes*, 45; Barrett, *Soldier Bird* (1876), 108; Dearing, *Veterans in Politics*, 84.

[17]Bryner, *Bugle Echoes*, 45.

[18]Milwaukee *Sentinel*, October 20, 1866.

[19]*Ibid.*, October 24, 1866; Dearing, *Veterans in Politics*, 94.

[20]Ross, *Empty Sleeve*, 97.

[21]*Wisconsin State Journal*, May 20, 1868.

[22]*Chicago Tribune*, May 20, 1868; see also Frank A. Flower, *History of the Republican Party* (Springfield, Ill., 1884), 293.

[23]*Ibid.*

[24]Ross, *Empty Sleeve*, 98; Milwaukee *Sentinel*, May 20, 1868; *Wisconsin State Journal*, May 21, 1868.

[25]McFeely, *Grant*, 277.

[26]Ross, *Empty Sleeve*; McFeely, *Grant*; Dearing, *Veterans in Politics*, 50.

[27]Lucius Fairchild to U. S. Grant, June 1, 1868, Fairchild Papers.

[28]*Soldiers' Record*, September 24, 1867.

[29]Barrett, *Soldier Bird* (1876), 93.

[30]*Ibid.*, 104; Flower, *Old Abe*, 73.

[31]Ross, *Empty Sleeve*, 114.

[32]*Ibid.*, 117; Dearing, *Veterans in Politics*, 94; Henry Casson, *"Uncle Jerry": Life of General Jeremiah M. Rusk...* (Madison, 1895), 156–157.

[33]*Soldiers' Record*, July 24, 1869.

[34]*Ibid.*, *passim*, 1869.

[35]Barrett, *Soldier Bird* (1876), 113.

[36]Milwaukee *Sentinel*, September 26, September 28, 1870.

[37]Ross, *Empty Sleeve*, 122

[38]Reunion Book of the Eighth Wisconsin Infantry, August 31, 1871, Weissert Papers.

[39]Milwaukee *Sentinel*, September 11, 1871.

[40]Barrett, *Soldier Bird* (1876), 114; Clark County *Republican*, October 10, 1871.

[41]*Wisconsin State Journal*, February 23, 1872; *Proceedings of the Sixth Annual Reunion of the Society of the Army of the Tennessee* (Cincinnati, 1872).

[42]*Proceedings of the Sixth Annual Reunion of the Army of the Tennessee*, 64–65.

[43]Ross, *Empty Sleeve*, 158.

[44]Milwaukee *Sentinel*, August 30, 1872.

[45]Ross, *Empty Sleeve*, 158.

21: The Centennial

[1]*Rpt. Adj. Gen. Wis., 1873*, p. 2.

[2]Charles E. Estabrook (ed.), *Records and Sketches of Military Organizations...Relating to Wisconsin in the Period of the Civil War* (Madison, 1914), 164.

[3]*Rpt. Adj. Gen. Wis., 1866*, p. 8; see also A. R. McDonald, Voucher for Eagles Feed, January 1, 1866–September 1, 1866, Wis. Q. M., General Correspondence, 1863–1889, box 19.

[4]*Rpt. Adj. Gen. Wis., 1867*, p. 443; Tuttle, *Illustrated History of Wisconsin*, 614.

[5]Barrett, *Soldier Bird* (1876), 91; see also *Rpt. Adj. Gen. Wis., 1869*, p. 114.

[6]Barrett, *Soldier Bird* (1876), 91.

[7]Annual Message of Gov. W. R. Taylor, January 5, 1874, in *Governor's Messages and Proclamations* (Madison, 1874), 9.

[8]*Wisconsin Legislative Manual*, 1875.

[9]Flower, *Old Abe*, 79.

[10]Barrett, *Soldier Bird* (1876), 112.

[11]*Ibid.*

[12]Chicago *Times*, May 14, 1875; Chicago *Tribune*, May 14, 1875.

[13]Barrett, *Soldier Bird* (1876), 117.

[14]*Ibid.*, 112; Milwaukee *Sentinel*, July 5, 1875.

[15]Dearing, *Veterans in Politics*, 212.

[16]Anna Butler, Emma C. Bascom, and Kathrine F. Kerr, *Centennial Records of the Women of Wisconsin* (Madison, 1876), 130–131.

[17]*Ibid.*

[18]*Ibid.*, 137; *Wisconsin State Journal*, July 7, 1875.

[19]Barrett, *Soldier Bird* (1876), 103.

[20]Milwaukee *Sentinel*, August 28, 1889.

[21]Report of the State Board of Centennial Managers, *Assembly Journal*, January 26, 1877, p. 72.

[22]State Board of Centennial Managers, *An Address to the People of Wisconsin by Some of Her Prominent Citizens On Their Interest and Duty Toward the Centennial Celebration and Industrial Exhibition to be Held in Philadelphia in 1876* (Madison, 1875); *Centennial Records of the Women of Wisconsin*, 185; see also Report of the Women's State Centennial Executive Committee of Wisconsin, *Senate Journal*, 1876, pp. 28–29.

[23]Barrett, *Soldier Bird* (1876), 120.

[24]Report of the State Board of Centennial Managers, 72–78; State Board of Centennial Managers, *The State of Wisconsin Embracing Brief Sketches of its History, Position, Resources and Industries and a Catalogue of its Exhibits at the Centennial at Philadelphia* (Madison, 1876), 85.

[25]J. O. Barrett to Governor Harrison Ludington, February 3, 1877, Exec. Cor. Civil War Mem.

[26]*Ibid.*; State Board of Centennial Managers, *The State of Wisconsin*, 85.

[27]Milwaukee *Sentinel*, February 25, 1876.

[28]Phillip T. Sandhurst, *The Great Centennial Exhibit* (Philadelphia, 1876), 539–543.

[29]Thomas L. Connelly, *The Marble Man* (New York, 1977), 66–67.

[30]*Ibid.*

[31]William Dean Howells, "Sennight of the Centennial," in the *Atlantic Monthly* (July, 1876), 102.

[32]J. S. Ingram, *The Centennial Exposition* (Philadelphia, 1876), 652.

[33]Sandhurst, *The Great Centennial*, 539–543.

[34]State Board of Centennial Managers, *The State of Wisconsin*, 85.

[35]Philadelphia *Palladium*, November 1, 1876.

[36]*Ibid.*; J. O. Barrett to Gov. Harrison Ludington, February 3, 1877, Exec. Cor. Civil War Mem.

[37]Ingram, *Centennial Exposition*, 686.

[38]Philadelphia *Palladium*, November 1, 1876.

[39]Howells, "Sennight of the Centennial," 104.

[40]*Ibid.*

[41]*Ibid.*

[42]William Dodge Horne, "Eagle Autographs" in the Milwaukee *Journal*, October 6, 1936; see example at G.A.R. Museum, Madison.

[43]R. C. Bierce to Edwin E. Bryant, May 7, 1877, Exec. Cor. Civil War Mem.

[44]R. C. Brice to Frank M. Putney, May 10, 1877, and Brice to E. E. Bryant, May 7, 1877, *ibid.*

[45]I. E. Troan to F. W. Putney, July 7, 1877, *ibid.*

[46]Rufus R. Dawes to Governor Harrison R. Ludington, August 10, 1877, *ibid.*; R. B. Hoover to Harrison R. Ludington, August 10, 1877, *ibid.*

[47]Maj. Charles D. Miller to A.A.G. Wisconsin, April 15, 1878, *ibid.*

[48]Williams, *Eagle Regiment*, 87.

[49]J. H. Campbell to Adj. Gen. Wisconsin, August 14, 1879, Exec. Cor. Civil War Mem.

[50]*Wisconsin State Journal*, March 28, 1881.

[51]Alexander H. Rice, Governor of Massachusetts, to Governor of Wisconsin, December 21, 1876, Exec. Cor. Civil War Mem.

[52]C. Alice Baker, *Old Abe, the War Eagle of Wisconsin* (Deerfield, Mass., 1903), introduction.

[53]*Ibid.*

[54]*Ibid.*; Flower, *Old Abe*, 82; Williams, *Eagle Regiment*, 86.

[55]George A. Goddard to Governor Rice of Massachusetts, December 4, 1878, Exec. Cor. Civil War Mem.

[56]Flower, *Old Abe*, 82; Williams, *Eagle Regiment*, 86; Baker, *Old Abe*, introduction.

[57]Baker, *Old Abe*, passim.

[58]Flower, *Old Abe*, 83.

[59]Milwaukee *Sentinel*, March 5, 1879.

[60]*Ibid.*, July 23, August 23, October 8, 1878.

[61]*Ibid.*, March 5, 1879.

22: Old Abe at Peace

[1]Flower, *Old Abe*, 101; Flower, *History of the Republican Party*; also see Flower, *Edwin McMasters Stanton: The Autocrat of Rebellion, Emancipation and Reconstruction* (New York, 1905); Flower, *The Life of Matthew Hale Carpenter* (Madison, 1883); Frank A. Flower Papers, State Archives; and Milwaukee *Sentinel*, May 21, 1885.

[2]Helen Ferris (ed.), *When I Was A Girl* [by Jane Addams] (New York, 1930), 184.

[3]*Ibid.*, 185.

[4]*Ibid.*; Milwaukee *Journal*, February 8, 1931.

[5]F. C. Bartlett to George E. Bryant, August 11, 1879, Exec. Cor. Civil War Mem.

[6]Chicago Union Veterans Club to Governor William E. Smith, August 16, 1870, ibid.

[7]Flower, *Old Abe*, 86.

[8]Mrs. D. J. Holmes to Governor William E. Smith, July 25, 1879, Exec. Cor. Civil War Mem.

[9]Milwaukee *Sentinel*, August 30, September 17, 1879.

[10]George Tonnar to Governor William E. Smith, September 14, 1879, Exec. Cor. Civil War Mem.; Milwaukee *Sentinel*, September 27, 1879.

[11]Martin Bean to Adj. General of Wisconsin, September 17, 1879, Exec. Cor. Civil War Mem.

[12]Flower, *Old Abe*, 87; William F. Vilas, "General U. S. Grant," in S. B. Fallows (ed.), *Liberty and Union* (Chicago, 1883), 248–250.

[13]Flower, *Old Abe*, 88.

[14]J. W. Strofe to Governor William E. Smith, Apr. 21, 1880, Exec. Cor. Civil War Mem.

[15]A. G. Weissert to Governor William E. Smith, February 26, 1880, *ibid.*

[16]Flower, *Old Abe*, 89; Milwaukee *Sentinel*, April 19, May 19, June 7–June 12, September 14, 1880, March 28, 1881; U. S. Grant to William Earnshaw, May 21, 1880, in *Proceedings of the National Encampment of the Grand Army of the Republic* (New York, 1880), 664.

[17]Samuel B. Smith to Quarter Master General of Wisconsin, July 24, 1880, Exec. Cor. Civil War Mem.; Flower, *Old Abe*, 80.

[18]Milwaukee *Sentinel*, August 24, 1880.

[19]*Ibid.*, August 25, 26, 1880.

[20]Flower, *Old Abe*, 90.

[21]*Wisconsin State Journal*, March 28, 1881; Milwaukee *Sentinel*, March 28, 1881; G. E. Bryant to Reuben G. Thwaites, January 8, 1903, State Historical Society of Wisconsin, Administration, General Correspondence, box 4, State Archives. Hereinafter cited as SHSW Admin.

[22]Milwaukee *Sentinel*, March 28, 1881.

[23]Flower, *Old Abe*, 91.

[24]Milwaukee *Sentinel*, April 19, 1881.

[25]*Ibid.*

[26]*Ibid.*, May 19, 1881.

[27]*Ibid.*, September 14, 1881.

[28]*Ibid.*, September 17, 1881.

[29]Flower, *Old Abe*, 103. The State Historical Society of Wisconsin did not occupy its present quarters until 1900, when its neoclassical headquarters building on State Street was completed.

[30]Milwaukee *Sentinel*, April 1, 1881.

[31]*Ibid.*, September 19, 1887. See also John G. Gregory, "The Story of Old Abe," in *West Central Wisconsin* (Indianapolis, 1933), 860–862; and William F. Bailey, *History of Eau Claire County* (Chicago, 1914), *passim.*

[32]Milwaukee *Sentinel*, January 31, 1889.

[33]Madison *Democrat*, March 25, 1892.

[34]Lafayette H. Bunnell, *Winona and its Environs on the Mississippi in Ancient and Modern Times* (Winona, Minnesota, 1897), 336.

[35]Washington *Post*, March 29, 1903.

[36]Milwaukee *Sentinel*, September 16, 1887.

[37]*Harpers Weekly*, (August 7, 1891), 619–620; Rossiter Johnson (ed.), *A History of the World's Columbian Exposition Held in Chicago in 1893, Volume I* (New York, 1897), 438.

[38]Hosea W. Rood, "Old Abe, the Wisconsin War Eagle," in C. P. Cary (comp.), *Memorial Day Annual* (Madison, 1904), 22.

[39]*Ibid.*; "Removal of Old Abe," in *Proceedings of the Wisconsin Historical Society* (1903), 36.

[40]*Ibid.*; see also Rood, "Grand Army Memorial Hall," in C. P. Cary (comp.), *Memorial Day Annual* (Madison, 1903), 23; George E. Bryant to Reuben G. Thwaites, January 8, 1903, SHSW Admin., box 4; Reuben G. Thwaites to G. E. Bryant, January 9, 1903, *ibid.*

[41]Rood, *Memorial Day Annual* (1904), 23; Chester W. Smith to Hosea Rood, April 16, 1904, in the Rood Papers, Correspondence, 1894–1923, G.A.R. Museum Archives, folder 5; Mary E. Aldon to Rood, April 13, 1904, *ibid.*; Rev. T. W. Chambliss to Rood, April 15, 1904, *ibid.*

[42]See photograph by G. Sutherland, Weissert Papers.

[43]Hosea W. Rood, "Story of the Eau Claire Encampment," Rood Papers.

[44]Fred L. Holmes, *Side Roads and Excursions Into Wisconsin's Past* (Madison, 1949), 92.

[45]C. J. Hasking to R. C. Henry, G.A.R. Memorial Hall Custodian, 1933, in Henry, "The Story of Old Abe," 5; Charlene Mason to Lynnette Wolfe, June 4, 1982, and telephone conversation, both in G.A.R. Memorial Hall Records.

[46]Rood (comp.), *Wisconsin at Vicksburg*, 12.

[47]*Ibid.*, 335.

[48]Holmes, *Side Roads and Excursions*, 92.

[49]Personal observation by author, 1981–1982.

[50]D. E. Fricker, J. I. Case Company, to Dennis K. McDaniel, May 20, 1975, G.A.R. Memorial Hall Records.

[51]Joe D. Huddleston, "Shoulder Patch with a History," in *Army Museum Newsletter*, Volume 19 (July, 1980), 32.

Bibliography

Manuscripts and Archives

Unless otherwise noted, these sources are available at the State Historical Society of Wisconsin, Madison. The Society's collections embrace both private manuscripts and the official Wisconsin State Archives.

Baker, Jeremiah. Papers, 1856–1874.

Brown, James E. Papers, 1861–1865. Chippewa Valley Historical Museum, Eau Claire.

Cronon, Edward. Civil War Letters, 1861–1865.

Demarest, Burnett. Papers, 1862–1874.

Department of the Executive, Administration.
———. Civil War Memorials Correspondence, 1861–1913.
———. Executive Journal, 1860–1873.
———. Military Returns, 1856–1901.
———. Telegrams Received, 1861–1873.

Dwight, Edward C. Diary, 1861–1863.

Fairchild, Lucius. Papers, 1818–1923.
———. Correspondence, 1826–1896.
———. Speeches and Miscellaneous Notes, 1845–1896.
———. Governor's Private Letter Books, 1865–1871.
———. Campaign Scrap Books.

Favell, Thomas R. (ed.). "Civil War Years: Thomas Favell and the 8th Wisconsin Infantry Volunteers." Transcript.

Flower, Frank A. Papers, 1818–1909.

Gould, Phillip H. Letters, 1860–1862, in the N. C. Gould Papers.

Heimstreet, E. B. "History of Old Abe, the Eagle Mascot of the Eighth Wisconsin Infantry, the Eagle Regiment," G.A.R. Memorial Hall Archives, Madison.

McLain, David. Papers, 1860–1976.

Palmetier, Charles. Letters, 1861–1864.

Perkins, John E. Papers, Chippewa Valley Historical Museum, Eau Claire.

Priestly, Thomas. Correspondence, 1856–1891.
———. Diary, 1861–1864.

Quiner, E. B. "Correspondence of Wisconsin Volunteers, 1861–1865," in 8 vols., in Papers of E. B. Quiner (unprocessed).

Root, Augustus. Papers, G.A.R. Memorial Hall Archives, Madison.

Root, Muncil V. Papers, G.A.R. Memorial Hall Archives, Madison.

Rounds, E. D. "Old Abe the War Eagle," manuscript presented to Chippewa Valley Historical Society, May 5, 1926, Chippewa Valley Historical Museum, Eau Claire.

Scrapbooks, G.A.R. Encampments, 1880–1936, G.A.R. Memorial Hall Archives, Madison.

Weissert, Augustus G. Papers, 1861–1923, G.A.R. Memorial Hall Archives, Madison.

Williams, John M. Diaries, 1861–1864.

Wisconsin National Guard, Office of the Adjutant General.
———. Regimental Descriptive Rolls, 1861–1865, Eighth Infantry.
———. Regimental Descriptive Rosters, 1861, Eighth Infantry.
———. Records of Volunteer Regiments, Eighth Regiment of Wisconsin Volunteer Infantry.

Wisconsin National Guard Records.
———. Quartermaster Corps, General Correspondence, 1863–1889.
———. Outgoing Correspondence, 1861–1873.

Governmental Publications

Adjutant General of Illinois. *Report of the Adjutant General of the State of Illinois*, Volume III, *Containing Reports for the Years 1861–1865* (Springfield, 1901).

Adjutant General of Missouri. *Report of the Adjutant General of Missouri, 1865* (St. Louis, 1865).

Adjutant General of Wisconsin. *Annual Reports of the Adjutant General and the Quartermaster General of the State of Wisconsin, 1860–1881* (Madison, 1860–1881).

Board of Centennial Managers. *An Address to the People of Wisconsin by Some of Her Prominent Citizens On Their Interest and Duty Toward the Centennial Celebration and International Exhibition to be Held in Philadelphia in 1876* (Madison, 1875).
———. *The State of Wisconsin Embracing Brief Sketches of its History, Position, Resources, and Industries and a Catalogue of its Exhibits at the Centennial at Philadelphia* (Madison, 1876).
———. Report of the State Board of Centennial Managers. *Assembly Journal*, January 26, 1877, pp. 72–78.
———. Report of the State Board of Centennial Managers. *Senate Journal*, 1876, pp. 29–33.

Governor of Wisconsin. *Governors' Messages and Accompanying Documents, 1864–1881* (Madison, 1864–1881).

Heitman, Francis B. *Historical Register and Dictionary of the United States Army, 1789–1903* (Washington, D.C., 1903).

Legislative Manual of the State of Wisconsin, 1861–1881 (Madison, 1861–1881). This publication was the predecessor of the *Wisconsin Blue Book*.

Morgell, C. S. *Battlefields in Front of Nashville Where United States Forces Commanded by Major General Geo. H. Thomas Defeated and Routed the Rebel Army under General Hood, December 15–16, 1864* (Topographical Engineers' Office, Dept. of the Cumberland, Chattanooga, 1865).

Rood, Hosea W. (comp.). *Wisconsin at Vicksburg. Report of the Wisconsin-Vicksburg Monument Commission: Including the Story of the Campaign and Siege of Vicksburg in 1863* (Madison, 1914).

Scott, Robert N. (ed.) et al. *The War of the Rebellion: A Compilation of the Official Records of the Union and Confederate Armies* (128 vols., Washington, D.C., 1880–1902).

Women's State Centennial Executive Committee. "Report of the Women's State Centennial Executive Committee of Wisconsin," *Senate Journal*, 1876, pp. 29–33.

Other Primary Sources

Andrews, C. C. *History of the Campaign of Mobile: Including the Cooperative Operations of General Wilson's Cavalry in Alabama* (New York, 1867).

Bascom, Emma C.; Butler, Anna; and Kerr, Katherine F. (eds.). *Centennial Records of the Women of Wisconsin* (Madison, 1876).

Brockett, L. P., and Vaughan, Mrs. M. C. *Women's Work in the Civil War* (Philadelphia, 1867).

Brown, A. F. "Van Dorn's Operations in Northern Mississippi—Recollections of a Cavalryman," *Southern Historical Society Papers*, Volume 6 (1878).

Bryner, Byron C. *Bugle Echoes: The Story of the Illinois 47th* (Springfield, 1905).

Bunnell, LaFayette H. *Winona and its Environs on the Mississippi in Ancient and Modern Times* (Winona, Minnesota, 1897).

Burdette, Robert J. *The Drums of the 47th* (Indianapolis, 1914).

Chicago *Tribune* (Chicago, 1861–1881).

Clarke, Norman (ed.). *Warfare Along the Mississippi: The Letters of Lt. Col. George E. Currie* (Ann Arbor, 1961).

Crandall, Warren D., and Newall, Isaac D. *History of the Ram Fleet and the Mississippi Marine Brigade* (St. Louis, 1907).

[Driggs, George W.] A Non Commissioned Officer. *Opening the Mississippi or Two Years Campaigning in the Southwest: A Record of the Campaigns, Sieges, Actions and Marches in Which the 8th Wisconsin Volunteers have Participated* (Madison, 1864).

Dyer, Frederick H. *A Compendium of the War of the Rebellion* (Des Moines, 1864).

Eau Claire *Free Press* (Eau Claire, 1862–1865).

Edwards, John N. *Shelby and His Men: or The War in the West* (Kansas City, 1897).

Eighth Regiment of Wisconsin Veteran Volunteer Infantry. *Proceedings of the Reunion of the Eighth Regiment of Wisconsin Veteran Volunteer Infantry* (Milwaukee, 1880).

Fallon, John T. (ed.). *List of Synonyms of Organizations in the Volunteer Service of the United States During the Years, 1861–1865* (Washington, D.C., 1885).

Fairbanks, Henry N. "The Red River Expedition of 1864," *War Papers*, Maine MOLLUS, Volume I (Portland, Maine, 1898).

Farley, Edwin. *Experiences of a Soldier, 1861–1865* (Paducah, 1918).

Ferris, Helen (ed.). *When I Was a Girl* (New York, 1930).

Fox, William F. *Regimental Losses in the American Civil War* (New York, 1898).

G.A.R. Headquarters, Department of Ohio. *Proceedings of the National Encampment of the Grand Army of the Republic*, Dayton, Ohio, June 8–9, 1880 (New York, 1881).

G.A.R. Headquarters, Department of Wisconsin. *General Orders, 1871–1884* (Madison, 1871–1884).

Gaylord, Augustus. "In and Out of the Wisconsin Adjutant General's Office, 1862–1866," *War Papers*, Wisconsin MOLLUS, Volume III (Milwaukee, 1896).

Grant, U. S. *Personal Memoirs of U. S. Grant* (2 vols., New York, 1885).

Greene, James H. *Reminiscences of the War, Bivouacs, Marches, Skirmishes and Battles* (Medina, Ohio, 1886).

Hoge, Mrs. A. H. *Boys in Blue or Heroes of the Rank and File* (New York and Chicago, 1867).

Home Fair Journal. Numbers 1–15, May 20, 1865—July 8, 1865 (Milwaukee, 1865).

Howells, William Dean. "Sennight of the Centennial," *Atlantic Monthly* (July, 1876).

Hubbard, Lucius F. *Minnesota in the Civil War and Indian War, 1861–1865* (St. Paul, 1890).

——. "Minnesota in the Battle of Corinth," *War Papers*, Minnesota MOLLUS, Volume VI (St. Paul, 1907).

——. "Minnesota in the Battle of Nashville, December 15–16, 1864," *War Papers*, Minnesota MOLLUS, Volume VI (St. Paul, 1905).

Ingram, J. S. *The Centennial Exposition* (Philadelphia, 1876).

Jackson, Alice F. and Bettina (eds.). *Autobiography of James Albert Jackson, Sr., M.D.*, (Madison, 1945).

——. *Three Hundred Years American: The Epic of a Family from Seventeenth-Century New England to Twentieth-Century Midwest* (Madison, 1951).

Johnson, Rossiter (ed.). *A History of the World's Columbian Exposition Held in Chicago in 1893* (4 vols., New York, 1897).

Lockett, S. H. "The Defense of Vicksburg," *Battles and Leaders of the Civil War*, Volume III, pt. II (New York, 1884).

Lyon, William P. *Reminiscences of the Civil War*, comp. by Mrs. Adelia C. Lyon (San Jose, California, 1907).

McClay, John H. "Defense of Robinette," *War Papers*, Nebraska MOLLUS, Volume I (Omaha, 1903).

McDonald, C. F. "The Battle of Brice's Crossroads, Miss.," *War Papers*, Minnesota MOLLUS, Volume VI (St. Paul, 1906).

McCall, D. *Three Years in the Service, A Record of the Doings of the 11th Reg. Missouri Vols.* (Springfield, Illinois, 1864).

McMorries, Edward Y. *History of the First Regiment Alabama Volunteer Infantry C.S.A.* (Montgomery, 1904).

Martin, N. (ed.). "Letters of a Union Officer, L. F. Hubbard and the Civil War," *Minnesota History*, Volume 35 (1957).

Milwaukee *Sentinel* (Milwaukee, 1861–1889).

Moore, Frank. *Women of the War: Their Heroism and Self Sacrifice* (Hartford, Connecticut, 1866).

Phisterer, Frederick. *Statistical Record of the Armies of the United States* (New York, 1883).

Porter, David D. *The Naval History of the Civil War* (New York, 1886).

Rosecrans, William S. "The Battle of Corinth," *Battles and Leaders of the Civil War*, Volume II, pt. II (New York, 1884).

[Rood, Hosea W.] One of the Boys. *The Story of the Service of Company "E" and the Twelfth Wisconsin Regiment of Veteran Volunteer Infantry in the War of the Rebellion* (n.p., 1893).

——. "Grand Army Memorial Hall," in C. P. Cary (comp.), *Memorial Day Annual* (Madison, 1907).

Roosevelt, Theodore. "Address, Madison, Wisconsin, April 3, 1903," in C. P. Cary (comp.), *Memorial Day Annual* (Madison, 1903).

Sandhurst, Phillip T. *The Great Centennial Exhibit* (Philadelphia and Chicago, 1876).

Scott, John. *Story of the Thirty-Second Iowa Infantry Volunteers* (Nevada, Iowa, 1896).

Scott, William F. *The Story of a Cavalry Regiment: The Career of the Fourth Iowa Veteran Volunteers from Kansas to Georgia, 1861–1865* (New York, 1893).

Selfridge, Thomas O. "The Navy in the Red River," *Battles and Leaders of the Civil War*, Volume IV, pt. I (New York, 1886).

Sherman, William T. *Memoirs of General William T. Sherman Written by Himself* (2 vols., New York, 1875).

Smith, Albert E. "A Few Days with the Eighth Regiment, Wisconsin Volunteers at Iuka and Corinth," *War Papers*, Wisconsin MOLLUS, Volume IV (Milwaukee, 1914).

Smith, Charles H. *The History of Fuller's Ohio Brigade, 1861–1865* (Cleveland, 1909).

Smith, E. Kirby. "The Defense of the Red River," *Battles and Leaders of the Civil War*, Volume IV, pt. I (New York, 1886).

Snead, Thomas L. "The Conquest of Arkansas," *Battles and Leaders of the Civil War*, Volume III (New York, 1884).

Society of the Army of the Tennessee. *Report of the Proceedings of the Society of the Army of the Tennessee at the Annual Meeting* (Cincinnati, 1862–1881).

Soldiers' Record (Madison, 1866–1876).

Staff Officer of the 8th Regiment Wisconsin Volunteers. *Army Life and Stray Shots by a Staff Officer of the 8th Regiment Volunteers, 15th Army Corps, 3rd Division* (Memphis, 1863).

Stanley, David S. "The Battle of Corinth," *Personal Recollections of the War of the Rebellion*, New York MOLLUS, second series, Volume LL (New York, 1897).

Taylor, Richard H. *Destruction and Reconstruction* (New York, 1879).

Vilas, William F. "General U. S. Grant," in Samuel B. Fallows (comp.), *Liberty and Union: An Encyclopedia of Patriotism* (Madison, 1883).

Walke, Henry N. *Naval Scenes and Reminiscences of the Civil War* (New Haven, Connecticut, 1877).

West, Emmet C. *History and Reminiscences of the Second Wisconsin Cavalry Regiment* (Portage, 1904).

Wilcox, Ephraim. "War Times in Eau Claire," *Daily Telegram* (Eau Claire, 1911).

[Williams, John M.] A Non Vet of Co. "H." *The Eagle Regiment, 8th Wisconsin Infantry Volunteers, A Sketch of its Marches, Battles, and Campaigns From 1861–1865* (Belleville, 1890).

Wisconsin State Journal (Madison, 1861–1881).

Woodworth, John C. *Reminiscences of 1861–1865* (Eau Claire, 1887).

Secondary Works

Bailey, Judge William F. *History of Eau Claire County, Wisconsin* (Chicago, 1914).

Barland, Lois. *Sawdust City: A History of Eau Claire, Wisconsin from the Earliest Times to 1910* (Stevens Point, 1960).

Boatner, Mark M. III. *The Civil War Dictionary* (New York, 1959).

Brisbin, James S. *The Campaign Lives of Ulyses S. Grant and Schuyler Colfax* (Cincinnati, 1868).

Carter, Samuel III. *The Final Fortress: The Campaign for Vicksburg, 1862–1863* (New York, 1980).

Castel, Albert E. *General Sterling Price and the Confederate Defeat in the West* (Miami, Florida, 1980).

Casson, Henry. *"Uncle Jerry": Life of General Jeremiah M. Rusk, Stage Driver, Farmer, Soldier, Legislator, Governor, Cabinet Officer* (Madison, 1895).

Connelly, Thomas L. *Army of the Heartland: The Army of Tennessee, 1861–1862* (Baton Rouge, 1969).

———. *Autumn of Glory: The Army of Tennessee, 1862–1865* (Baton Rouge, 1971).

———. *The Marble Man* (Baton Rouge, 1972).

Current, Richard N. *History of Wisconsin. Volume II: The Civil War Era, 1848–1873* (Madison, 1976).

Dearing, Mary R. *Veterans in Politics: The Story of the G.A.R.* (Baton Rouge, 1954).

Dillon, John. "The Role of Riverine Warfare in the Civil War," *Naval War College Review* (March–April, 1973).

Eau Claire Leader-Telegram. *Our Story: The Chippewa Valley and Beyond* (Eau Claire, 1976).

Flower, Frank A. *History of the Republican Party* (Springfield, Illinois, 1884).

Freeman, Douglas S. *Lee's Lieutenants: A Study in Command* (3 vols., New York, 1944).

Gosnell, H. Allen. *Guns on the Western Waters* (Baton Rouge, 1949).

Hay, Thomas R. *Hood's Tennessee Campaign* (New York, 1929).

Horn, Stanley F. *The Decisive Battle of Nashville* (Baton Rouge, 1956).

Hurn, Ethel A. *Wisconsin Women in the Civil War* (Madison, 1911).

Johnson, Ludwell H. *Red River Campaign: Politics and Cotton in the Civil War* (Baltimore, 1958).

Jones, Archer. *Confederate Strategy from Shiloh to Vicksburg* (Baton Rouge, 1961).

Klement, Frank. "The Soldier Vote in Wisconsin During the Civil War," *Wisconsin Magazine of History*, Volume 28 (1944).

———. "Wisconsin in the Civil War." *Wisconsin Blue Book, 1962* (Madison, 1962).

Love, William De Loss. *Wisconsin in the War of the Rebellion: A History of All Regiments and Batteries the State Has Sent to the Field* (Milwaukee, 1866).

Mahan, Alfred T. *The Gulf and Inland Waters*. Volume III of *The Navy in the Civil War* (New York, 1883).

Mahon, John K. "Civil War Infantry Assault Tactics," *Military Analysis of the Civil War by the Editors of Military Affairs* (Millwood, New York, 1977).

Mattern, Carolyn J. *Soldiers When They Go: The Story of Camp Randall, 1861–1865* (Madison, 1981).

McFeely, William S. *Grant: A Biography* (New York, 1981).

Milligan, John D. *Gunboats Down the Mississippi* (Annapolis, 1965).

Mollenhoff, David. "Rowdies in Blue: Madison as a Civil War Town," *The Journal of Historic Madison*, Volume IV (1978).

Monaghan, Jay. *Civil War on the Western Border, 1854–1865* (Boston, 1955).

Moore, John G. "Mobility and Strategy in the Civil War," *Military Analysis of the Civil War by Editors of Military Affairs* (Millwood, New York, 1977).

Nesbit, Robert C. *Wisconsin: A History* (Madison, 1973).

Pratt, Fletcher. *The Civil War on Western Waters* (New York, 1956).

Quiner, E. B. *The Military History of Wisconsin: A Record of the Civil and Military Patriotism of the State in the War for the Union* (Chicago, 1866).

Rappaport, Armin. "The Replacement System During the Civil War," *Military Analysis of the Civil War by Editors of Military Affairs* (Millwood, New York, 1977).

Reed, Rowena. *Combined Operations in the Civil War* (Annapolis, 1978).

Ross, Sam. *The Empty Sleeve: A Biography of Lucius Fairchild* (Madison, 1964).

Shannon, Fred A. *The Organization and Administration of the Union Armies* (2 vols., Cleveland, 1928).

Shea, William L. "Battle at Ditch Bayou," *Arkansas Historical Quarterly*, Volume 39 (1980).

Tuttle, Charles P. *Illustrated History of the State of Wisconsin* (Boston and Madison, 1875).

Warner, Ezra J. *Generals in Gray* (Baton Rouge, 1959).

———. *Generals in Blue* (Baton Rouge, 1964).

Wiley, Bell I. *The Life of Billy Yank* (Indianapolis and New York, 1951).

Williams, T. Harry. "Badger Colonels and the Civil War Officer," *Wisconsin Magazine of History*, Volume 47 (1963).

Weller, Joe. "The Logistics of Nathan Bedford Forrest," *Military Analysis of the Civil War by the Editors of Military Affairs* (Millwood, New York, 1977).

Wright, Gavin R. *The Political Economy of the Cotton South: Households, Markets, and Wealth in the Nineteenth Century* (New York, 1978).

Publications Relating to Old Abe the War Eagle

Baker, C. Alice. *Old Abe the War Eagle of Wisconsin* (Deerfield, Massachusetts, 1904).

Barrett, Joseph O. *The Soldier Bird! History of "Old Abe" the Live War Eagle* (Chicago, 1864).

——. *The Soldier Bird Old Abe: The Live War Eagle of Wisconsin, That Served a Three Year Campaign in the Great Rebellion* (Madison, 1876).

Bennett, K. W. "Old Abe the Wisconsin War Eagle," *Creative Wisconsin*, Volume 8 (1961).

——. "The Eagle and the Iron Men," *The National Guardsman* (May 1, 1957).

Bradish, Sarah P. "Old Abe," *Little People of the Air* (Boston, 1884).

Bradford, A. M. *Wisconsin's War Eagle, Patriotic Song and Chorus* (Milwaukee 1905).

Brownell, H. H. "The Soldier Bird," *Union Fifth Reader* (New York, 1867).

Brunell, Henry H. "The Eagle at Corinth," *War Lyrics* (Philadelphia, 1880).

Carlisle, Norman. "Yankee Bird of Battle," *True Magazine* (February, 1961).

Carson, Gerald. "The Glorious Bird," *Natural History* (October, 1979).

Chapin, Earl. *Tales of Wisconsin* (River Falls, 1973).

Castigan, Arthur. "Old Abe the War Eagle," *Civil War Book Exchange*, Volume 9 (1983).

Catton, Bruce. "Old Abe the Battle Eagle," *American Heritage* (October, 1963).

Crofutt, B. B. "Old Abe, the Battle Eagle," *Boy's Life Magazine* (July, 1923).

Davis, Bette J. *Freedom Eagle* (New York, 1972).

Dietz, J. Stanley. *The Story of Old Abe the War Eagle* (Madison, 1946).

Dodge, Margarite C. *Old Abe the Wisconsin War Eagle* (n.p., 1930).

Flower, Frank A. *Old Abe the Eighth Wisconsin War Eagle* (Madison, 1885).

Gard, Robert E. *This is Wisconsin* (Madison, 1969).

Gilbert, Kenneth. "The Bird That Led an Army," *Western Story Magazine* (January 10, 1930).

Gore, Leroy. "Old Abe, Bird of Battle," *Yarns of Wisconsin* (Madison, 1978).

Gregory, John G. "The Story of Old Abe," *West Central Wisconsin* (Indianapolis, 1933).

Henry, Charles H. *The History of Old Abe the War Eagle* (Madison, 1933).

Hill, Lee. "Old Abe, Bird of Battle," *Wisconsin Week End* (April 30, 1975).

Holmes, Fred L. "They Knew Old Abe, Wisconsin's Civil War Eagle," *Side Roads and Excursions into Wisconsin's Past* (Madison, 1949).

——. "Old Abe the War Eagle," *Eagle* (June, 1944).

Huddleston, Joe D. "Shoulder Patch with a History," *Army Museum Newsletter* Volume 19 (July, 1980).

King, Madeline Favell. *The Story of Old Abe* (King, Wisconsin, 1970).

Lindemann, Georgianne. "Old Abe the Union War Eagle," *Civil War Times Illustrated* (January, 1985).

Lindop, Edmund. *War Eagle: The Story of a Civil War Mascot* (Boston, 1966).

Madison Public Schools. "Old Abe the Civil War Eagle," *Instructional Materials About our Community* (n.d., n.p.).

McLain, David. "The Story of Old Abe," *Wisconsin Magazine of History*, Volume 8 (June, 1925).

Merk, Frederick. "The Story of Old Abe," *Wisconsin Magazine of History*, Volume 2 (1918).

[Miles, Samuel C.] Selim, C. S. *The Eagle of the Regiment, An Epic on Old Abe, the War Eagle* (n.p., 1892).

Miller, R. Russell. "Some New Notes on Old Abe—The Battle Eagle," *Military Collector and Historian*, Volume 15 (1963).

Nelson, C. P. *Abe, the War Eagle* (Lynn, Massachusetts, 1903).

"Old Abe: Fact and Fiction," *Badger History*, Volume 25 (November, 1973).

"Old Abe, Bird of Battle," *Wisconsin Tales and Trails* (Spring, 1961).

"Old Abe, War Eagle of the Eighth Regiment Wisconsin Volunteers," *30th Star*, Volume 4 (December, 1958).

Prueher, J. G. "A Tribute to Old Abe—Famous War Eagle," *The Wisconsin Magazine*, Volume 6 (1928).

Rauschenberger, John. "Old Abe: Wings of Victory," *Exclusively Yours* (October 6, 1981).

Rood, Hosea W. "Old Abe, the Wisconsin War Eagle," in C. P. Cary (comp.), *Memorial Day Annual* (Madison, 1904).

Sherwood, Lorraine. *Old Abe: American Eagle* (New York, 1946).

Smith, Beatrice S. "Old Abe," *Vista For Adults*, Volume 64 (1970).

Stewart, Charles D. "Old Abe's Shield," *Wisconsin Magazine of History*, Volume 36 (1953).

Todd, Maria P. "Old Abe War Eagle of the 8th Wisconsin," *Military Collector and Historian*, Volume 4 (1952).

Weissert, Augustus G. "Story of Old Abe, the War Eagle," in H. W. Rood (comp.), *Wisconsin at Vicksburg, Report of the Wisconsin-Vicksburg Monument Commission* (Madison, 1914).

Woodworth, John. *Old Glory: Song and Chords* (Elgin, Illinois, 1905).

Young, Patrick. *Old Abe: The Eagle Hero* (Englewood Cliffs, New Jersey, 1965).

U.S. Navy Department

Supreme Commander Dwight D. Eisenhower talks with troopers of the 101st Airborne ("Screaming Eagles") on the eve of D-Day, 1944.

THE AUTHOR

RICHARD H. ZEITLIN is Curator of the Grand Army of the Republic Memorial Hall, housed in the state capitol in Madison, Wisconsin. He was born in New York City in 1945, where he did his undergraduate work at Queens College. He earned both a master's degree and a Ph.D. in American History at the University of Wisconsin, the latter in 1973. He worked for Old World Wisconsin, the State Historical Society's outdoor ethnic museum, between 1973 and 1977. He is the author *Germans in Wisconsin*, published by the Society in 1977.